D1139154

YESTERDAY'S FARM

Life on the farm 1830–1960

by **Valerie Porter**

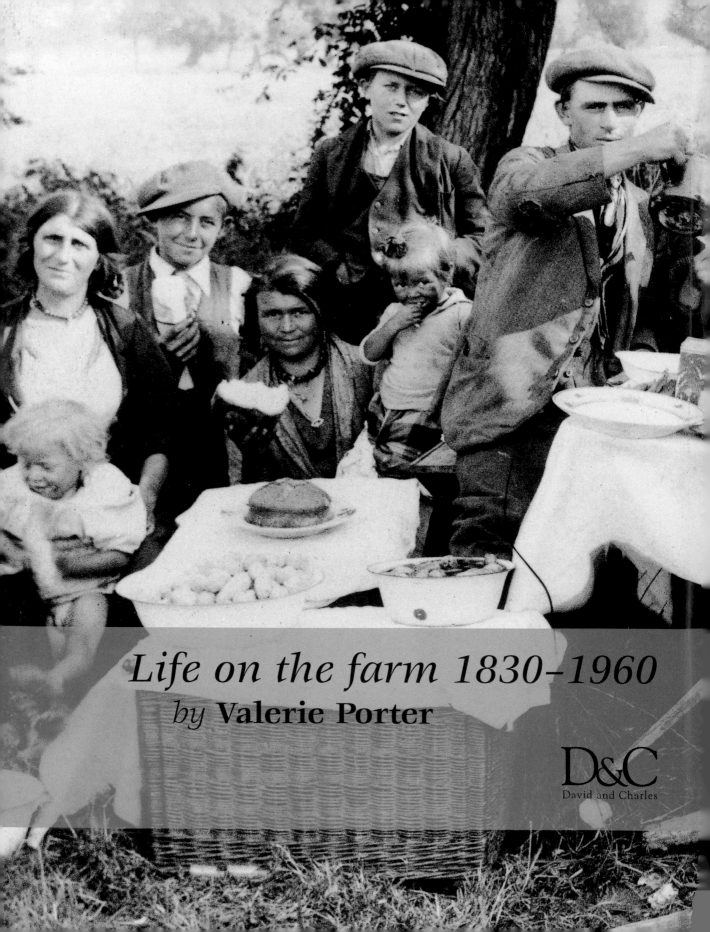

Life on the farm 1830–1960
by Valerie Porter

D&C
David and Charles

Yesterday's
FARM

Previous pages: Working family's field picnic under the hedge.

Right: Bob Tanner of Upperton, Sussex. He started his long working life on the land as a boy of 11 at East Tisted, Hampshire, in about 1870.

Front cover images courtesy of: EH Donovan and Friends of the Lake District

A DAVID & CHARLES BOOK
Copyright © David & Charles Limited 2006

David & Charles is an F + W Publications Inc. company
4700 East Galbraith Road
Cincinnati, OH 45236

First published in 2006

Text copyright © Valerie Porter 2006

Valerie Porter has asserted her right to be identified as author of this work in accordance with the Copyright, Designs and Patents Act, 1988.

The publisher has endeavoured to contact all contributors of pictures for permission to reproduce.

A catalogue record for this book is available from the British Library.

ISBN-13: 978-0-7153-2184-3
ISBN-10: 0-7153-2184-6

Printed in China by SNP Leefung
for David & Charles
Brunel House   Newton Abbot   Devon

Commissioning Editor Jane Trollope
Editor Jennifer Proverbs
Head of Design Prudence Rogers
Designer Sue Cleave
Production Beverley Richardson
Project Editor Joan Gubbin

Visit our website at www.davidandcharles.co.uk

David & Charles books are available from all good bookshops; alternatively you can contact our Orderline on 0870 9908222 or write to us at FREEPOST EX2 110, D&C Direct, Newton Abbot, TQ12 4ZZ (no stamp required UK only); US customers call 800-289-0963 and Canadian customers call 800-840-5220.

Contents

Introduction

Some of these would have been common sights within living memory. But now? The teams and herds and flocks have been ousted from the lanes by motor traffic. The families working in the fields have given way to a massive machine with a lone driver, isolated in his safety cab and insulated from the life in the soil he tills, the dust and aroma of the crop he harvests and the joy of the birdsong that surrounds him, and without companionship.

Farming has always been a process of change but, during the 20th century, the pace of that change accelerated way beyond the imagination of earlier

When did you last see the fields alive with local village families working together, talking, laughing, singing and swearing together, sharing a picnic and ale and cider in their al fresco lunch break taken during work that progressed at a human pace: hard physical work, sweaty work, dirty work, achingly exhausting work in drenching rain, bitter cold or blazing heat, day after day after day? In fact, when did you last see anybody on their legs in the fields? Or even working manually in the farmyard?

When did you last meet a tired, steaming team of plough horses ambling homewards with boys astride their broad backs, or even a herd of dairy cows meandering along the lane between meadow and milking parlour, or a sea of sheep bleating down the road in response to a couple of silent, eye-bright, chivvying collies?

generations. What happened and what was yesterday's farm really like? Was it a better place than it is today? Was it really the 'good old days'? Or has nostalgia warped the reality?

Over the years I have listened to many a farmer and many a farmworker harking back to earlier times in their own lives and also recalling the tales of their parents, their grandparents and beyond, memories rolling back into the 19th century when the rural world was a very different place. In the intervening decades farmers and their workers have had to adapt rapidly and learn many new skills.

Above: Fine bull, docile enough to be led by a very small boy.

Opposite: Apple pickers in Buckinghamshire, 1930s. The fruit went by rail to London along with local plums, damsons, Aylesbury ducks and sheep.

Left: Cornish farmstead at Porthmeor.

They have adapted above all to scale, mechanisation and technology and their ramifications – a great speeding up of all aspects of rural life, a substantial reduction in the labour force, an overwhelming increase in the use of chemicals and artificial fertilisers, controversy over pollution and over genetically modified organisms, a huge increase in bureaucracy and paperwork and safety regulations in the morass of European legislation, the different demands of new markets and the loss of old ones, the heart-rending horrors of mass slaughter in the face of livestock diseases, the inability to control farm-gate prices, and pressures on the countryside and the rural way of life from incomers from the towns and a feeling of alienation from the urban majority who no longer remember their own familial rural roots. The alienation

Above: Each man to his horse: three Suffolk men well matched with their charges.

is compounded by an increasing sense of isolation, in particular with the loss of the informal companionship that went with being part of a larger group in the workplace, whether the extended family or farm employees. The suicide rate in the farming community is now alarmingly high.

Back in the early 1970s, a landowner told me quite seriously that he could see no point in keeping his farm in good heart for his sons, as he firmly believed that, before they became of age, his land would be taken from him by nationalisation and he therefore had no incentive to treat it with the respect he felt it deserved.

It didn't happen and it seems highly unlikely to happen in Britain in the foreseeable future. But the loss of faith in the future of farming is now very serious indeed, particularly among those who would have expected future generations of their own family to continue their good work. When a farm becomes *only* a business, and no longer a way of life, it ceases to be a living entity and its land becomes a mere commodity, as lifeless as a packet of biscuits on a supermarket shelf.

Setting the Scene

Farming today would be almost incomprehensible to the great-grandfathers of present day farmers. They would not understand modern attitudes, let alone modern techniques and practices. A Victorian farmer dropped into the 21st century would be wide-eyed with envy and disbelief, with possibly a dash of disgust at the lack of concern for future generations.

The traditional family farm is close to extinction in many parts of Britain. Its time as a purely agricultural unit is almost over. To survive at all, most family farms are busily diversifying. They offer bed-and-breakfast accommodation, convert the yard buildings into holiday cottages, organise farm tours for townsfolk to come and see cows being milked and lambs being born, or they turn some of the land over to pick-your-own fruit. They smarten up the old stables for livery customers; they launch into keeping exotic animals such as Angora goats, Asian water buffalo, South American camelids, and ostriches. They might turn the whole place into a farm park for tourists, or they go for 'added value' by selling their own cheeses and ice creams and smoking their own farm-reared meat; they dip a toe into the water of the nearest farmers' market or set up a farm shop selling a lot more than their own produce. They are fizzing with ideas and are crestfallen when dreams do not match reality. The modern farmer needs to be skilled in marketing, as well as production of food, and some are not cut out to be salesmen.

Back Along

A historical framework of the past century or two gives
a context to the story of farming and how (and why)
it has changed so radically – especially since Queen
Victoria was crowned in 1837, two years after the death
of that well-known pamphleteer and rural rider, William
Cobbett, and two years before the founding of the Royal
Agricultural Society of England (RASE).

By the 1830s farming was already feeling
the breeze of revolution: plough oxen had
largely been replaced by horses, men were
inventing all sorts of implements to make
the most of horse power, and railways
were beginning to make what would be
a decisive mark on the country. Steam
was also generating its first tentative
chugs and whistles which would send
the faithful farm horse into permanent
retirement a century later. The population
of the country was soaring: in 1821 there
had been 12 million people in England
and Wales; by 1881 there would be 26
million, all needing food.

Farming has always had its ups and
downs, its periods of prosperity and of
depression, and the Great Exhibition
of 1851 seemed to mark the start of an
upward curve that filled farmers with
optimism, boosted by the power and
promise of the steam engines that were
exhibited at Crystal Palace that year.
There were important horse-powered
implements too, with the horse rapidly
replacing human labour in some of the

Above: Land reclamation in 1874 on 2,000 acres of Scottish moorland at Strath Ferry, using Fowler steam engines, here with a 'toothpick'.

Top left: Photographer Barclay Wills chatting with 'Old Shep' Sheppard at the Findon Sheep Fair.

Left: Teams returning from the fields in Yorkshire. Ploughmen typically rode home sitting sideways on their horses rather than astride.

more arduous tasks such as threshing and reaping.

This period of optimism continued through the 1860s, which saw the real start of some eight decades during which the change from manual labour and animal power to the fully mechanised age would be made. It was an exciting time and farmers in the 1860s felt they were moving up in the world.

It couldn't last. It never does in farming, though farmers, with their eye on the seasons, never quite grasp the inevitability of the cycle of long-term ups and downs. Across the Atlantic and in Australasia, new farmers were making gigantic progress in their wide-open spaces and it was not long before the steam power on their own railways and ships combined to make the transport of grain, wool and meat a relatively simple and cheap matter to distant Europe. By

the mid 1870s, Britain was importing produce on a massive scale and the price of home-grown wool, grain and dairy produce tumbled alarmingly, causing an agricultural depression that was to last more or less up to World War I. To add to farmers' woes, appalling weather in the late 1870s and early 1880s led to harvest losses and extensive outbreaks of livestock disease. Farmers were being bashed from every side. Some left farming altogether, or let their land go to scrub and weeds, and many of their sons seized the opportunity to leave it all behind them and emigrated.

Meanwhile horses used purely for agricultural purposes continued to go from strength to strength, reaching a peak population of 937,000 in 1911, but their time would not last either. The first British tractor was made as early as 1902.

Two World Wars

World War I came at the moment when many of the big landed estates were breaking up, the agricultural industry as a whole had only half the number of farmers and farmworkers as a century earlier, and many farms were looking scruffy or even derelict.

Above: Troop manoeuvres in a Sussex lane during World War I.

Right: A Lancashire hill farmer in the 1950s, symbolising 'dog and stick' farming.

The Great War

With Germany doing its best to blockade Britain into starvation, the government needed British farmers to come to the country's rescue. The government offered them the carrot of guaranteed prices for farm produce and promised that it would continue to support the agricultural industry even when the war was over. The farmers believed it. Despite the logistical problems caused by horsemen and farm horses being commandeered for war service, the farmers started ploughing up old grassland as they were bid and did their very best.

After the war, people began to return to farming confident in the government's promises and many raised substantial mortgages to buy farms at a time when land prices were rising. They really should have known better. By 1921 the government had decided it could no longer afford to guarantee prices and by the mid 1920s the bottom had dropped out of British farming and many farmers simply could not cope. Farming slid rapidly backwards into another depression, with farmers reverting to the old-fashioned 'dog and stick' methods that meant employing as few men as possible and running store cattle on rough grazing under the watchful eye of the farmer himself (and his dog), which required very little capital input. Others gave up altogether and some migrated into the towns. Some went further away, just as they had in earlier depressions, and started a new life overseas.

Here and there people were experimenting with machine milking and the like but men and horses (often remounts obtained from the army) remained the major source of power on

the farm. The war had changed many aspects of life in the country, especially social attitudes: the old class divisions were crumbling and farmworkers were bolder in their complaints about poor cottages and poor wages. Their horizons had been broadened by the war and by the post-war influx of newcomers into the countryside in the form of commuters and tourists – ramblers and leisure motorists pootling along country lanes – many of them trying to escape the general economic depression of the time. But the farming industry was rolling back into near-destitution, with millions of acres of land lingering uncultivated.

Some farmers pulled themselves together and started to modernise their outlook. Although most still relied on horses, the use of tractors began to increase and the first combine harvesters had been seen in British fields by 1928. In the late 1920s a few farmers were beginning to specialise in more intensive

Above: Wartime Yorkshire farming family, clearly tired from their labours and with not much to spare to feed their horses.

Above: An early tractor, the International Titan 10-20 imported from America, ploughing with a Ransomes four-furrow riding plough during World War I.

methods with poultry and pigs and by 1939, 15 per cent of the nation's cows were being milked by machine rather than by hand.

Livestock became far more important than cash crops and the acreage of pasture increased throughout the decade. The Milk Marketing Board was established in 1933 and there were livestock improvement schemes to encourage the development of pedigree herds. British farmers were in love with cattle, especially dairy cows. And Britain, as a nation, was importing huge amounts of food, especially meat, grain and vegetables.

War Agricultural Committees

As early as 1937 the threat of a new war was being taken seriously and, once again, the government realised that it had been neglecting its farmers but was about to need them desperately. It set up local War Agricultural Committees to tell farmers how to do their job.

The committees' powers were considerable: they could direct a farmer's efforts, instruct him on what crops to grow, tell him how to manure them, what animals to keep, what labour to employ and, in extreme cases, they could evict

him from his farm and either work it themselves or let it to someone else. There was no appeal against their decisions.

Donald McCullough knew all about the War Ags, as the committees came to be known. In the latter years of World War II he joined one of them in Leicestershire, the once-grassy county famous for hunting but which, during the war years, found that the area under plough was increased by a thousand per cent. The chairman of Donald's committee was 'one of the best and heaviest (he weighs over 18 stone) farmers in the county'. The members set off at 10 o'clock one morning to a farm miles from anywhere, in company with a single official. The committee members were all on first-name terms with the farmers whose farms were the focus of their visits.

First they called on Bill, who did not receive them too kindly: he demanded to know what they wanted, using a few swear words to indicate his displeasure, saying, 'Haven't we farmers got enough trouble on our hands without chaps like you hanging about?' The committee stood on their dignity and explained that all they wanted was another ten acres of grassland to be ploughed up and that they were trying to look four years ahead. 'There's no need,' said Bill, after a pause, 'for you fellows to look four years ahead. You'll be burned in the market place long before then.'

The next call was to a progressive gentleman farmer who, before the war, had his own circus as a hobby, though his circus building was now crammed with tractors, ploughs and disc harrows. When the committee mentioned acreages, he responded, 'Why, of course, delighted. Just see my secretary.' The third visit of the day was to a younger farmer, who told them he had no grass left to plough. Then came the 'best farmer of the day – a quiet man with a handsome, kindly face', who assured the committee that he *wanted* to plough up as much as he could, but he was already very short of grass and needed to wait until new grass had taken. Next was the manager of an estate, the house on which had been taken over to be a hospital; he told them he was 'going mad' for lack of workers. The committee asked him why he didn't have landgirls. 'You ought to know by this time,' he said, 'that if there are wounded soldiers about you can't get anyone to worry about farming.'

Finally they visited their toughest farmer of the day, who told them he had done all he was going to do, that he was fed up with War Committees and would be greatly obliged if they would 'get to hell'. The committee explained to him tactfully that the country had asked the Minister to undertake a job and that this was the share that the country reckoned this particular farmer could do. 'Why didn't you say that at first?' he exclaimed, 'I'm not here to be insulted! I can do *twice* that.' Game, set and match to the committee, who retired gratefully after having motored more than a hundred miles to talk, beg, persuade, threaten and joke non-stop with hard-pressed farmers for seven hours.

The Battle for Food

As with World War I, the government's main aim was to increase the amount of arable land, moving away from livestock to grain, sugar beet, potatoes and vegetables. Once again, this meant asking farmers to plough up grassland and once again the farmers did what was asked, but to a degree that was almost impossible to imagine.

Below: Soldiers stationed locally helping with the harvest in Cheshire in 1939, bolstering a workforce depleted by so many farmworkers being called up for military service.

The farmers did Britain proud in World War II and indeed the nation owed them as much as it did the armed forces. The Battle of the Atlantic was crucial, but so was the battle of the land though no one gave any medals to the farmers and their workers. In 1939, about 1.5 million families were making their living directly from farming. There were as many farmers in Britain as there had been in 1880 but only half as many labourers. There were only 150 combine harvesters in the whole country and about 15,000 tractors. Although there were still eleven farm horses to every one tractor, those tractors provided two-thirds of a farm's mobile power. While farming still relied heavily on the muscle power of horses and humans the war had altered that situation forever. British farming would – indeed had to – become fully mechanised at top speed.

So began the race to increase production. It was a marathon, not a sprint: farming cannot be changed overnight, however 'industrial' it might seem. It took a lot of hard graft and determination, helped by government promises (as ever) that not only would farmers be paid good prices for their crops and given an extra element of profit to encourage them to plough up more land – they would also benefit from guaranteed income levels for at least a year after the war was finished.

The first wartime harvest in the summer of 1940 gave high yields but had some unusual problems. First of all, there was a shortage of manpower. The Women's Land Army came to the rescue and would have more than 80,000 women working on the land by 1943. Secondly, the glorious summer weather encouraged tourists into the countryside intent on watching the air battles in the skies and trampling all over the crops looking for crashed planes and bomb craters. Thirdly, many farmers

had joined what was at first known as the Local Defence Volunteers (renamed that summer as the Home Guard) and had to fit in their voluntary duties as well as working flat out on the land.

In the winter of 1940, the government was demanding an extra 2¼ million acres of arable land to be wrested from pasture and increasingly from less likely tracts that had not felt the blades of a plough

for centuries, if ever. In the spring of 1941 there were fleets of imported heavy tractors moving earth, reclaiming unlikely land and draining marshy tracts. By the following year they were gradually moving up the slopes of the downs and hills, while at the same time some land was beginning to be lost to new airfields, troop camps and munitions factories deliberately placed in rural areas. The crucial harvest of 1942 saw more than a thousand combine harvesters helping to cut and thresh a bumper crop of grain from some 8.5 million acres.

In 1943 the land was positively bursting with produce, helped by another long spell of good weather in June and July. Then in 1944 came another invasion of the countryside – not by tourists but by huge numbers of soldiers and their

A FARMING FORECAST

The farmers of 1942 had a secret weapon: their own encoded weather forecast issued by the Air Ministry to help them time their harvest and mobilise their workforce quickly at the right moment. Encoded? Yes, to make sure that the Luftwaffe didn't pick up broadcasts of fine-weather prospects that would encourage them to make air raids! Rather charmingly, though not always fairly, the forecast codes were DOG (good), HORSE (fair), COW (doubtful), SHEEP (poor) and PIG (bad), with the further outlook being BUY (settled), FAT (uncertain) or SELL (unsettled). The word pabulum (meaning food, or food for thought) began the forecast, which was followed by the county name, the outlook, and finally the forecast. For example, you might be informed 'Pabulum Kent Sell Pig'. It would reach the farmer by a roundabout route: the Air Ministry prepared the coded forecast and it was telephoned at about 5pm every evening to Whitehall's Ministry of Agriculture, who in turn forwarded it to the War Agriculture Committee headquarters, who filtered it through various channels down to the relevant War Ag member, who would then decode the forecast and tell the local farmers in strictest confidence what weather to expect. One can imagine it turning into a game of Chinese whispers, with Kent searching for a fat horse instead of selling a pig ...

Below: A wet wartime harvest, decidedly 'Pabulum PIG'!

equipment moving southwards for the build-up to the D-day landings. Country roads in southern England became dedicated convoy routes; the local woods were crawling with soldiers and their equipment, moving silently under cover of the trees like swarms of jungle ants. The harvest looked promising but then there was heavy rain over the whole country in August and September, followed by wet autumn gales and, in the southeast, a persistent rain of flying bombs and rockets to be dodged. By now farmers were running out of basic essentials such as sacks for storing the crops, churns for holding milk and grass for grazing dairy cows to produce that milk. The fertility of the overworked land was being affected and there were shortages of the heavier machinery that had originally been imported from the Americans, who now needed their machinery output for their own farmers. Mechanisation had come on apace, of necessity, which was just as well since they were also running out of labour, again, though in the middle and later years of the war those willing women of the WLA had been joined by another unlikely workforce – prisoners of war.

Then at last the war was over. The farmers had kept the nation fed, and the nation appreciated it. The government began to shift the emphasis slowly back to livestock; the national populations of pigs, poultry and cattle were expanded and the prices farmers received for milk, eggs and meat animals and for potatoes and sugar beet began to rise.

What about those who had helped the farmers throughout the war? Many land-girls, who had come to the countryside from the towns not knowing one end of a cow from the udder, had given precious years to farming. They had joined up when they were perhaps 18 to 20 years old, when life should have been full of fun and opportunity, and they had found themselves out in the sticks, knee deep goods and with a great deal in the way of experience. But with all those men coming home from their time in the armed forces and wanting to settle back on the land, would there be room for the women as well?

in mud and muck, up to their elbows in tractor oil, their hair full of straw, their skin sunburnt, wind-whipped and grimy, their muscles honed and toned by physical labour. Many of them wanted to carry on, perhaps finding a small farm of their own or continuing to work on someone else's farm. They had left the Land Army with very little in the way of material

As for the prisoners, some decided to stay rather than return to their own homeland: they married local girls and settled into the British countryside quite happily. A large number of Poles, many of them having taken up arms to serve Britain during the war, also remained and made a go of a new life on the land.

Above: The Women's Voluntary Service sold 1½ million pies a week to farmworkers in the fields, with the encouragement of the Ministry of Food from 1942.

Changes on the Farm

Farming practices had been altered radically by the Battle for Food. The government had discouraged the keeping of pigs and poultry but encouraged milk production and there were incentives to produce more liquid milk, which was deemed to be such an important food for humans that dairy farmers were actively discouraged from making on-farm cheese and butter and prohibited from selling cream.

By 1946 there were 3,200 combine harvesters, three times as many as in 1942, and the number would treble over the next four years, rising to 50,000 in 1960. The internal combustion engine was also playing a major role as a static source of power: there had been 120,000 engines on farms in 1939 and this increased to 200,000 by 1952, while the number of electric motors rose from 11,000 to a quarter of a million. Mains water and electricity were reaching rural areas at last, though in 1951 only two-thirds of the nation's dairy farms had piped water and only half had electric light.

There had been a move away from mixed farming and towards specialisation as a result of the war and those who specialised in pigs and poultry would be a long way along the line of intensification by 1960. Arable farmers had discovered the joy of bagged artificial fertilisers (so much easier than muck spreading) and of chemical pesticides, freely sprayed to

Above: Landgirl ploughing during World War II.

TRACTOR NUMBERS

Statistics about the number of tractors in the country at different times vary wildly but in 1945 it was firmly stated that there were 200,000 of them in Britain, a huge rise from 21,000 in 1925. With the tractor and its implements, and particularly with the combine harvester, came the need for much bigger fields and the increasing importance of the farm workshop, where farmers and their staff could play at being mechanics. A big drawback to tractors was that farmers could not grow home feed for them: fuel had to be purchased. By 1960 British farms were using more than a million tons of fuel a year and tractor drivers were beginning to forget what legs were for.

rid crops of insects and weeds; they also tended to practise monoculture, rather than rotating crops in the field to break pest cycles. Dairy farmers were milking with machines, usually in parlours. Grass farmers found new ways of drying their grass crop or made silage rather than hay; and grain farmers were starting to dry their grain artificially.

The most obvious change brought about by the war years was the status of the farm horse. Before the war, a farm of 350 acres working a crop rotation on average soil might need a dozen horses in its stables. Now the era of the horse was virtually at an end, supplanted by the iron horse of the fields: the tractor. In 1944, only on a small percentage of British farms was all the work (including farm haulage) being carried out by tractor; large numbers of small farms still had no mechanical equipment, though the farmer might bring in a tillage contractor for tractor ploughing or cultivation. The larger farms had a combination of tractors and horses but the rapid development of small general-purpose tractors during the war meant that mechanisation was spreading to smaller farms as well. The theory in 1944 was that, if the farm needed more than four horses for its work, the farmer should consider partial replacement by a tractor or tractors.

The post-war years became something of a boom time in the countryside. Farmworkers had far more options in life; they could find better paid jobs in the towns and cities. It worked both ways; there were those in urban areas who, liberated by the growth in car ownership, decided to make their homes in the villages and commute to their urban work. At the outbreak of the war there were only two million private cars in the country, by 1966 there were seven million, rising to 30 million by 2005. The new villagers came into a different social world than that which had existed even between the wars, let alone before World

War I. The squire had gone and along with him the patriarchal benevolence and involvement in the village that his type had often practised from a sense of public duty which was virtually in his blood.

In the farmyard, the changes in the late 1940s and the 1950s were there for all to see. Grant aid and technical advice encouraged farmers to build, build, build, largely with harsh factory-made materials such as concrete, corrugated iron and asbestos cladding. Proud old buildings were swept aside as they were no longer suitable for post-war farming. Life was good for farmers and in the mid 1950s they were pocketing ten shillings out of every pound spent on food in Britain. Today it is a mere 7½ new pence (less than two shillings).

It was in the 1960s that the first flickers of doubt appeared. Farming, on a wave of prosperity, was increasingly driven by advice based on technical research, rather than on the practical experience of people who knew and worked with the land and livestock. All this progress was wonderful, all this energy and science and technology and growth, but there was a cost. In 1962 Rachel Carson published *Silent Spring*, pointing out that heavy use of pesticides could do harm as well as good. DDT, first produced in 1874, was famously persistent, but no one thought through the ecological effects of its persistence.

Above: Farmland being lost under concrete during aircraft runway construction by the American army in 1943.

COUNTRY IDYLL?

Throughout the 1970s I was living in a small cottage completely surrounded by the fields of a large arable farm and began to be alarmed at the practices that I witnessed. Increased use of heavy machinery, crop spraying and stubble burning all took their toll on the land around me. The land was heavy clay yet huge tractors were being used, their weight creating a solid, impenetrable pan and crushing the old reliable system of land drains. The farm manager also took to night ploughing, and the tractors' powerful headlights and the sound of their engines penetrated even the thickest bedroom curtains. Frequent spraying was matter of course and, worse, included aerial spraying – a system in which nearby gardens were invariably sprayed just as much as the crops. Local people noticed that the goldfish in their garden ponds were dying, and we all made very sure that we thoroughly washed our organically homegrown fruit and vegetables before eating them. Another problem for cottagers at the time was the practice of stubble burning after the harvest. First we were choking on thick black smoke, and then surrounded by scorched black acres until ploughing time. The fields were already large, with the old hedges having been gouged out so that the combines could operate unimpeded, and the winds whipped across them with glee, fanning the hedge-singeing fires and flinging sparks and burning fragments of straw in every direction.

Squeezing the land

Farmers in the 1970s were doing what they had been encouraged to do since 1939, squeezing the highest possible yields out of the land. At the end of the war, a farmer in Huntingdonshire was mightily pleased that his ploughed grassland yielded a 'most impressive' two-hundredweight of threshed wheat to the acre. By 1982 a well managed winter-sown wheat crop would yield 2.8 tons per acre and by 2004 it would shoot up to four tons per acre (10 tonnes per hectare) on the most productive farms. By then, the number of people employed in agriculture in Britain was a quarter of the number it had been in 1939.

In 1973, the year in which Britain entered the European Economic Community as the EU was then known, Colin Buchanan made a speech accusing farmers of mismanaging the countryside, of spraying chemicals with abandon, of blighting rural areas with ugly buildings, of pushing livestock beyond their limits. Gradually, in spite of the advantages of cheap food in the shops, the general public began to question the wisdom of farming practices and looked at what was happening to the environment in the name of progress, high production levels and efficiency; what was happening to animal welfare; what was happening to the pace of life. Long before the controversies over genetically modified organisms and distressing diseases such as bovine spongiform encephalopathy (BSE), farmers were being turned into the bad guys, bit by bit, in the eyes of the public – and there is no world war to turn them back into the nation's saviours.

Farmers All

There is really no such creature as a typical farmer, and Brian was not typical of what most people imagine farmers to be. He was not brawny, or bucolic, or rustic, or rosy-cheeked with straw in his hair. He did not drawl. He did not ride to hounds, or go to the markets, or keep a pocket watch, or dress in cords or even, in the early 1970s, in a waxed jacket. He was a man brimming with energy, famous for sprinting around the farm (never walking, let alone welly-trudging), always in a hurry, always full of wild ideas and actions, a man who had never really grown up and was just loving the childish fun of playing at being a farmer.

On Monday mornings he would assemble his workers at seven sharp and issue instructions for the coming week, bouncing restlessly on the balls of his feet and popping peanuts into his mouth from his jacket pocket (he said they gave him energy). Then he would climb into his helicopter and take off for the city to earn his living, so that he had the money to continue to play farmer. During harvest he would fly home eagerly, leap from the helicopter and jump on to the combine for a few roaring circuits round a field, more often than not causing a breakdown and leaving the stranded, straw-jammed machine to be coddled back to life by his cursing workforce after he had lost interest in the toy.

The Farmers

In much of Sussex and neighbouring counties, city men with wealth to spare have been taking over the farms for several years and it has become increasingly rare to find a 'dirty boots' farmer whose father had farmed the same land before him, and even his grandfather and great grandfather too. City men sometimes value wealth above a pride in good farming.

Top: Cotswold yeoman farmer Humphrey Porter in the mid 1880s.

Above: Edwardian family at Manor Farm, Holwell, Oxfordshire.

Brian farmed about 500 acres and added to the land whenever the opportunity arose, especially if it was suitable for his other passion, shooting. He had already removed many of the hedges, making the fields more suitable for his big machinery: the field rolling down to my cottage was called Chilbeams, and aptly so as the wind whistled across its open 30 acres. On old maps, and from hints in the soil, you could see that it had originally been many small fields, sheltered by hedges. But Brian told me his vision was one of 'rolling acres of golden corn, as far as the eye could see'. Fortunately, his latest gamekeeper explained that pheasants liked hedges and so the grubbing out stopped.

The family that owns the land surrounding my present cottage, where I have lived since 1980, are of the Brian type but the locals have given me vivid descriptions of the good old Sussex farmers who had farmed it before World War II. This 120-acre farm, which dates back in the records at least as far as the 13th century, was at one time in the hands of a genuine Farmer Giles, who had married the local village schoolteacher, Bertha Lintott, whose own parents had worked the farm before him. 'Young' Bill Tull, who was born in 1920 and whose title differentiated him from his dad, horseman 'Old' Bill, remembered that in his schooldays:

I used to go down the farm at weekends and work with them, used to go with my father and help make hay and this, that and other. Then the school teacher got married to Giles, on the Christmas, and I went down there to help her mother because we had to milk ten or twelve cows by hand while the teacher went on honeymoon. Jerseys and Guernseys, the cows were, twelve or fourteen of them. Got up at five o'clock, milking had to be done by seven, turn out the cows – that was over the Christmas holiday from school. Mrs Lintott was a nice old lady. That was the school teacher's mother (the old man died when I was small). She was a big stout old lady and always wore a black man's cap and white apron. We used to milk and then have breakfast

*indoors there. My granddad said she
was always watching him, watching
the work; he didn't go much by her. He
was working down there and when I
left school he partly retired and I took
over his horses.*

A famous woman farmer was Mrs Heelis,
better known as Beatrix Potter. She
owned several Lakeland farms from
the 1920s onwards, gradually acquired
with the profits from *The Tale of Peter
Rabbit* and her other children's books.
She became deeply involved with farming
and showing sheep – especially the local
grey and white Herdwicks. She was
described at the time as an autocratic,
resolute, strong-willed little woman, who
wore clogs and liked the old-fashioned
ways. She could be rather severe with
those who didn't do as she wished, or who
annoyed her.

Mrs Heelis, as all the locals called her,
was highly respected as a farmer and
kept her farms firmly in hand; she was
very much a dirty boots farmer. Jack, an
old Westmorland drainer, recalled that
she and he had walked up the rough
fellside together to check on one of her
farms. They came to a beck and Jack
wondered whether he ought to offer to
carry her across. Before he could make
the gesture, 't'owd body slipped off her
clogs and paddled through t'beck and
niver said owt about it, and it must hev
bin gey caald,' he recalled. When she died
in 1943, at the age of 77, she bequeathed
her 14 farms, totalling 4,300 acres, to
the National Trust with instructions
that they should continue to maintain
purebred Herdwick sheep there.

*Right: Beatrix Potter, known locally as farmer
Mrs Heelis of Troutbeck Park and Hill Top
Farm's Castle Cottage, near Sawrey,*

Rachel Knappett worked as a land-girl during World War II and wrote an immensely detailed and funny account of the farm work that she undertook. She found herself posted to Bath Farm, in southwest Lancashire. Knowing nothing about farming, she cycled into the farmyard on the morning of April Fool's Day, 1940, and was met by the boss, the two horsemen Bill and Billy, Barney the Irishman, Joe the tractor driver and Tommy, who was a combination of pig-man, pony-man and hen-man. 'The boss', Doug, was the exact opposite of the conventional idea of a farmer:

Instead of being stout and having apple cheeks and shiny leather gaiters, he is tall, lean, alarmingly active and wears, of all things, pince-nez. He has a reputation, which he encourages with delight, of being quite mad. He takes his glasses off when he reads, his teeth out when he eats, and he celebrated his sixtieth birthday by standing on his head in the middle of the road. …

It seems to be absolutely impossible for the boss to sit still; he chases about from morning till night, on his legs or in his motor car; he talks very fast, and is the most restless person I have ever met; he always seems to move in the middle of a whirlwind.

After the long, hard, hot work of harvest one year, Rachel was looking forward to a time of rest and recuperation. She heard Doug remarking with great energy and satisfaction, 'Now we've getten shut of that bloody stuff, we can start work.' Timidly, she asked, 'When do you expect to finish?' He laughed, and told her, 'Tha

Below: Farmer Thomas Brown of Horley, Surrey, stacking hay in about 1910.

n'er 'as finished, not until tha in a long box and we clod earth at thee.' After five years on the farm, she learnt the truth of that remark. 'End, in the language of a farm, is another word for beginning. Work without end. Amen.'

Peter Ditchfield, the rector of Barkham in Berkshire, wrote several books between the wars about village life and the characters he came to know well. He liked farmers. He saw them as brave men facing their 'stupendous difficulties' with a gallant spirit in the days of the 1920s depression. His praise was fulsome but he also saw their faults. One of their problems was that, having been born and bred on the land, they could only farm and were not usually able to turn their hand to other careers. Nor were they good businessmen and seemed to put themselves entirely in the hands of their dealers. Finally, they were averse to co-operation with each other for mutual advantage:

> In the early morning you may see cart after cart conveying cans of milk to the railway station for transport to London. It does not occur to the farmers to unite in sending this precious freight, and so saving the time of many men, the wear and tear of horse and cart.

Aubrey Seymour was a farmer who wrote books about his life. A schoolmaster had told him that he was 'only fit for hoeing turnips' and he duly became a farm pupil. But he had his own farm before he was 20 years old and by the time he died in 1972, at the age of 85, he had become not only a farmer but also a naturalist, sportsman, the author of three books and an artist. So much for schoolmasters.

Seymour was 'Warwickshire born, Warwickshire bred, as firmly rooted in Warwickshire soil as any of its hedgerow

Left: Essex farmer Katherine Courtauld, whose father gave her the 243-acre Knights Farm, at Colne Engaine, when she was 21. She gradually increased her holding to 2,000 acres and by 1899 had a staff of 15 men and boys but still attended livestock sales to buy all of her own cattle, sheep, pigs and poultry. Many women were efficient and successful commerical farmers long before they were allowed to vote.

AN UNLIKELY FARMER

At Churt in Surrey, an unlikely farmer was the Liberal MP and coalition prime minister Lloyd George, who, according to JW Robertson Scott, had an 'ineradicable rusticity' and was a countryman through and through. He was so full of zest for seeing things grow that a colleague on the Land Committee claimed that, despite his Welsh nonconformity, he was surely a sincere pagan at heart 'whose natural expressions would have been in fertility rites'. He was a morning man, awake and alert early and ready to pour out ideas as he strode across the heather. (In Wales, he was apparently able to get over a hedge 'without leaving a trace of passage'.) At Churt, he owned fields that had been cultivated but also many up the hill towards Hindhead that had been allowed to run to waste in the past, and these he cleared by putting in pigs to root around and fertilise the ground, before using bulldozers to take out the bigger scrub. He was delighted that his cleared sandy wasteland became bountiful, though it had probably cost him a small fortune to make it so.

elms'. His father, a businessman but a countryman at heart, kept a house cow, poultry and pigs, and Seymour kept his own Old English game birds as a boy. Having left school at 15 to become a farm pupil, at 18 he became a tenant farmer near Kineton for two years, after which his father bought him his own farm. Farming was only 'change for a shilling' at the time and it was easier to lose money than to make it; if it had not been a way of life, the countryside might have become derelict. It was during the agricultural depression that lasted right through to World War I and there were many properties on the market, going cheap. He gradually built up his new farm with plenty of good animals, especially beef cattle and pigs; he worked the land with horses and began to rent or buy more and more land. Then came World War I and suddenly the farmer was everybody's friend. Something of a pioneer, he bought his first tractor and, in the days of hand-milking and taking churns to the station by horse and cart, he signed a contract with a London firm to supply winter milk. He increased his sheep flock, but he also

Below: Canvas home near Ongar, Essex, for a demobbed soldier and his family in 1920.

ploughed up more and more land with his new Fordson tractor, as instructed by the local war committee.

Like so many farmers, Seymour discovered that the good times immediately after World War I did not last. By the mid 1920s he was getting only 30 shillings an acre for his grazing, rather than £5, if he could let it at all. He made his living elsewhere but in World War II the good times came again and he carried on farming until he was 78 years old.

Not all farming families were so lucky during World War II. All over the country the War Ags were supposed to encourage – or indeed, instruct – farmers to do what was believed to be necessary during the war to feed the nation. War Ags were told to deal firmly with farmers who did not make the best of their land through neglect or incompetence, and even to evict them if necessary and requisition the land. Nearly 1,400 farms in England and Wales suffered from this indignity during the war. In Hampshire, a man who had been born on his farm, which had been

TURNED OUT

Among the farmers that came up against the War Ag were an unlucky Warwickshire family turned off their farm and out of their house. The family ended up living in a disused hen-roost, where the farmer's eldest son found them when he returned home on leave from the army. Another victim was a 67-year-old Northumberland farmer, whose son and only help on the farm had been called up. He struggled to manage the farm in his son's absence and then shot himself when the War Ag ordered him out.

farmed by his father before him, was ordered by the local War Ag to plough up a field for crops but he refused, as he knew his own land better than they did. They immediately gave him notice to quit, which he refused to do; instead, he bolted his doors against the police and retreated upstairs with his shotgun. The police threw in teargas, then fired a few shots and broke in, shooting the farmer dead when he resisted them.

In the summer of 1945 that venerable pocket-sized quarterly magazine *The Countryman* (subtitled 'A Quarterly Non-Party Review and Miscellany of Rural Life and Work for the English-speaking World', and founded and edited by JW Robertson Scott) published the second issue in its 31st volume. It was bound between dark green paper covers and full of statements by optimistic advertisers promising a return to normal supplies 'when restrictions are removed, and who knows, the lean years may be nearly over by the end of 1945'. Printed on war-grade paper, the magazine included an article by FC Hynard about his farming experiences.

From being the owner of a successful draper's shop in London he had emigrated to British Columbia at the age of 36 in 1920 to become a fruit farmer but then returned to England to take on a 21-year lease on a derelict Kent farm of some 250 acres. The previous tenant had become bankrupt but there was a good house with fine views, albeit the land itself was in poor shape. Locked into the lease, Hynard became submerged in the depression of 1925–6 on a farm that initially was 'without man, beast or implement' and with himself knowing nothing at all about farming and also in poor health.

He found himself a working bailiff, engaged some farmworkers ('necessarily a poor lot because no good men were out of jobs') and planted potatoes, barley, wheat and ten acres of soft fruit, working alongside his men to learn their jobs as he went along. He tried, unsuccessfully, a

Above: Selecting the best; apple picking in the 1940s.

small herd of milking Jersey cows ('some of my cottagers preferred milk out of a tin to fresh Jersey milk at 1d a pint'), he tried a little pig breeding with half a dozen Middle Whites and then reverted to buying in store pigs instead; he ran a flock of sheep, again unsuccessfully, and tried to fatten a dozen store bullocks over winter but sold them for £60 less than they had cost to buy. He lost more money with his wheat, barley and potatoes in sharply falling markets, but he did manage to market his apples successfully, carefully handpicking the best as samples and taking them personally to West End stores like a commercial traveller. He tried savoy cabbages, beans and heaven knows what else. And he almost eliminated horse work, using crawler tractors instead.

Finally, with the war nearly over, he was winning. He had excellent health and had reared seven children. He had converted a derelict waste into a fertile valley and for many years had earned 'more than a competency'. He now owned 330 acres of Kent, 'including wartime battle scars from two doodle bugs, thirty-five high-explosive bombs and hundreds of incendiaries. What more could one want?'

Smallholders and Labourers

It is important to remember that the term farmer included not just the aristocrat and his estates and the yeoman with his many acres but a huge number of lesser farmers, especially many smallholders who often had another business or trade besides.

Above: William Playfoot and helper mending sacks, 1933.

Left: Taking milk to the dairy.

Mary French, an author and farmer's wife (and much more than that), wrote about the Cornish parish and village of Quethiock. She described how, when the big local estate of the same name was on the market in 1919, there were 16 smallholders. Among them were a publican, a retired farmer, a miller, a carpenter, a blacksmith, a wheelwright, a mason, a widow, a shopkeeper, a sawyer and several farm labourers. They were part-timers on their holdings, but they could still claim to be farmers, though it was usually the wife who was milking the cows, pegging out the goats, feeding the pigs, caring for the poultry and maintaining the orchard as well as doing all the cooking, washing, cleaning and other domestic jobs, while her husband earned his living in the village.

But a smallholder could rise. A man named by Mary French only as 'E-H' was born in 1881 on a small farm at Little Larnick, near Looe in east Cornwall, and told her his story when he was 91. He married in 1908 and the couple had a cottage with the traditional three acres and a cow. E-H was an employee but he was also an opportunist, never slow to seize a chance of bettering himself. In due course he was employing a dozen men, whose main task was to harvest bark for a tannery in Launceston. He gradually accumulated animals and land, until by 1927 he was owner of one of the finest farms in the area; he was still farming it until his retirement in 1942, when he handed it down to his son.

The lucky few were able to graduate from being an agricultural labourer to being a farmer in their own right. James West, born in 1840 in Bepton, West Sussex, was a splendid character with a flowing white beard who eventually died just a few weeks short of his 100th birthday shortly after he and his wife, born in 1847, had celebrated their 75th wedding anniversary. This was an achievement seen as a record at the time and was enough to bring national newspaper journalists flocking to their pond-side cottage.

Longevity was in the family genes: his father had reached 96 (despite having been deported to Australia for 15 years for sheep stealing) and one of James's many sons achieved his century. James started his working life as a bird-scarer when he was a 'bit of a shaver no higher than a kitchen table', earning threepence a day. He became a farm servant ('my first job in service I went just for my board, and my parents were glad to have me go for my board'), graduating to general farm work, including

using what he termed a thrashing frail and over the years progressing to a horse thrashing machine and finally a steam traction thrasher. (The old terms thrashing and frail were gradually standardised as threshing and flail.) He had also mown grass with a scythe and cut corn with a hook before the farm became mechanised. As a young man he would be out in the field scything grass at six in the morning and would then go to farms up to 20 miles away to hoe turnips and help with harvesting. His wife would rise at four to make his breakfast on the days when he went thrashing at a farm some six miles away, to which he might walk or go by cart. When he was out harvesting, he 'never saw a bed'; he would sleep on some straw in a handy barn.

Young West worked his way up carefully, learning the skills he would need in agriculture, and was earning 12 shillings a week as a labourer when one of his masters 'took a fancy to me and lent me the money to set up in a farm'. He

was 26 years old and that was when he married Maria Blunden and they moved into her grandfather's farm in 1866. James ran the farm himself, looking after the cows, doing the ploughing and so on with his three horses, while Maria ran the dairy and the house.

Above: James and Maria West with a dozen of their 14 children in 1913. James farmed all his long life, and several of his sons became successful farmers as well.

SELF-SUFFICIENCY

James West and his wife grew their own wheat, took it to the mill to be ground and then Maria baked all their bread from it. 'Everything we ate we grew, except such things as tea and sugar. When our family was growing I killed 120 stone of meat a year for us.' Their meat was mainly from their own few pigs, though they had the occasional rabbit, and 'hedge-poking' sometimes produced a pheasant for the pot. Maria would get up at three in the morning to churn their milk for butter, producing up to 80 pounds a week in summer. She also made cheese and brewed their own beer – indeed James claimed that never in his whole life had he drunk 'raw water', believing beer to be much better for him, as long as it was home brewed.

Above 'Work was our pleasure' – James and Maria West in their 90s.

WORK WAS OUR PLEASURE

When a journalist asked what this hard-working couple used to do for pleasure, the response from the then 97-year-old James West was incredulous.

Pleasure? It was all pleasure. Our work was pleasure. I had my cows to look after, and she made butter and cheese, and at night when it was dark and there was no more work I could do I'd sit by the fire and she'd sit across from me sewing and darning socks and we'd talk. That was pleasure. You can take it from me, that was pleasure – work.

The couple put their good health and longevity down to hard work and wholesome homemade fare.

He continued to work his way up carefully, rearing his growing family of 14 on what became a hundred-acre farm with cows, pigs and working horses. The boys helped on the farm as soon as they left school and several went on to become farmers themselves. At one stage James was employing 30 men on his farm.

James West saw many changes in his long farming life, especially mechanisation. 'I went through all the changes,' he said, 'and they were for the best.' He had some regrets, of course, such as the disappearance of the old custom of local landowners killing a bullock or two at Christmas for the estate employees. But he was certainly old enough to remember the bad times, such as lanes where the ruts were so deep that the bottom of the cart scraped the road surface, and his own lack of schooling – he had never learnt to read. He remembered cutting turf from the common as fuel for their winter fires and the pleasure of baking potatoes 'practically every night'. In 1913 the farm was put up for auction and the stock included three active and powerful young cart horses, a yearling cart colt, an active nag mare, nine Shorthorn and Guernsey cows, a dozen heifers, a roan Shorthorn bull, a Sussex sow and seven fat hogs and 50 head of poultry. The animals were listed by name – the horses included Flower, Captain, Smiler and Topsy, and the cows had the classic names such as Daisy and Rose. The long list of agricultural equipment included as the star lot a set of traction threshing tackle by Tasker & Son, with a 7hp traction engine, 54-inch threshing machine, stacking elevator and clover cleaner, alongside an assortment of wagons, manure carts, market and dog carts, ploughs, cultivators, harrows, drills, reapers and self-binders, mowing machines, rollers, swath turners, horse rakes, tedders, turnip cutters, cake crackers, chaff cutters, rick poles, harness, blacksmith and engineering tools and a portable forge – everything a farmer needed.

Making it work

In 1938, William Kerr migrated from Scotland to East Anglia to try his luck. Like several Scottish farmers at the time, he used a mixture of thrift, hard work and a shrewd business sense to make a success of farming where the locals had failed. He left Ayrshire to rent 400 acres at Easton in Suffolk, finding the farm in a shocking state. In that first year he planted 70 acres of sugar beet, a crop he had never grown before. Come the war, like many other farmers he found opportunities for expansion, especially in supplying milk for the retail market as a sound basis from which he could expand his business into cereals and vegetables. He long remembered the big step of buying his first combine harvester and replacing his Suffolk horses with Fordson tractors. By 1954 he was able to buy two farms that he had been renting, amounting to 640 acres. By the late 1980s, after adding other 'bits and pieces', his family owned 1500 acres and farmed another 2500 acres under various leases, management agreements and consultancies. William's son John was running the business then and growing mainly winter wheat and winter barley – and still growing lots of sugar beet, along with potatoes, and also field vegetables for freezing. They milked a herd of 250 dairy cows, fattened 30,000 turkeys a year and had a successful farm park attracting more than 50,000 visitors annually. They employed 27 full-time workers and many more casual and seasonal ones, and they featured in Howard Newby's six-part television series, *The Countryside in Question*, as an example of how farming was changing at a time when only two per cent of the British population was engaged in farming. Canny people, those Scots.

So are Yorkshiremen. In the West Riding, before World War II, 57 per cent of all the dairy farmers who had registered with the Milk Marketing Board (created in 1933) were milk producer-retailers in thickly populated districts. Most of this type of farmer would depend heavily on bought-in feeding stuffs and were thought of as 'wasters of cows', buying them when in full yield and selling them when they were worn out. But not all were like that. During the war ER Greenwood was farming at Poplars Farm, virtually in the city of Bradford. The land that he farmed

Below: Farmer ER Greenwood of Poplars Farm, Bradford, in the early 1940s.

LONDON'S DAIRY FARM

In 1945 there was a dairy farm within a mile of St Paul's Cathedral in London, just behind the Mint in Swedenborg Square. Here, David Carson (known as Dave to everyone in the London docks) had a small retail milk shop facing the street. Behind it he had a byre in which he kept about a dozen cows and above each stall was a name: Doll, Maude, Alice, Mary, Kitty and so on. They were all kept in fine condition and were groomed daily; the byre was frequently mucked out and its brick floors sluiced with plenty of water to keep them dairy-clean. Of course Daisy and the gang never saw a field, nor did they stay with Dave for long: his method was to buy in middle-aged cows, keep them for about nine months (the length of a cow's pregnancy, incidentally) and then dispose of them. He had started working in this dockland dairy at only nine years old, for the then owner William Jones. During the war, with the continuous air raids of 1940, incendiary bombs often fell into the cowshed and one night seven high-explosives and a land-mine fell within an area of about 200 square yards. There is no mention of what happened to the cows under this rain of fire and one can only wonder what the onslaught must have done to their milk yields and general welfare.

was by nature poor and acid, on millstone grit, watered by a gentle rain of soot from industrial Bradford, and set on very steep slopes – hardly ideal for dairying. During World War I, Greenwood had served three years in the army and by the time he got home he found there was no room for him on the family farm. He found Poplar Farm, more or less derelict at the time, and he became a tenant of 30 acres. Off he went to Otley and bought six heifers, driving them home himself as he couldn't afford to pay for someone else to take them. By that weekend he had his first milk cheque, for £14, and from then on he never looked back.

In 1924 Greenwood took over his brothers' milk business, with a round of 50 gallons a day, still relying on the 30 acres at Poplar Farm. For five years he had to battle against a rash of dairy combines that seemed determined to drive small farmers such as himself off the city streets. They beat his round down to 25 gallons, but he was not a man to be beaten. He had attended winter night classes at Leeds University from 1921 to 1923 and got to know Professor McGregor. With his milk round declining, he called on the professor and other experts for advice, and they suggested he should offer something that the others had not got; he should, in effect, find a niche market. His niche turned out to be the new Grade A milk and he quickly won back his trade. In 1929 he and his wife (who did all the cooling and bottling) won the Yorkshire Clean Milk Competition. Being a sound marketing man, he shouted about his competition success to all and sundry and sent a charabanc into the city every Wednesday afternoon with big placards saying: 'Come to Greenwood's – showing the milking.' Mums and their children would come to the farm in the charabanc and someone from the university would talk to them about milk. From then on, the Greenwoods had more customers than they had milk.

There are many different types of farmers, and many different types of farms. Around the time of World War I many of the large old estates were being sold off, often broken up into smaller and smaller chunks. With their disappearance there vanished a major source of social cohesion in the countryside. The estate was in effect an extended village; the majority of the local rural population worked either for the estate itself or for its tenant farmers, and often the actual village had been built or rebuilt by the owner of the big estate. Some estates had been handed down within the families of lords for several generations; others had been built up more recently by men who had made their wealth in industry, some of whom became good squires and looked after their tenant farmers as well as those who worked for them direct on

the home farm or as domestic servants. Others cared little for the villagers and smallholders and farmworkers; the estate was their plaything, a place where they could show off their wealth and influence, a place where they could build

Above: Rick building on the Cornish Quethiock estate.

Opposite: John Demmol milking at Swedenborg Square, London, 1943.

LAST COW KEEPER IN LIVERPOOL

In 1975 the last cow keeper in Liverpool went out of business. He used to feed his cows on grass at Everton Football Club's training ground. Also in the 1970s there was a dairy farm, milking Guernseys, if I remember rightly, in Petersham Meadows beside the Thames at Richmond, Surrey. It was a popular attraction for Londoners, who would stream in to watch the cows being milked twice a day. No doubt it made city folk believe, for just a short while, that they were out in the countryside far, far away from the traffic, noise and hurry of town life.

Above: Colonel Algernon Bonham Carter (wearing a tie) examining the prize-winning hops on his estate at Buriton, Hampshire. Hops were grown locally for about 150 years but production finally ceased in the late 1960s.

themselves a grand house, a place where they could enjoy a country lifestyle but escape back to the city whenever it palled.

In 1893 Richard Heath published a book that brought together various papers he had written for different periodicals between 1870 and 1884. He had undertaken a series of 'pedestrian tours' in various parts of the country in the early 1870s, during which he chatted with all sorts of 'English peasants'. One part of Heath's book was entitled *The Cottage Homes of England*, written in 1870 when rural workers' cottages may have appealed to artists but were 'in most other respects a scandal to England'. This was at a time when farmers and landowners still felt prosperous and reasonably confident of the future – so much so

that in 1870 WH Hall created a colony of 150 small farms or allotments near Cambridge, and similar experiments were being set up by others elsewhere. Perhaps they had read Heath's wry comment:

There are times when the yearnings of humanity claim to be heard, and when those who, from any motive, good or bad, have allowed themselves to be carried away by the tendencies of the day, will be forced to exclaim with the greatest of modern English agriculturists, 'It is a melancholy thing to stand alone in one's country. I look around, and not a house is to be seen but mine. I am the Giant of Giant Castle, and have eaten up all my neighbours.'

The Farmstead

The farmstead was an organic creature – an apparently haphazard collection of buildings created at a farmer's whim to meet an immediate need, but somehow evolving into a cohesive whole, settled comfortably in the landscape, however disparate the styles and materials of each structure.

This is not always true, of course. The Victorian era (1837–1901) started with the birth of the railway network and tiptoed into the very beginning of the age of the internal combustion engine on the farm, passing along the way through a period of great agricultural prosperity and a contrasting one of depression. It was also a period in which the builders of new farmhouses, farm cottages, farmyards and any other structure in the countryside began to lose touch with the vernacular and created buildings that were irrelevant to their region and often inappropriate to their environment. Modern farmyards, especially those developed since World War II, seem alien in their setting, too hard in their lines, too much like rural factories, with too much concrete surfacing and industrial materials, and not even a nod in the direction of the vernacular.

The Farmhouse

In some parts of the country, farmhouses used to be in the heart of a village. In the 1960s there was still a working farm right at the heart of the coastal South Hams village of Thurlestone and it was typical of its kind: a dairy farm, with stone cowhouses clustered close to the stone farmhouse. Villagers could buy their milk fresh from the cow, warm, creamy, yellow and frothing. For those who had left the village but yearned for the tastes of memory, the local shop would helpfully send cartons of clotted cream from the farm by post and include a hand-written note updating them on local gossip. Now, that was service!

There was a delightful old farmhouse on the other side of the large area of woodland from my cottage in the 1970s; its frontage was Georgian, but behind the tidy façade was a much older farmhouse. This old house, known as Songhurst, had been displaced as the main farmhouse by a smart new one built at the top of the hill in the 1920s.

The old farmyard had crumbled but the vintage cider-apple orchard still produced an abundance of fruit, to the delight of one particular cow in the farm's milking Ayrshire herd: she would gorge on windfalls in the early autumn and became quite tiddly on the fermented apples. The farmer fed sound apples to the rest of the herd as a treat anyway, believing that they did wonders for milk yields. Half a century later, the widow of the farmer who had built the new house still liked to wander down the lane to the old house with a small milk-can in her hand, so that she could collect warm milk fresh from the udder in the milking

Bobbolds farmhouse, Milland, set within a courtyard of barns and other farm buildings.

parlour. It was not as she remembered it in her youth, of course: the old farmyard had been replaced by modern buildings, including a vast Dutch barn that an airline pilot told me he and his fellow pilots used as a landmark when they were flying into Gatwick.

Naturalist, farmer, sportsman and author Aubrey Seymour, born in the last years of the 19th century, found himself in a rambling old farmhouse in Warwickshire when he was 20 years old. It was a hodge-podge of a place, built of stone and with wisteria scrambling right across its face. The centres of the steps to the cellars were saucer-shaped, worn down by generations of barrels of farm-brewed cider, and on the damp floor of the cider cellar were lots of newts. The previous occupant had used some of the rooms in the house as granaries

and he had also stored the wool clip from several years of shearing in one of the bedrooms (he couldn't be bothered to sell the wool, because he didn't need the money). Seymour was lucky; there are farmhouses where, in difficult times, farmers have stored much worse stuff than grain and wool in their homes. A Welsh farmer used to keep calves in his Cotswold drawing room in the days of the agricultural depression in the 1880s. The Grange, a fine Queen Anne house opposite the castle in the Surrey town of Farnham, once showed evidence of manure having been stored in what is now a splendid panelled drawing-room. My own humble Victorian farm cottage was used within living memory to shelter pigs, with barn owls contentedly roosting upstairs.

Top: Farmstead at Slinfold, Sussex. The farmhouse fits seamlessly with adjacent farm buildings, built with the same materials and structural style.

Inset: A fine medieval manorial farm building, Hawkshead Courthouse, in the Lake District. The farm had once belonged to Furness Abbey. It was given to the National Trust in 1932 and was a forestry depot when this photograph was taken in the 1950s.

Above left: Interior of a Kentish farmhouse.

Above right: Inside an old Welsh farmhouse kitchen.

The backside

Many a mid-Victorian farmer added a drawing-room wing to his house in prosperous times and often there was a dining room or parlour. The dining room was rarely used for dining, except on big family occasions; it became the farm's office and often remains so today. It was the back of the house where life was lived, especially in the big family kitchen. The back rooms usually included a scullery, a larder, the wash-house with its copper or boiler, perhaps a pump house with a big sink, and in many old farms a dairy and a salting house with granite troughs for salting pig meat, which might later be hung in the farmhouse bacon-loft to be smoked over the wood fire.

The kitchen was the warm, living heart of the farmhouse and its fire was often the only source of heat: it was always alight, even if only glowing from a great big log at the back of the fireplace that could be sparked into life when necessary by a puff of the bellows. By the end of World War I some farms had enormous iron kitchen ranges as well, which heated up more quickly than the open fire and did not need so much attention to keep them going. Here the farmer's wife cooked not only the household's meals but also potatoes and meal for the poultry, pigs and calves.

The all-in-one

Before the huge advances in agriculture from the 18th century onwards, one of the main principles of farm buildings was to put everything under one roof – including the farmhouse. The longhouse is typical of this arrangement, particularly in the West Country, but the idea of housing livestock in a building that was integral to human housing was widespread throughout the country for many centuries.

Brickkiln was a magical derelict farmhouse hidden away in sunlit sheltered meadows surrounded by many acres of woodland and approached by muddy paths. When I first discovered it

CHIMNEY FIRES

When a good fire had been kept going for some time in the farmhouse's big open fireplace, there would often be a build-up of soot that would quietly burn and smoulder away to itself for days until somebody sniffed a problem. The solution was instant: a shotgun was fired straight up the chimney. Less dramatically, a large holly bush was pushed up and down the inside of the chimney to clean it, or bunches of goose feathers.

in 1970, all that you could see was a big scramble of ivy reaching skywards as it surrounded an invisible chimney; the rest of what remained of the building was completely engulfed in brambles and shrubbery. Over time, I gradually worked out what lay beneath the cloak of undergrowth. The most obvious structure was a boastful brick farmhouse with a large inglenook at either end and quite an imposing front door set above two or three brick steps. Stairs to the upper floor were almost climbable but the roof tiles had long since been removed to deter squatters and the upstairs rooms were open to the skies. There was a crumbling wooden stairway down into a cellar dairy; there were long slate-topped benches in this cool, damp room, lit at one end by a half-window at ground level. The house had clearly been built to impress in a time of agricultural prosperity. All those hopes and aspirations now lay in ruins.

Far more interesting was the original small home to which this brick showpiece had been added. The newer brick house formed the top bar of a T but the leg of the T was a very old structure indeed, with wattle-and-daub walls in a timber framework. It had the worm-holed remains of a tiny, steep winding staircase leading up to a sleeping loft. There was a single downstairs room and a superb roof (originally tiled or thatched) that swept almost down to the ground at the back and side, wrapping the old cottage in a warm embrace – warm, indeed, as part of the roof covered what had clearly been housing for the animals. A door near the staircase led directly from the main room into the cattle shed.

Such close proximity of the farming family with their animals persisted in some parts of the country into the 20th century. Originally, there would have been very little between house and housing. Cows would have peered over a partition into the kitchen, the gentle steam of their breath mingling with the steam of the cooking pot and the smoke of the inglenook fire; chickens would have wandered freely into the family's quarters. Over the centuries dwellings gradually pulled away from their cowhouses, blocking out the cows' prying eyes, shutting out those wandering hens, and in the end the farmhouse did not share even a party wall with the animal buildings, which became further and further removed as the farmhouse retreated from the farmyard.

Below: Thatched longhouse (in Tolpuddle, Dorset, in the 1940s), originally designed to shelter livestock as well as the farmer's family under one roof.

LIVING TOGETHER

In Devon and Wales you can still find longhouses with evidence of mangers in one part of the house, and you can so easily imagine the comforting sounds and smells of the cows that used to live so close to the family.

In some areas the family quarters were also right next to hay and grain storage areas, which must have invited too close companionship with rodents. This arrangement was typified in the 'laithe barns' or 'laithe houses' of the northern counties, and in a different dimension in the byre-houses of Durham and the 'bastle' of the Borders: these two-storeyed buildings had the cattle on the ground floor, with the farmer's family living above them. The idea of 'all-in-one' buildings persisted in the north within living memory and new ones were still being built in the early 19th century.

The Farmyard

The farmyard is the beating heart of a working farm and it is here as much as out in the fields that the huge changes in farming over the past century or two can best be seen. On the bigger farms and the grand estates the buildings were designed to enhance the property and proclaim the landowner's wealth and prestige.

Above: Cottage and cartshed between the wars at Houghton, Sussex.

Below: A typical smallholding in the early 1880s.

Among them were the various model farms of the 18th and 19th centuries, sometimes with buildings so fanciful and elegant that the animals and their stockmen felt almost embarrassed to use them. They were usually designed by London architects, who had surely never muddied their boots or mucked out a cowshed, cut the curd or boiled up pig swill, turned the handle of a root cutter or pitched a forkful of hay up into the loft.

Long before Queen Victoria became a grandmother, farmyards were beginning to be seen as industrial units, the 'farmer's manufactory', and in the 1860s there was a more scientific approach to their design: as livestock breeding improved, the buildings to accommodate the animals also improved. Many old farmyards, however, remained ramshackle collections of buildings that simply evolved, bit by bit, to suit the farmer's needs (one of the chief characteristics of farmers is their ingenuity and their ability to create something useful out of whatever happens to be to hand). Yet they were often the essence of vernacular architecture and gave a strong sense of local identity. Built of local materials, they were thoroughly practical, often with little heed to their visual impact in the landscape but somehow part of it, growing out of it and disappearing back into it when they finally collapsed.

Muck and middens

A wandering lane runs quietly between two hamlets some four miles apart, through a soft English lowland landscape of pasture and arable fields broken occasionally by lone stone cottages. A handful of these cottages – no more than three or four – makes a loose cluster near a small rural church that otherwise appears to be in the middle of nowhere. The church is next to a rather beautiful old farmyard, with a large old stone and timber barn, forming one side of

a courtyard of stone and timber farm buildings under mossy mellow tiled roofs. As you approach from the lane, you can see on the far side of the yard an archway through the buildings leading the eye up a long, straight garden path to the heavy wooden front door of a fine old Jacobean three-storeyed stone farmhouse that was once the home of an ironmaster.

Close to the centre of the yard is an octagonal stone structure, its walls perhaps three feet high, with big, age-bleached oak uprights supporting an octagonal tiled roof. This is a midden – a somewhat fancy but originally practical place for storing dung from the cowhouses surrounding the cobbled yard.

Today there are no carthorses or haywains in that middened farmyard but it has not yet suffered the fate of so many, which is for all the yard buildings to be turned into desirable residences or holiday cottages, or, more often, into granny annexes, playrooms, swimming pools, private squash courts and the like, where the big barn itself has been converted into an expensive house and the old yard has been paved, planted and primped into a courtyard garden around an ornamental pond. The ghosts of cattle and poultry that used to roam there, along with the farmworkers who worked there, are quietly cackling and tittering to themselves at the sight of the aspiring classes lounging where there used to be muck.

Above: A timeless farmstead in Snowdonia.

Shants, shippens, garners and clobber

During World War II, landgirl Rachel Knappett worked on a farm that had a wonderful jumble of buildings fairly typical of many farmsteads of the time. She had never seen any yard with so many convenient places for dumping what the men on the farm described as 'clobber'.

Most of the buildings lay along the yard on the far side from the house. The block attached to the back of the house consisted of the shant, the garner, the cellar and the pony's loose-box. The shant was an old slate-roofed brick building with a big fireplace and chimney in one corner, a sloped floor paved with stone, big beams festooned with cobwebs and one small window. It was the farm's central meeting-place, where the men ate their dinner perched on forms surrounding a wooden table.

Every inch of wall in the shant was taken up by hanging clobber: saws, spades, rakes, ropes, trowels, scythes, harness, bits of machinery, hats, coats, waterproofs, scarves, old boots and

waterproof trousers, and shelves that held dozens of paint pots, brushes, animal medicines, balls of string, hammers and boxes of nails, mostly covered with dust and all kept 'just in case'. Next there was an equally useful cellar for storing things, and above the cellar was the garner, up a few shallow steps from the level of the yard. In theory a garner is a place where corn is kept, but not on this farm. Whenever Rachel had finally given up looking for something in the shant, one of the men would say, 'Well, go and 'ave a gradely look oop garner.' In the garner she might find a few sacks of corn for the horses but she would also find drawers full of carpenter's tools, bits of harness, decaying machinery and derelict pieces of rusty metal parts that might come in handy some time.

The shant, garner, cellar and loose-box stood in a compact square and were all of the same age, whereas the rest of the buildings that rambled along on the other side of the yard were a complete

Below: A fine three-storey Jacobean farmhouse at Linch, Sussex, photographed in 1950.

mishmash of styles, shapes and ages. The two modern Dutch barns, one large and one small, were 'practical, convenient and hideous' in comparison with the inconvenient but beautifully proportioned old mellow brick barn with its high pointed roof on enormous, rough-hewn oak beams. This barn would be stacked to the eaves with sheaves of corn at harvest.

Tacked at right angles to the back of the barn was a long building divided by brick walls into three: two stables and a shippen. Each old-fashioned stable contained three stalls, and these were impregnated with the smell of generations of horses. Above the stables was a hayloft, and in the loft above the shippen seed potatoes were stored in winter. The word shippen, or shippon, is not a loose pronunciation of sheep pen but is generally a building for cattle. This particular shippen was a big, square brick-floored area with a low-beamed ceiling and divided by a narrow passage known as a raunge, complete with gutter to make mucking out easier. It had been built to house a dozen cows tied by chains attached to iron stakes and stone slabs but had been used for storing clobber for years, as the farm had ceased to be a dairy farm.

The space between the brick barn and the stable was known on the farm as the 'proven place' and was said to be an old threshing floor harking back to the days of flails: there was a gap in the barn's brick wall through which sheaves would have been thrown to the flailers in the proven place. It may or may not be coincidence that, in Rachel's time, the proven place was used for storing the horses' provender, along with a small engine for chopping their hay, a bin for their oats and an old bath in which their food was mixed.

At the back of the farmhouse the yard had a wooden boiler house with a corrugated-iron roof. Beside it was a stone trough where the tiny chat potatoes

Above: 'Uncle Perce' Heath thatching a farmyard shed with coppiced chestnut shavings.

for the pigs were washed before being boiled in the old brick copper and then 'pummered' in an old iron bath and mixed with pig meal. In a dark corner was a collection of drums and cans containing paraffin, dirty tractor oil, petrol, lubricating oil, and a large pile of rags. Next to the boiler house was a row of pig-cotes, only one of which contained pigs. The rest contained yet more clobber – logs, coke, coal, bags of sand, shale, sawdust, hoes, forks, wagon wheels, old car seats and the like.

The cart shed was a large three-walled brick building, with its open front facing the yard. The floor had been covered with clay 'to make it smooth' but this turned into sticky mud when the rain blew in. Next to the cart shed was the farm office, which had recently been used as a farrowing pen for the sows. On the other side of the shed was a lean-to known simply as George's Place, in honour of a blacksmith and wheelwright who had been dead for many years but who had once worked the old forge and bellows that still stood there. George's Place was 'the greatest of all clobber places'.

The barn

As mechanisation increased, the older buildings had to be adapted and the barn is a good example. Originally a barn (the word actually means barley house) was where corn was hand-threshed by men wielding flails while working up a good old sweat. It required a suitably paved or boarded floor, cover overhead to keep the grain dry during the work, and large doorways on either side of the big central threshing area to provide a good winnowing draught. The doorway on one side was high enough to admit a laden wagon; the one opposite could be lower, as an exit for the now-empty cart. Threshing

barns usually had bays on either side of the central area where the crop could be stored, piled ceiling-high. Sometimes a bay had a loft, used as a granary or even as somewhere for farmworkers to sleep. When flails were replaced by travelling steam threshing gangs, the barn became a quieter place, used simply to store hay and straw, and it remained in that role after the combine harvester took over from steam and did everything from cutting the crop and separating out (threshing) the grain to binding the straw into bales, making the farmyard hayricks and straw ricks but a memory.

There were as many different designs and styles of barn as there were farmers to invent and adapt them to their own needs. The essence of a barn is size and any carpenter will tell you the joy to be found in examining the basic wooden framework needed to support a large area of roof. When you look closely at the wooden skeleton of a barn, you can only marvel at the combination of simplicity and engineering brilliance of

Below: Thatched timber Sussex barn and a well-loaded manure cart.

BARN CONSTRUCTION

*Barns were constructed in bays, each bay being the
area between the paired principal posts or uprights that
ran from the ground up to the eaves and the horizontal
timber ties that kept the sides of the barn from collapsing
inwards. The sides might be of local stone, flint, cob,
brick, timber boarding, or wattle (with or without
daub), or a combination of these materials, and the
huge roof was very often thatched, partly because
thatch was less weighty (and cheaper) than tiles.
Some barn roofs are gloriously organic, rippling and
sweeping smoothly and seamlessly over high door
porches and hips, sometimes rolling down almost
to the ground to cover side aisles or outshots where
the farmer might keep anything from implements
to animals. The flow of the roofline is halted where
harsh modern materials such as corrugated iron
have replaced the original roofing – and even
where local stone or mellow clay tiles have been
used they somehow detract from the feeling of
oneness with the setting if the roof has been
freshly raftered and lathed and looks all neat
and tidy and straight.*

*Above right: Barns
being demolished at
East Hanney in the
Vale of the White
Horse, revealing the
skill of the original
carpentry.*

*Right: Fourteenth-
century tithe
barn at Bredon,
Worcestershire.
Note the bailiff's
'solar' above the
south-facing porch,
approached from
the outside by a
stone staircase.*

the construction and you will probably be reminded of timber-frame domestic housing and also of the great wooden ships that helped the British to colonise large parts of the world and to protect their own shores from invaders. You might also be reminded of churches and cathedrals, and in some cases fortresses: those slits that are so often a feature of barn walls might simply be for ventilation, or they might, if you find that they are wider inside than out, have been a sharp-shooter's defence post many centuries ago. They also offer useful nesting crannies for birds and were sometimes deliberately designed to allow rodent-hunting owls good gable-high access to the barn. In some solidly built barns, the mason or bricklayer has used his creative skills to produce ventilation gaps in interesting shapes and patterns, rather than simple slits.

The granary

Where grain is stored, there are bound to be rodents. That is one reason why purpose-built granaries were usually set up off the ground, supported by mushroom-shaped staddle stones or by brick pillars a few courses high topped by an overhanging stone or sheet to deter the animals from climbing into the building. The air gap beneath the floor also served to keep the building dry, so that the grain did not go mouldy in storage.

Thus a granary is basically a building on legs, and it might look like any old wooden shed or might be a more robust structure, sometimes built in brick or stone, perhaps based on a timber-frame building whose walls were originally infilled with wattle-and-daub but later with something more solid. Quite often granaries were hexagonal (especially on model farms or where a large estate took an interest in its tenant farmers' yards) and many were thatched. Sometimes the concept of legs is extended by incorporating a granary as another storey on top of, say, an open-fronted cart shed, or less often over a stable or cowhouse, and usually approached by outside steps at the top of which a small landing, one step down from the level of the base of the granary door, jutted out over the step to deter rodents. As an added precaution, there might be a cat-hole in the door and perhaps somewhere under the steps for the farm dog, who would also guard the treasure from human thieves (a reason why quite a few small granaries are built close to the farmhouse).

The engine house

With the coming of mechanisation in the farmyard, men with flails were no longer needed in the barn and by the early 19th century their muscle power was replaced by other sources of energy such as water, wind, steam and horses. Sometimes a wheelhouse, horse track or engine house, in which the 'engine' was horse-driven, would be tacked against a barn, usually at the back (it was also known as a gin gang or pound house when the engine was used for purposes other than threshing, such as crushing cider apples). At first as many as four to six horses or oxen were needed to power the threshing engine, which was basically a wooden or iron wheel on an upright spindle connected to a horizontal overhead shaft that ran into the barn. The machine itself inside the barn worked on the principle of a peg-studded drum revolving within a concave cover so that the grain was beaten off the straw as it went round. The grain dropped into a bin and the straw was separated away, while the horses continued to trudge round and round in circles to turn the wheel. By the

Above: Thatched cart shed in Hampshire, about 1900.

nature of their work, the engine house was usually circular or polygonal, with a conical, polygonal or pyramid-shaped roof – quite an elegant little building. By about the middle of the 19th century, most of these horse-powered threshing machines were being replaced by the power of steam, or by water-driven wheels.

Where steam was used in the farmyard an iron chimney pipe, or sometimes a more elaborate and boastful towering factory-like chimney of stone, slate and tile, was needed to carry away the hot smoke and especially the fire's sparks, highly dangerous around straw and hay. Portable steam engines were more popular than stationary ones needing their own building. Like a modern tractor, portable steam engines could be used to drive a belt, which turned a wheel and rotated the shaft of whatever machine the engine was driving.

The cart shed

Cart sheds were invariably open-fronted and usually open on at least three sides. They needed hard, dry floors (beaten earth, paving and so on) and eaves high enough to allow horse-drawn carts to

Opposite top: A Tudor granary being re-erected at the Lackham School of Agriculture in Wiltshire, presented by the Marquis of Bath.

Opposite bottom: An 18th century granary re-erected at the Avoncroft Museum of Buildings. The large space beneath the granary served as a cart shed, and dog kennels were built into the brick stairway.

Right: A typical old cow 'hovel'. Today this farmyard's extensive barns and buildings have been converted to residential and leisure use.

move easily in and out. They often served two purposes, having a loft above for storing hay, straw or grain. When horses gave way to the internal combustion engine, tractors were equally grateful for the shelter of a cart shed and the floor would be concreted so that the shed could double up as a workshop. As tractors and implements got bigger and more complicated, they also became more expensive and needed more care and maintenance; the old open cart shed was no longer good enough, nor were its eaves high enough.

LONESOMES

One of the most beautifully simple cart sheds I have seen was out in a field known as Lonesomes, tucked in the corner by the woods. It was no more than some very substantial oak pillars, possibly recycled from a ship and weathered by the oceans, supporting a gently undulating raftered roof of old clay peg tiles. There were no walls of any kind and there was not a nail in the place: all the joinery was by means of good fit and wooden dowels. Sadly, rabbits had been burrowing for at least a century under its dry earth floor and the whole structure was slowly subsiding. There was no sign of it when I returned to Lonesomes a quarter of a century later.

The stables

When plough horses, and before them oxen, were the big muscle power on the farm, stables were an important feature of the farmyard. Stables were more likely than cowhouses to have an airy loft, as much to insulate these precious working animals against extremes of heat and cold as a place to store hay and bedding straw, and with much more head space between the animals and the loft ceiling than in cowhouses. In many ways, stables were similar to cowhouses: they had wooden partitions making stalls for individual horses, or sometimes pairs, but the stalls were roomier than for cows. There were head-high hay racks and low feeding troughs, and they were fitted with tethering rings at the front of the stalls. There would be a tack room or recess where harness equipment was hung on wooden pegs and a wooden corn bin held the horses' fodder. The floor would usually be of slabs, cobblestones or brick, with drainage channels to take away urine. On some farms the horses had looseboxes, where they were not tied as in stalls and which gave them more space to mooch about. In others, they might have access to a yard, much like cattle, so that they could have even more freedom. A 'nags stable' was home to the farmer's lighter horses for driving and riding, not the big workhorses of the fields.

The cowhouse

Very often there was a low building tacked on to a barn, perhaps aligned with it at one end but more often at right angles. This might be the stable block, or might be where cattle were housed. Such a building was sometimes known as a hovel and might be no more than a long three-sided building with its open front, broken by posts supporting the roof, facing into a cattle yard so that the animals had the option of taking shelter from rain, snow, wind or hot sunshine or enjoying the fresh air. Other hovels, or stock sheds, adjoining barns might be fully enclosed byres, clad with timber or built of local stone or brick. Between them, the barn and the hovel made the beginnings of a yard.

TAKING SHELTER

It was in an open-fronted hovel that I used to hand-milk my Jersey cows in winter by the light of a camping lamp. Very cosy it was in there under its old tiled roof, snuggling against a cow's flank while the warm milk purled into the bucket. I was allowed one bay of the three-bay building, each bay separated with chunky oak rails, and here the cows would remain snugly warm during winter nights. The shed was a deep one and they could retire to its inner depths, or bask in the winter sun at the railed south-facing front of the shed if they had to be kept in for a while to avoid 'poaching' the meadow into a hoof-printed quagmire. We shared the shed with the gamekeeper's ferrets, skittering amongst themselves in hutches in the furthest bay. Chickens and pheasants wandered in and out as they pleased, scornful of the caged predators and very happy to mingle with the cows and their calves. Owls sometimes peered down from the rafters, bats and moths flittered in and out at dusk, and ivy crept through cracks in the walls.

Left: Old cowhouse in about 1850. The combination of top hats worn with smocks was common among farmworkers of the time.

CALF PENS

*On the dairy farm where I worked in the 1970s, calves were
kept with their mothers for the first four days in a makeshift
loose-box – no more than a corner of an old rather dark
cowhouse fenced off with hurdles. After four days the cow's
yellow colostrum turned into ordinary saleable milk and the
calf was removed from the mother, who went back into the
herd for normal milking in the parlour. These very young
calves were then transferred to the calf house, which was
simply an airy shed in which individual 'houses' were made
for them from straw bales, giving them a snug and secret
home of their own in which to recover from the shock of
losing their mums. In the wild, calves would anyway lie up,
hidden in undergrowth or long grass, while the cows returned
to the herd to graze, visiting at intervals to suckle the calves.
In the calf house, they would be suckled by a human-held
bottle or would be taught to drink their milk from a bucket.
As they grew a little older, the calves would be put into pens
to mingle in groups of the same age and learn to accept hay
and concentrates instead of milk. This was the start of their
very own herd and, as dairy heifers, they would probably
form bonds with the same group for the rest of their lives,
even when they all became part of the larger dairy herd.*

A couple of miles from my cottage was
the remote and derelict yard of a long-
vanished smallholding. Here, cows had
been kept in byres for the entire winter,
with never a chance to stretch their
legs; they were tied to their stalls, with
a manger at the head and just enough
slack in the chains to allow them to lie
down. A Polish friend told me about the
cows in her native land between the wars
who were kept in for the winter, but in
enclosed cowhouses with no natural light
at all. When the time came for the spring
turnout into the fields, their legs could
hardly support them and their eyes were
almost blind, yet they still tried to do
what all cows do at turnout: dance and
scamper and kick and buck with joy, their
udders swinging with gay abandon.

The bull pen

Bull pens began to come into their own
shortly before World War II, when cattle
breeding was increasingly scientific and
progeny testing was introduced. Progeny
testing meant calculating the breeding
potential of a bull by measuring the
performance of his offspring, especially the
milk yields of heifers. Before then, the bull
had run in the field with the herd or had
a stall within the cowhouse, or perhaps
his own box somewhere in the yard. After
the war, there were greater efforts to
give a bull a better life: he had access to
shelter, a yard of his own for a modicum
of exercise (albeit sometimes attached by
his nose ring to a chain sliding along an
overhead rail), a special box in which he
could perform his bullish duties, and all
sorts of safety devices to ensure that he
could not harm his handlers.

The dairy and the cheese room

The farm dairy was where the milk was
taken to be cooled, contained and where
appropriate processed. On the family

farm, the dairy tended to be a room within the farmhouse, often a cellar, where the farmer's wife and daughters performed their magic to turn liquid milk into something that would keep for longer than a couple of days before pasteurisation and refrigeration.

By the early years of the 19th century the farmhouse dairy was often designed and built for its purpose, with the need for hygiene and coolness in mind. There remained the problem that the dairy was some distance from the cowhouse, which meant that buckets of milk had to be carried across the yard, usually with the aid of a yoke across the shoulders, risking contamination along the way. Milk attracts bacteria in no time at all and from the mid 1880s a positive plethora of regulations sought to reduce this risk by firstly bringing the dairy closer to the cowhouse and secondly improving hygiene standards within the dairy itself. By the mid 1920s, many dairy farms had bowed to the regulations and their dairies were equipped with corrugated milk coolers and steam sterilisation. The milk was transferred into churns, which

Above: Taking the morning's milk from the cowhouse to the farm dairy.

were then taken to a roadside platform for collection by a commercial dairy company or transported by horse and cart to the railway station. The whey from cheesemaking was generally fed to the pigs and a few ingenious farmers installed underground pipes to carry the whey straight to the pigsties.

The pigsty

Pigs were common on dairy farms, slurping their way through the whey and other waste products, and they were also kept at the bottom of most cottagers' gardens. In the farmyard they might roam about at will, hoovering up all manner of waste, but usually they were confined

BULLY BOYS

By 1960 farm bulls were rapidly being replaced by men wielding artificial insemination tubes. The stud bull on my 1970s farm was luckier: the dairy farm did call in the AI operative for some of their cows, but they still liked to use a well-bred Jersey bull and some of the cows refused to have it any other way. It was noticeable that so-called 'silent heat' cows were more likely to display the characteristic signs of being in season if they could meander past the bull on their way to the milking parlour and say good morning.

to simple sties: a low run of small pig houses, each perhaps four to six feet square, with outdoor runs accessed by way of low doorways. Less often an open-plan, open-fronted house led directly into a small pig yard. In both situations the pigs could wander freely into their yard as and when they pleased. The same type of sties persisted well after World War II, though by then pigs were rarely seen in ordinary farmyards. Most had become part of a specialised pig industry and were either housed in arks of corrugated iron (and later igloos) in the fields or kept intensively in large factory-like buildings, where they might be crowded together indoors in communal strawed pens or, as sows, in narrow individual stalls where on the whole they had no room to turn around or to stretch out when lying down.

In the 1930s there had been a major period of expansion in Britain's pig industry, which inevitably meant increased intensification. The permanent indoor systems of the period included the popular Scandinavian or Danish design of completely enclosed buildings, with a central feeding passage running between long rows of pens and manure channels at the rear of the pens. Some preferred simple looseboxes with thick, warm walls and a ceiling or well-lined roof. An alternative permanent system was to add a small yard to the pighouse, or the pigs could use a partially covered yard with a roof covering about a third of the yard and supported on three sides by substantial walls, but with the front of the covered area open to the yard.

The logical extension of this system was to have access to a grass paddock directly from a covered pen, but this usually turned into a trampled quagmire – a problem that could be avoided by housing pigs in huts out on pasture. The huts might be built from straw bales and poles with a natural roof of straw, reed, heather or bracken and the whole thing could be burnt down every few years to get rid of any build-up of pests and diseases. More often the field huts were of metal, which would last well enough if galvanised or painted. Typically the huts were circular, making them stronger and easy to move: you simply tipped them on to their sides and rolled them to a new position. One farmer, pioneering a system of pig tethering out on pasture, ingeniously used the bodies of old cars and trucks for his sow houses but his fields looked rather like a scattered scrapyard.

The poultry yard

Chickens and other poultry – ducks, geese and turkeys – often had the freedom of the farmyard and scratched about in fields and the farmhouse garden, laying their eggs in unlikely places and perhaps roosting in the barn if they felt so inclined. If the farmer's wife wanted an easier life, laying birds would be encouraged to use wooden arks and portable wire runs in the field so that at least she could find their eggs. The serious producer wanting more than mere pin money might adapt an existing farm building to provide a poultry loft, perhaps over the pigsties or in the cow shed, with or without a little pop-hole and hen-sized ladder to give the birds access to the

Below: Corrugated iron pigsties with their own small yards.

great outdoors. Birds for fattening for the table were often kept in semi-darkness in quiet, warm houses of their own. It was after World War I that the poultry industry became more truly specialised and intensified.

Intensive livestock

Intensive livestock housing is not a modern idea. Even in the late 18th century a Northumberland farm was mass-producing eggs from a special building for its laying hens and was sending hundreds of thousands of eggs to London by way of Berwick-on-Tweed. By the turn of the 18th century some farmers were cramming hundreds of beef cattle into purpose-built housing and fattening them on factory-made oilcake, often imported. In the early 19th century veal calves were being reared on slatted floors in calf pens in Gloucestershire, lambs were fattened for Christmas in long, narrow housing on farms around London, and pigs in Essex were in pens so small that they could not turn round within them.

It was mainly in the cities that intensive housing was used for livestock. In London there were 8,500 dairy cows

in the Regency period and the capital was also fattening more than 50,000 pigs a year and a large number of beef cattle. The cows spent most of their time tethered in stalls within dark hovels knee-deep in manure, though they might be let out for a few hours during the day to exercise in yards, and this was their miserable life until the time they were slaughtered. The delightful idea of transporting cattle to pasture fields in wheeled cattle houses running on iron rails never caught on. Most of the dairy herds were in the vicinities of Gray's Inn, King's Cross, Paddington and Tottenham Court Road and no doubt the locals became inured to drinking milk produced under such filthy conditions.

Above: Somerset farmer's wife with her hand-reared livestock, Wincanton, Somerset 1900.

WIMPOLE

For the Wimpole estate, in Cambridgeshire, Sir John Soane (1753–1837) conceived a grandiose semicircular poultry yard that included a small house for the 'poultress', a fountain, a duck pond, a roosting house and hen house. This splendid concept was never built, nor was his 'Dove Cott' or his planned 'rustic' dairy, 'the front to be with wood'. Undeterred, he built a dairy at Betchworth in 1799, designed to look like a Greek temple (despite its thatched roof) with creeper-clad pillars. It was the style of the time to make country buildings look classical but it was not just flights of fancy and prettiness. The layout of model farms of the period aimed to make everything as labour-saving as possible.

Above: Farmers found many uses for old railway carriages. In the 1950s, when many railway lines were being closed, an imaginative employee of the Inverurie Locomotive Works sold off surplus carriages to local farmers in Aberdeenshire and the idea spread to other parts of Britain.

The farm office

Many a field on a livestock farm would have field shelters of various kinds for animals too far from the farmyard to come under cover in bad weather. But quite a common sight, especially after World War II, was that of apparently abandoned railway carriages in the fields, or even next to the farmyard buildings. They had a variety of uses: you could put chickens in them, roosting in the luggage racks, or use them to house seasonal farmworkers, or shepherds at lambing time, and, of course, you could store all manner of clobber inside as well.

Occasionally a railway carriage, complete with its scenic pictures, faded window curtains and comfortable upholstered seats, was used as what increasingly became one of the most important buildings on the farm – the farm office. Many farmers continued to use their dining-room table for their paperwork, but as the paper mountains increased along with the miles of red tape and regulations the larger farms needed proper accommodation for it all and for that new employee, the farm secretary or book-keeper, whose job it was to put everything in order once a week. Sometimes a whole room within the farmhouse became the office, but often a special office was built as part of the farmyard – a place where staff came to discuss matters with the farm manager, where field maps were spread out on tables, where commercial reps came to flog their wares, where telephones jangled and where, more and more, computers became standard equipment for farmers. Computers were also being used to identify cows, wearing transponders around their necks, so that they were automatically fed the correct ration for their stage of lactation and yield, as well as to hook them up to the milking machines. Who needs stockmen?

Working the Land

Out in the fields, the seasons hold sway and farmers continue to be dominated by daily weather fluctuations and the annual cycles of preparing the ground, sowing the seeds and then nurturing the crop through its stages of growth until it is ripe enough to be harvested and can be removed from the field so that the whole cycle can then start again.

In terms of what is actually grown, we still rely heavily on the big three: wheat for bread and other staple human foods, barley for brewing and for feeding to livestock, and oats for porridge and horses.

But crops are so much more than corn. Root crops, for example, have been important for generations, feeding both humans and livestock. Many a traditional farm has a hand-turned root chopper rusting away at the back of a shed, and I can still remember the aroma of mangolds growing in Wiltshire fields for cattle, the more delicate fragrance of turnips and the orange of the mashed swedes we were given for lunch as children.

The Crops

Today some of the older crops have become increasingly rare; some have become increasingly common and in many parts of the country the eye is blinded by the violent chrome yellow of oilseed rape, the scent of its honey-heavy flowers spreading headaches and hayfever to the vulnerable.

Hemp was once grown on a large scale as a fibre crop for rope making and was important in Lincolnshire and Norfolk. Linseed, or flax, is a soft haze of blue flowers in the morning and then, when you next look, the blue has vanished until tomorrow. Pulling flax and the subsequent retting processes (soaking to soften and partly rot the fibrous stems) were labour-intensive until the invention of mechanised pullers. In 1934 only 1,311 acres of linseed were grown in the whole of England and Wales and it was a difficult crop: it was tough to cut, even though by then it was being cut by horse-powered mowers rather than by hand, and the horses, as well as the blades on the mower, had to be changed frequently.

In the 1930s they were growing pyrethrum in Sussex: the crop was harvested by binder and taken direct to a factory at Billingshurst to make Keating's Powder. Teasels, the thistle-like heads of which were used for combing cloth, were grown in much of Somerset and occasionally in Yorkshire. Liquorice used

Above: Cutting linseed in 1935. The crop could be crushed for its oil and to make linseed cake as a feed for livestock.

Right: Women hand-pulling flax (the fibre from which linen is made).

to be grown in Lincolnshire and saffron in Cornwall as well as around Saffron Walden. Woad was still being grown on a farm at Boston in Lincolnshire up to 1930 for the dye market (especially for policemen's uniforms), though Ernest Pulbrook wrote in 1922 that the famous woad farm and factory at Parson's Drove, near Wisbech, had been closed. Peppermint was grown for its oil as a small local crop, expensive to cultivate. Mustard was grown in great yellow swathes across Norfolk and Cambridge. Brussels sprouts were familiar in Bedfordshire in particular, rhubarb around Leeds, asparagus in the Evesham vale, watercress in favoured places, early flowers in the Scilly Isles, flowers grown for seed in bright patchworks round Kelvedon and Coggeshall, fruit in Kent – there was always some crop waiting for help with the harvest. It might be whortleberries, or daffodils, or acorns for farmers' pigs, or apples and pears and raspberries, or wild rose hips for syrup, or elderflowers. Jennie Kitteringham, a student at Hull University in the early 1970s and the daughter of a dairyman, lived in the village of Ivinghoe Aston as a

child and remembered the vans that used to come to the village to collect the bags and bags of elderflowers that she and other children had picked.

One of the most important crops in some areas was potatoes, especially during World War II when they were deemed essential to the national diet, but in the early 1920s the British crop of the moment was sugar beet. It had taken its time: attempts had been made to introduce the growing of sugar beet in Britain half a century earlier but it was not until the government freed home-grown sugar from excise duty in 1922

Top: Fruit pickers in the Wisbech district, fresh from the London train, in the mid 1930s. The main local crops were gooseberries, plums and apples.

Above: Harvesting pyrethrum with an old binder (originally a horse implement) in 1937.

Above: Carting mangolds in 1938. The lifted roots were placed in heaps in the field and then covered with leaves to keep the early frosts away until they were ready for carting to the yard.

Below: A load of sugar beet on a fenland lighter at Nordelph in 1933.

that the situation began to change, and three years later substantial subsidies were introduced by way of encouragement to grow beet. The crop was grown on contract for the factories that soon sprang up. It was an expensive crop in terms of hand labour, with the fiddliness of singling the young plants and then the heavy work of lifting the crop. Bill Tull, in Sussex, recalled the labour of sugar beet in the 1930s, all of it 'manhandled':

Used to get all the ground ready, drill 'em and then you had to get out there and hoe and set them all out, and when it was ready to pull you had to pull 'em all by hand, three rows at a time, lay them in rows, leaves one way one row and leaves to leaves, chop 'em off, you had to put 'em in heaps, shovel 'em all up in a trailer and then take 'em to the railway station. Sometimes the fields was bad you had a job to get out. Then they found a way to lift them for some reason or other, wasn't so bad pulling then, all soaking wet, used to have sacks tied all the way round your legs. And of course to get a truck on, you only had two days to load this truck. The old station master if he knew he had a truck to come in he would put it all right down so that we were standing there and the truck was right up there … all we had to do was chuck it downhill.

Wartime farmers described this government-promoted sugar-producing crop as 'an infernal nuisance' (or something stronger). You didn't even feed it to your livestock, with the benefit of returning some of its goodness to the soil in the form of manure; sugar beet all went away from the farm to the sugar factories. The crop's chief merit was that it came with that government subsidy attached.

Tools

A huge range of tools and implements for use on the farm has fallen out of use, lingering in the back of sheds and barns or relegated to museums. When most farm jobs were done by hand a tool was devised for each task and some defy identification.

In the early 1930s, T Hennell had been touring farmyards all over the country for many years recording all the 'lumber' that accrued in piles. He was intrigued by all the 'wormy and twisted forms with their crust of fowl-dung', so jumbled that it was hard to work out their original character. He spent many a leisurely hour extracting the information he sought 'from a welter of daily common-places, the genial warmth of fire and beer bringing them ripely from the dwindling memories of the third generation back'. His book, *Change in the Farm*, published in 1934, chronicles what he learnt about the days when tools were simple and you could often make them yourself.

Not long after World War II, Edward G Bolton, a schoolmaster in Rutland, and his class were studying the Agricultural Revolution. To enliven the dustiness of book learning and classroom talks, he came up with the idea of a school museum. He realised that almost every farm and cottage in the area would have old bits and pieces tucked away in corners and the children started collecting. They gathered crooks, ointment horns, sheep-bells, turnip dobbers 'with one or two prongs for picking up the roots for trimming with a chopper', pecks, root-slicers, cooperage tools, cobblers' tools, thatchers' tools, wheelwrights' tools, horse brasses, dairy and kitchen equipment, lace-making and tatting paraphernalia, love-spoons and knitting sheaths made by sweethearts, skirt holders and goffering irons, sweathrakes, a wide range of dock lifters, draining scoops and crescent-shaped graft spades. They made recordings of his craft by one of the last of the local skilled dry-stone wallers and collected corn dibbers, saw-edge barley sickles, gathering rakes, stook-shifters, three-tine barley pitching forks, threshing flails, hummellers for removing barley awns, wooden barn-shovels, hicking barrows for humping filled sacks, bushel strikes for measuring corn, millstone nibs, a penknife for sharpening goose-quills, a working pole-lathe, a Kentish turn-wrest plough with large wooden wheels, a local wooden-beam plough and a heavy painted Lincolnshire wagon nearly a century old. They were most proud, though, of a mystery tool: a carved piece of iron, sweated on to a stem and set into a handle made from a piece of deer antler.

Below: Group of farmworkers in Loddiswell, Devon, with the tools of their crafts.

TOOL TALK

Around the farm there was talk of swingers, latten-bells, monkey-boxes, skidpans, oxbows, hermaphrodites, bavin-trucks, mufferers, mophrodites, bob-wheels, cheps, pillows, rice, shelve-ristes, one-way zuels, seed scuttles, fiddles, dodgers, unicorn teams, sneaths, nibs, tangs, brittle-bats, ripe-stricks, tumbling Jacks and tumble-down Dicks, pea-swaps, drashels, vliels, fringels, whangs, scries, hummellers, dashiel stabbers, louping staffs, spittles … ah, the richness of the language!

It was only when they discovered, quite by chance, that it had come from what had once been the home of a harness-maker that they realised it had been a useful tool for packing the stuffing into a horse-collar or saddle. For the children, the collection brought history to life.

Cultivations

Cultivation embraces everything that is done to the soil by a gardener but on a bigger scale. It is all that unglamorous work of preparation, without which the excitement and satisfaction of harvest cannot happen.

Major evolutions have taken place in cultivations within the last century or so, especially with the change from back-breaking handwork to horse work and from horses to machinery driven by steam and the internal combustion engine, and finally the replacement of some of the implements by spraying with chemicals.

Ploughing

Ploughing is the most basic of cultivations: it loosens and breaks up the ground and then inverts the topsoil so that all the trash and weeds are buried. This second stage of the plough movement is no longer so essential in these days of using herbicides to kill off the weeds, and for a while the antisocial practice of stubble burning after the harvest was another way of getting rid of the trash that earlier farmers might have considered to be useful organic matter that improved the soil's structure and fertility.

Ploughing is more than a skill; it is an art, in the sense that its traces are left on

Above: Horses and an iron-wheeled tractor working in harmony between the wars.

Right: Mrs Parham at work, with her chickens in attendance. There were ploughwomen as well as ploughmen, even before WLA girls took up the challenge.

Opposite: A Norfolk plough photographed in about 1880.

PLOUGHS AND PLOUGH PARTS

Just for the record, and for the joy of words: whippletrees or whiffletrees and swingle- or single-trees were the coathanger-like bits between the plough and the horses that distributed the load evenly and were connected to the horses by the trace chains; the pommeltree was the section at the front of the whippletree and had a chain running back to the hake, bridle or muzzle; the stilts were the handles by which the ploughman controlled the plough; the beam was mainstay of the whole implement, running from front to back; the coulter was the iron 'knife' that cut vertically into the soil, separating the new furrow from the unploughed land; the share was a triangular piece of iron with a sharp edge to make a horizontal cut, separating the furrow slice from the soil beneath it; the mouldboard or breast, which had a twist to it and was immediately behind the share, turned the furrow slice over; the slip land-cap or landside plate slid against the newly cut face of the furrow and stopped stones and loose soil falling into the body of the plough; the sole or slade slid along the bottom of the furrow and helped to support the plough.

A wheel plough usually ran on two wheels, occasionally only one, whereas a swing plough had no wheels at all and needed a highly skilled ploughman. There were double-furrow and three-furrow horse ploughs but it would need a tractor to make best use of multiple ploughs: steam tractors could plough up to a dozen furrows at a pass. There were turn-wrest ploughs, designed to turn the furrow in one direction only; there were horse-drawn balance ploughs, paring ploughs to slice off turf, ridging ploughs useful for potatoes, deep-digging gallows ploughs, ride-on or pole ploughs, three-wheeler 'flying dutchman' sulky ploughs, subsoil ploughs to break up the panned soil under the furrow and mole ploughs for land drainage.

That was just the horse-powered ploughs in Britain; there were plenty of other types in the colonies and in North America, and then a host of new plough designs once tractors became the drawing power. There was a whole lexicon of terms connected with ploughs, with plenty of local dialect versions of them as well, not to mention another host of terms to describe ploughing methods and patterns, furrow and ridge shapes, and measurements connected with ploughing and the implements used to make those measurements. It is perfectly possible to read an old agricultural implements catalogue purely for the pleasure of the vocabulary and the inventive phraseology of those seeking patents for their wares.

Above: A steam pulley plough in action, dragging the plough across the field.

the landscape for all to see, and it is also a statement of the vernacular. You used to be able to tell what part of the country you were in by the style of ploughing. Every ploughman had to take account of the shape of the field boundaries, the direction of the natural drainage, the depth of the soil, the needs of the crop and countless other variables that governed not just the pattern of the lines but also the type, shape, angle and size of the furrows and ridges. Ploughing was

a highly technical, almost mathematical challenge and it is not surprising that good ploughmen were among the cream of the farm's labour force.

Steam ploughing

Heavy land used to be described as three-horse or four-horse, referring to how many horses were needed to pull a single-furrow plough through it. Lighter soils would be two-horse land. In the early years of the 20th century, when horses were still ploughing the land, it was estimated that only about an acre could be ploughed in a normal eight-hour day. Plough horses averaged a speed of 1½ to 2 miles per hour and the ideal length of a furrow for horses was about 250 yards. A furlong (originally a furrow long) is 220 yards.

Horses had been competing with steam ploughs to some extent since the 1850s and 1860s. These were originally stationary engines at the edge of the field that simply reeled the plough towards them on a cable: one engine at one end of the field to haul it one way, and another opposite it to haul it back again, and then both engines had to be moved along the headland to start on the next haul. A typical steam plough could work at least a dozen acres a day (compared with the one acre of a horse plough), partly because it was faster and able to plough up to six furrows in one pass, and partly because it could work much longer hours than a horse. On a thousand-acre farm you needed two 16-horse-power ploughing engines and 900 yards of steel rope; these engines were capable of doing 10–15 acres

of ploughing or 15–20 acres of cultivating in a day. Very few farmers could afford the capital outlay required for their own steam ploughing sets and so they tended to rely on contractors.

The staff of a double-engine outfit usually consisted of a foreman, two drivers, a ploughman and a cook boy, all living in a caravan on site. The farmer would supply a horse and tumbril for carting coal for the engines and another two horses and a man for the water cart. Everybody recognised the whistle code: one short sharp blast meant stop, two shorts blasts for go ahead, and a long continuous note calling for more water or coal. The ploughman had his own signalling system to his mates on the engines: an arm held out horizontally meant go slower, a swinging arm told them to speed up and holding both arms up said stop.

Stationary steam cable ploughing continued within living memory. It was

Above: Steam ploughing, with a woman in the driving seat, at the Cambridge University Farm in 1917.

Left: Draining and ploughing the newly enclosed Viverdon Down in Cornwall. The project, started in 1890 by local squire William Coryton and intended to counteract mass local unemployment, took ten years to complete and provided much-needed work for displaced miners. A large number of hefty ploughs were made locally, each requiring a team of six horses and three men.

Opposite: Driving a tractor in World War II and not a safety cab or pneumatic tyre in sight.

a natural step to mobile steam-driven cultivation with traction engines and some mighty beasts were developed, such as the Hornsby steam caterpillar built in 1909 and actually designed for a coalmine in the Yukon. This splendid engine looked something like a railway engine bolted on to an army tank and in fact the design probably influenced the makers of the first tanks in the coming Great War.

All sorts of dramatic accidents happened with all that steam power, some of them very nasty indeed. Anyway, the steam frightened the horses and, as one farmworker complained in the hearing of an engineer from the firm of Hornsby: 'I've fed yer, I've give you a drink, and fathered yer and mothered yer – and now yer – yer 'oont go!' On the engine's cylinder lay a piece of bread, a handful of grass and a costrel of beer.

Motor ploughs and tractors

During the 1970s, the cornfields surrounding my Sussex cottage were alive to the joyous, lilting peewit call of lapwings, indulging in their glorious aerobatics. Back in 1934, D Johnson of Hereford was also particularly fond of peewits. In those days he was cultivating his fields with the help of horses and one of the joys of the work was being in contact with what was happening all

around. The birds made their rough and ready nests by scratching out a slight hollow in the soil of his arable fields. Just about the time they had laid their eggs in early May, the horses would come along to roll the corn as part of the regular cultivation cycle. There were two horses abreast, pulling the roller, and behind them was the horseman, controlling them with his lines. The horseman was always on the alert for the nests – but so were the horses. They would make a little sideways movement when they approached a nest and he would immediately stop them. As they stood patiently he would go under the horses, place the eggs to one side, move on a short distance, stop the horses again and replace the eggs in their nest. Never once did a horse tread on an egg.

By the 1970s, horses were no more than a memory in the fields and tractors had no such sensitivities towards eggs or anything else. Tractor drivers whom I knew in the 1960s were still alert to the other inhabitants of the fields and would leap off their vehicles to move eggs or transplant interesting seedlings, but then came the era of the compulsory safety cab, which isolated the driver from his surroundings and made it much more difficult for him to see or hear what his tractor was destroying. No wonder lapwings have become rare in many areas.

But it's all so much quicker with a tractor. Even before World War I the power and speed of steam was being challenged by oil and petrol motors, which could 'be adapted to any farm work, on about the same scale as horses'. These early tractors, often known as motor ploughs, moved across the field with the plough, just like horses, but it was a two-man operation: one to drive the tractor and another perched on the plough to operate levers controlling the depth of the ploughing and to steer the thing. At the time the most convenient was a paraffin-driven machine with a speed of 2–3mph, able to plough up to five acres in a day

Below: A big 25hp Mogul tractor, imported during World War I and made by the International Harvester Company of Chicago.

Above: A rare sight in 1933 – pneumatic tyres, on a Fordson tractor on display at the West Sussex County Council's demonstration farm near Chichester.

A BLINKERED VIEW

Ernest Pullbrook was perhaps wearing blinkers when he wrote in 1922:

Many regret the general introduction of machinery, declaring that all the poetry has gone from field operations. Certainly the tractor plough is not picturesque, especially one of those bluff nosed models which resembles some uncouth monster as it heaves into sight out of a hollow, enveloped in a cloud of vapour and shaking with stertorous breathings, but it is better than the steam plough pushing its many furrowed way across a large field like a huge spider. It will be a sad day when the teuf-teuf of the motor replaces the jangle of harness and the pleasant hiss of the plough cutting the furrow, and the reek of petrol is but a sorry substitute for the scent of newly turned earth. No doubt the hayfield lost something of its beauty when the line of men advancing with scythes flashing in the sunlight was supplanted by the mowing machine, but few can maintain that the progress of the harvesting machine, drawn by its team with tossing heads, throwing aside sheaf after sheaf in regular line, is a less pleasing sight than a group of men laboriously reaping with a sickle.
However, it will be long ere the team is banished from the field, and those with time to idle may still watch its varied work through the year ...

drawing a three-furrow plough. During the war there were already more than 30 makes of motor plough and then Henry Ford shipped 5,000 tractors across to England in 1917 after a plea for help from Lloyd George.

Tractors with internal combustion engines had largely been developed in the United States in the early days, although at the start of the 20th century a three-wheeled petrol-driven tractor was developed in Britain. In 1906, Henry Ford built his first 24hp petrol-engine tractor and the rest, as they say, is history. The impetus to use tractors was provided by the two world wars, in both of which Britain was fighting potentially severe shortages of food. By the end of World War I new tractors had been invented that did away with the plough-riding second man and the whole job could be done by the tractor driver on his own. It was the beginning of the final death knell for steam ploughs and for plough horses and would also lead to the disappearance of men working in groups in the fields. During World War II, large numbers of steam traction engines suffered the indignity of ending up as scrap metal, though a few were converted into oil-powered engines. By the end of the war, the tractor had triumphed.

It was quite a sudden conversion. Avice Wilson now lives in Canada but she has had a lifelong association with the Wiltshire area of Cocklebury and remembers how it was when she worked on the farm during World War II:

At the outbreak of the war, all the farm machinery, such as the haymaking equipment, the drills and harrows, and the carts and wagons, were pulled by horses. There was an old tractor, used for moving the hay elevator and other heavy jobs, and a milking machine ... Ten years later, in 1949, there were four tractors. All the horses had gone ... Cocklebury had become mechanised.

Big advances had already been made before the war. For example, in 1936 there was a demonstration at Colworth Farm, near Chichester in Sussex, by the International Harvester Company, who showed how just one tractor could complete everything from ploughing to harrowing in the freshly sown seed in one smooth operation: there was a three-furrow plough, a three-wheel presser, a three-row seed drill and a set of harrows, one after the other behind what by today's standards was one very small tractor.

By the 1970s, four-wheel-drive tractors had become common and a huge range of implements was available for all sorts of tractors. By the early 1980s a tractor and plough could plough at the rate of up to two hectares per *hour* for every 100kW of power.

It all seems rather impersonal. Tractors don't run on oats and they don't reproduce themselves either, let alone notice lapwing nests. Nor can you talk to a tractor and get a whickering reply or a soft warm snort. And what about the dreamy stable smell of leather, dubbin, horse and manure? The smell of tractor-shed diesel fumes simply cannot compare. Yet many

a farmworker remembers his first tractor with some fondness.

Russell Baker was born on a Devon farm in 1929, when his father Jack had a threshing and agricultural contracting business. Mechanical matters had always appealed to Russell and on leaving school during the war he was fortunate that 'tractors were coming about and that was what I was interested in, working on that type of machinery and not horse stuff'. He joined a firm that had started with two-wheeled Trusty tractors guided with handles. Russell was with the firm when tractors were being imported from America on the lend-lease scheme:

> They were in crates and had to be assembled; the majority were MM's and Olivers. They came down on the train to Ivybridge station and delivered up to Cantrell. We had to put on the spade lugs on the wheels and get them out to the farms.

Other farmers remember that the first combine harvesters seen in Britain also came in bits in crates and had to be built on the farm, which must have been quite a challenge even with the handy instructions in the box.

Many farmers thought that tractors

Above left: An ingenious time-saver in 1936, this International 10/20 tractor is hitched to a three-furrow plough with a three-wheel presser and attached seed box, followed by a set of harrows so that it is ploughing, sowing and covering the seed all in one pass.

Above right: Photographer George Garland described this monster Gyrotiller as 'the largest and most fearsome machine I have ever seen'. It was one of only 15 at work in Britain in 1934. Its ploughing 'claws' were driven round and round under the soil by a 150hp oil-powered engine and it was fitted with caterpillar wheels to prevent it from getting stuck under its own weight. Powerful lamps enabled the Gyrotiller to work through the night.

would be too costly to run but, as Russell pointed out, you didn't have to feed the tractor when it wasn't doing anything – you could just get off and leave it.

Rolling

Rollers drawn by horses, or later by tractors, might be used to knock down clods and firm up a seed bed, or to level grassland – getting rid of hazards such as molehills, cow prints and frost-lifts that might impede haymaking equipment later in the year. In theory, rolling could destroy pests such as wireworm as well. Rolling also left elegant, broad stripes, like an exaggerated garden-lawnmower effect, and many a horseman prided himself in making perfect stripes.

Rollers used to be made of wood or even stone, but these had been replaced by cast-iron in the early 19th century. There were rollers for specific purposes,

such as spiked rollers, disc rollers, turnip rollers, drill rollers, furrow pressers, clod crushers and, invented in the middle of the 19th century, the efficient clod-crushing Cambridge ribbed ring roller.

In his diary for May 1865 Derbyshire farmer William Hodkins recorded that, on 17 May, he harrowed in the forenoon and washed sheep in the afternoon ('a very fine day'); he harrowed the fallow the following morning before going into Edensor to pay his rent and, with the fine weather continuing, he was harrowing and dragging the fallow all the next day as well. On 22 May it was 'spike rooling the fallow till it began to rain'; two days later he finished spike rooling and went to get his carthorse shod; the next day it was more harrowing of the fallow and a week later he was ploughing 'a great piece for rape' during the day and clipping five sheep at night. The next day he finished ploughing that piece and 'sowed 5 bags of manure on it' while his father-in-law sowed part of the field with rape: 'he sowed 5lbs of seed then he rowled all he

Below: Chain-harrowing to smooth out grassland lumps in a Keswick hayfield.

had sowed'. That same day they finished clipping their own sheep and then set about clipping other people's.

Manuring

A familiar sound from the fields around my cottage in the 1970s was the clattering racket of the muck-spreader, its flailing chains flinging the muck sideways out of a tank on to the soil. In earlier tractor-driven muck spreaders a revolving chain conveyed the manure so that a spiked bar propelled the stuff out from the back, not the sides, and most farmers with this type of spreader had simply converted what had originally been a horse-powered implement.

Muck, of course, was essentially animal manure, which was treasured and managed as carefully as any crop. Dorinda Jeynes, remembering her Devon hill-farming days between the wars at Bremridge, recalled how the big heap of manure in the corner of the stable yard would be taken out by horse and cart and put on the land in heaps, to be spread later. It was not just cow dung, sheep dung, pig manure and chicken manure. One year there was also a heap of billy-goat manure: they spread it on the fields and grew 'mangolds as big around as the black kettle. Never were such sizes grown before, nor since.'

Lime was used to protect against insect pests and root diseases, and also to kill off weed seeds and other undesirables in barnyard manure. Many a local map still shows evidence of farm limekilns, built into a steep slope or near the roadside so that loads of chalk could be easily deposited, but most had gone out of use by the mid 19th century. The kilns were generally fuelled with bundles of furze, or gorse, from nearby fields and these are often marked on old maps.

Above: Farmyard manure being forked out of the dung cart into the furrows before the crop is sown.

Above: Landgirl trainee Miss M Haslam, formerly a riding instructress from Southport, spreading manure in Suffolk in 1939.

Below: Muck-spreading with a Massey-Harris manure 'coffin' spreader behind a Fordson tractor in the 1930s.

Muck spreading was hard work. On the Lancashire farm where landgirl Rachel Knappett worked during World War II, potatoes were grown on fields that had carried hay the season before and in winter the horsemen would plough them; in spring they cultivated the furrows with a splendid homemade tractor-drawn contraption on legs. Then Billy the horseman would trudge steadily up and down drilling: locally the potatoes, cabbages and similar crops were grown in drills, each drill being a ridge of soil with a furrow (known to the men as a rigot or rein) on either side. Billy used a 'three-rudger' or ridger to make three drills at a time. The farm being on the cusp of changing from horses to tractors, there was rivalry between horseman Billy and tractor driver Joe. Some of the drilling was done by tractor and if a drill was a little off-line Joe would blame 'them bloody 'orses' and Billy would state that 'it's all along of yon bloody tin lissie!'

After the drilling, farmyard manure was carted from the midden in a horse-drawn two-wheeled muck cart and spread at the rate of 20 tons to the acre, which is a lot of muck. The stuff was dropped in forkfuls at frequent intervals along the furrows – not an easy job for those with the forks, bouncing along in the tilting, jerking cart and always at risk of tumbling head-first into its steamy contents. The muck-carters were followed by the muck-knockers, who had the gruelling task of knocking the neat little piles of manure into the bottom of the furrows with their forks.

The knocker walks crabwise on the ridge and bends nearly double to hit the muck with his fork in the furrow. Sometimes the muck is light, dusty stuff, mostly sawdust, and one wallop

More Than Muck

Manure also included materials such as ashes, soot, white greasy chalky marl, slaughterhouse waste, sheep's trotters, horn shavings, leather scrawings, hog's hair, fellmonger's poake, sugar-baker's scum, soap-boiling ashes, pigeon guano, human night-soil (carted in from the nearest large town), fish waste, seaweed, woollen rags, cotton shoddy and more.

with the fork sends it flying to the next pile in a most encouraging way. This sort of muck, beloved by the knockers and cursed by the boss because its value as manure is negligible, is very rare. It is usually heavy, sodden and rich, and has to be shaken and persuaded and bullied into going in the right direction.

Muck-knocking for anything up to eight hours on end inevitably brought on searing backache and aching muscles. And the job went on for weeks and weeks. Bag-muck, on the other hand, was 'sown' with the aid of a horse-drawn sower, on top of the real muck. Then the horseman used a single ridging plough to split the original ridge in two, with half falling over to cover the muck in the furrow on one side and the other half on the other, creating a new ridge over the muck. And into this new ridge the seed potatoes were planted.

Bag-muck

It was much easier when 'artificial' fertilisers came in. You could amble beside the horse as it slowly plodded along, pulling an implement like a seed drill, with nice clean fertiliser pouring through the coulters. On Rachel's farm, a grimy dusty group of fellow workers would arm themselves with spades, riddles and brushes and assemble in the cart-house for 'mixing bag-muck'. Bag-muck meant artificial manure. Before the war, some firms sold bag-muck ready mixed with varying proportions of the different nutrients, but during the war deliveries became erratic and many farmers went back to buying minerals separately and mixing them on the farm.

In the years of the great agricultural depression from the mid 1880s, George Baylis had been farming 240 acres at Bradfield in Berkshire since 1866 and had steadily lost money, despite being backed by the long farming experience of his father. He decided to experiment and see whether his corn could be grown without dung and without being folded by sheep. Instead, he used ammonia and phosphates as artificial manures. By the end of the century he was farming 3,440 acres and had clearly demonstrated that it was more than possible to make a profit from growing corn without the help of livestock and their muck.

Yet many farmers refused to buy artificial fertilisers and stuck to muck,

Above: While a horse-drawn ridging plough prepares this potato field near Cockermouth, two men spread heaps of farmyard manure in the furrows. The farmer himself is spreading 'bag-muck' (artificial fertiliser) by hand from a bucket.

or at best would only buy fertilisers if the contents of the bag smelt like ripe manure. In the 1930s virtually all of the older generation of farmers still swore by muck and abominated 'artificials'. They firmly believed that chemical fertilisers made the crop grow too fast for its own good and left the soil exhausted, which meant that you had to keep on adding more chemicals to revive the land, and more and more, year after year.

During World War II, farmer OK Peacock at Broughton, Huntingdonshire, was a great believer in using muck on his heavy clay land, saying that if artificials were applied year after year the land would get 'sad and livery', whereas with regular mucking the clay broke up and was much easier to work. 'If my land requires humus and I want a beef steak,' he said, 'I don't see how we're to get them without muck and cattle.' Mind you, he still spent a few hundred pounds a year on artificials, finding that they did not actually *harm* the land at all – as long as it was full of muck. As for his horses, they led a gentleman's life for most of the year, out at grass in summer and in a yard over the winter, and available for drilling beet or as a standby for working the land if the weather turned wet. It was a gentle way of easing his working horses off the farm in favour of post-war tractors.

In the 1970s, although bagged fertilisers had made a big difference to labour needs and to crop yields, it was beginning to be appreciated that some of the modern high-yield hybrid cereals needed lots of fertiliser to perform well but that the fertiliser also made the weeds grow and so farmers needed to spray lots of herbicides. By killing the weeds so efficiently, the aphids were given a clear view of their cereal targets and so insecticide spraying was essential. All this often meant that tractors were passing over the field nine or ten times in the growing season, compacting the soil each time they did so (and the structure of the soil was already being affected by the lack of organic matter that would have been provided by muck). Then came the problem of all these chemicals seeping into the aquifers and running off into the streams and rivers. The ultimate irony was that farmers were having problems in disposing of slurry (liquid manure) from their livestock, because they were no longer using it to fertilise the land.

Sowing

To convert a two-acre patch of stubble into pasture for house cows, I harrowed the field (with the aid of a venerable Fergie tractor, not a horse), put a grass-and-clover seed mixture into a pouch slung around my waist and spent a happy time rhythmically broadcasting the seeds. I set up marked sticks on the headlands to give me a line across the field, in

DUNG BOYS

In 1872 Richard Heath was making his way through southern Warwickshire, on a pilgrimage to Barford to see Joseph Arch, leader of a famous agricultural workers' rebellion. He was enjoying the 'truly English' landscape of roads lined with elm and beech, green parkland, ancient Tudor mansions glimpsed between the trees, medieval beamed and thatched cottages in flowery gardens, wildflowers along the lanes, pleasant arable farms. His first companions on the road were two little lads driving a dung-cart. One of them claimed to be 12 years old and said he had been working for four years, giving up school entirely when he was eight. He worked from six in the morning to six in the evening, and always took a companion with him as sometimes the horse 'ran away'. As Heath pointed out, accidents were frequent when such young children were allowed to act as carters, and they worked long hours with insufficient food. The boy asked Heath for something to drink, preferably alcoholic to still the cravings of his empty stomach.

Left: Charles Kilham sowing by hand in the 1930s. He had worked at the same farm at Bury, Sussex, for more than 60 years.

Below: Frederick V Dixon using a fiddle to sow seeds. The seed fell into cups, from which it was spun out evenly across the ground by moving the fiddle's 'bow'.

time-honoured fashion, and then kept an eye out for pigeons and other scavengers. Unfortunately, this was the spring of 1976 – the year of the great drought – but at least the clover did well.

Had I been sowing a crop other than grass, I would have first ploughed the field so that there were furrows into which the seed would fall in neat lines, then I would have raked or harrowed the crests of soil over the seed. Harrows always reminded me of an old-fashioned sprung bedstead, with vertical iron tines that act like a series of rakes. As with ploughs, there were (and are) numerous different designs for harrows for different purposes, including disc harrows in which the tines are replaced by rows of vertical discs. Larger harrows, or drags, could be used to break up clods, rake out couch-grass and generally prepare a seed bed. Heavy wheeled harrows known as cultivators, or scarifiers, grubbers or scufflers, with substantial moveable teeth or tines, were used from the early 19th

century to refine the ploughing and rip out the weeds.

Even in the 1930s farmworkers in the west country, northern England and parts of Scotland were still broadcast sowing by hand, regulating their pace and their swinging throw to ensure that just the right rate of seed was delivered in just the right place. Some might have been using a fiddle where the seed was in a hopper, flowing into cups or paddles whirled around on a spindle spun by a fiddle-like bow. And they might even have still been sowing to the calendar, rather than to the actual weather: winter wheat in the 'darks of November' to grow with the moon, for example, or oats at Septuagesima, or potatoes planted in the afternoon on Good Friday (and I know of several octogenarians who still insist on planting their potatoes on Good Friday, regardless of whether it falls in March or April).

An improvement on hand broadcasting

groove. Bigger and more complicated drills
could also 'sow' manure, at the same time
or separately. Horse-drawn seed drills
were still in use in the 1930s: the lucky
rode on the drill, guiding the horses, while
the less lucky walked beside the drill to
steer its front wheels (keeping a perfect
line, bearing in mind that the evidence of
his tidy rows would be visible to all until
the crop was harvested and its stubble
ploughed in) or walking behind to check
that the coulters had not become blocked.

Above: Jack Miles and his horse Punch sowing with a long-barrow corn-drill in 1939. This apparently unwieldy implement could be folded to pass through gateways.

Right: Women planting potatoes during World War II. They were lucky to have the help of mechanisation: most gangs during the war planted potatoes by hand and on foot.

Opposite: A robot transplanter in the early 1940s. The four operators are feeding plants into rubber-protected metal fingers that carry the plants by means of an endless chain to the ground, which has been prepared by the furrow-opener. The fingers release the plants just as the furrow is being closed by converging roller wheels behind the delivery point.

was the seed-barrow, a long seed-sowing trough resting on a simple wooden large-wheeled barrow frame. As the barrow was pushed, the wheel also turned a brush-covered spindle within the trough to sprinkle the seed through a series of small holes at the base of the trough.

The horse made seed sowing easier, especially after the invention of seed-drills in the 18th century. A drill has a row of coulters that make grooves in the soil. Behind each coulter is a hole or chute through which the seed is ejected into the

Dibbling and planting

Dibbling is making holes at regular intervals and then dropping one or more seeds into each hole. It was a labour-intensive method that had faded out long before the end of the 19th century in most places. You used an iron rod, about a yard long, with a spade handle at one end and a pointed knob at the other, and you carried one in each hand. Then you walked backwards over the field dibbling two rows of holes six to eight inches apart, giving a twist as you poked the dibber into

the soil so that the hole was a clean one. Women and children followed, stooping quickly to drop seeds into the holes.

Dibbling was also a method of planting out, by popping seedlings and young plants into the holes rather than seeds. Manually setting out young plants, such as mangels, was truly back-breaking work and very reliant on plenty of cheap labour.

There were dibbers (the dibber is the tool; the word dibbler is usually reserved for the person using it) for every occasion: single dibbers and double dibbers for sowing seeds, spring-loaded corn dibbers, hand dibbers for transplanting, potato dibbers (rammed into the ground with your foot like a bulb planter), dibbling wheels and so on.

Weeding

An ongoing task with any crop is weeding. Jethro Tull became a hero to many a labourer when he invented horse-hoes so that the horses did the work instead of the field workers, but these implements could only be used where there was enough space between the rows. Otherwise it remained a matter of hoeing by hand and then hand weeding and pulling out thistles and the like, and hand-roguing any wild oats. What a deal of *work*, as Cobbett would have cried, but what a wonderful opportunity for the ingenious to devise a hoe for every possible occasion: narrow hoes, broad hoes, square hoes, triangular hoes, double-pointed hoes, triple-bladed hoes, mattocks …

There is a wonderful collection of recorded memories in the Essex Record Office, including those of Mrs E Turvey. She left school in 1887 at the age of eleven 'and did odd jobs on a farm with my mother, such as cutting out thistles from the corn with a weed hook, singling mangold, stone picking, etc.' Her mother was paid 1s 6d for collecting 21 bushels of stones and putting them in rows near the field gate. Edith Mary Sargent, born

OLD ANNIE

On a potato farm, there was a lot more to sowing the crop than simply delivering seed into holes, whether by dibbler or by seed-drill. The 'spritted' potatoes had to be set-cut, an art by which each potato is cut into sections, each section bearing a sprit or several sprits, according to personal preference of the farmer. Set-cutting was quite peaceful work but it left your fingers stained with ingrained greenish-brown potato juice and the occasional cut.

Old Annie was a famous set-cutter at Bath Farm in southwest Lancashire during the war. She was Irish, with a shrill, piercing voice, and she always wore a shapeless long flowing black garment down to her ankles, topped by a very large and very old man's topcoat. Her straggly wisps of grey hair were mainly tied back in a bun but she covered her head with a man's cloth cap. In the fields, she draped herself from head to toe in sacks. And she was usually smoking a fairly smelly old clay pipe, which she had been known to fill with tobacco from other people's discarded cigarette stubs, grubbed out of the gutter. She was also very partial to beer and generally managed to spend most of her wages at the pub on the way home. But she was an expert set-cutter.

Above: Frank, John and Tom Bainbridge thinning and weeding turnips by hoe and by hand at Stonethwaite in 1944.

in Essex in 1880, went stone picking as a child: they made heaps of them, which would then be 'carted in a tumble marked with chalk and we had to pick a load for 1s 6d and then we picked up acorns and sold them at 1s a bushel and oh it did take a lot of them to make a bushel.' Another Essex woman, Mrs Field, recalled her first job in the market garden district near Tiptree:

I went out to work when I was nine, working for … a seed grower. In winter we worked inside a shed cleaning out peas and beans and getting pips from marrows and cucumbers. In summer we collected carrot and parsnip seeds … The very special thing we did was picking up Canary Creeper seeds from rows. It was the first that had been grown and was very precious … I earned 3s a week and I gave it all to my mother for my father was ill and could not work … I used to pick watercress growing wild and had to go right into the pond to get it, I bunched it up and sold it and once I got enough to buy my father a tin of crab … We used to go to

Totham a long ride with Mr Parrish in a wagon, doing all sorts of jobs in the fields – mostly 'twitching' we walked behind the ploughs and picked up every little bit of white root and burned it. We took all our food to the fields, cold tea to drink, and bread with something homemade or a bit of cheese. I worked there until I was 14.

In her memories of childhood in the Croyland district of the Fens in the 1850s, published in 1931, Mrs Burrows recalled how she had worked as part of a gang from the age of eight, doing a 14-hour day in the fields with 40 or 50 other children of whom she was the eldest:

We were followed all day long by an old man carrying a long whip in his hand which he did not forget to use. A great many of the children were only five years of age … We always left the town, summer and winter, the moment the old Abbey clock struck six … We had to walk a very long way to our work, never much less than two miles each way, and very often five miles each way. The large farms all lay a good distance from the town, and it was on those farms that we worked. In the winter, by the time we reached our work, it was light enough to begin, and of course we worked until it was dark and then we had our long walk home. I never remember to have reached home sooner than six and more often seven, even in winter. In the summer, we did not leave the fields in the evening until the clock had struck six, then of course we must walk home, and this walk was no easy task for us children who had worked hard all day on the ploughed fields.

She could remember terrible days working in a cold east wind laden with sleet and snow, eating her cold dinner in the meagre shelter of a hedge and so numb with cold that she could hardly move.

Rachel Knappett remembered the agony and sweat of weeding out couch grass (also called twitch or wicks) from the potato crop. There had been weeks of rain, making hoeing and other methods of weed control impossible and the wicks got themselves thoroughly entangled in the potato roots and shoots. Then came a spell of dry, hot weather, and the sight of:

… a row of nine behind ends, as seven men and two girls crawled, cursing, on hands and knees, up and down the drills. Up and down we 'scrawled on wer bellies', as the men put it. Our backs were burnt red through our shirts, we wiped the sweat out of our eyes with soil-coated hands, and we came home at night looking as if we'd 'bin oop chimney back'. As for the wicks, as soon as our eyes were off them, they calmly ingratiated themselves once more with the earth and made up for lost time. The weeds, that year, had 'over-got' us.

And then someone invented weed-killing sprays and life became so much simpler for the workers and for the farmer, if not for the environment.

Below: International 'Farmall' tractor-hoe, working in a sugar beet field.

Pest Control

In 1919, Primrose McConnell's encyclopaedic and essential publication *The Agricultural Note-Book*, by then in its ninth edition, contained a thoroughly practical table of 'Principal Insects, etc., Injurious to Farm Crops', with a column for 'Treatment Recommended'.

Above: Spraying the potato crop with Bordeaux mixture, near Rickling, Essex, in the 1930s.

The pests included a wide range of weevils, beetle, fleas, wireworm, sawflies, moths, aphids, thrips, assorted flies, midges and their maggots, nematodes, millipedes, slugs and spiders and in nearly all cases the treatment was based on good husbandry: crop rotation, hygiene, liming, dusting the soil with soot, feeding the plants so that they were strong enough to resists attack, ensuring 'clean' cultivation, burning off stubble, good drainage, green manuring, rolling, deep ploughing and so on. Rarely was there a recommendation to use sprays and powders; for example, spraying (but only as a last resort) with paraffin or sulphur against flea-beetle, turnip fly, mangold fly, onion fly, bean and pea weevils, turnip saw-fly, carrot fly and the like; or dusting hellebore on damp carrot leaves to deter carrot-blossom moth or, better still, interspersing the carrot rows with parsnips, which the moths preferred; or spraying brassicas with Paris green against cabbage white butterflies, or with soft-soap solution or tobacco infusion against aphids.

BOB FLY

Between the wars, Fred Stillwell found himself leading his horse across the field dragging a line of sacks behind it. The sacks had been treated with a potent mixture of tar and paraffin to deter bob fly and Fred was lucky that the horse was doing the work: quite often the pram-wheeled ten-foot bar carrying the sacks would have been pulled by a man with a rope over his shoulders. Or he might have found himself dragging an elder bough over the land, the aim being to cover the soil with a smell that the flies did not like.

Bird-scaring

Many a farmworker began his career as a bird scarer, including William Cobbett. Even in the late 19th century, most agricultural labourers considered that their sons would do much better to get a day's work scaring off rooks in the field for a few pence than wasting a day at school. He might simply yell or yodel at them and clap his hands, or ring a bell, or he might be armed with a wooden clapper or rattle or some pebbles shaken in a tin. He could make his own pair of clappers – just a couple of flat wooden bats loosely linked by a leather thong. Rattles were more complicated, and quite often had a beautifully turned handle and an elegant design: the cogged wheel against a sprung piece of metal could create an awesomely ear-splitting noise that probably led to early deafness. At the age of perhaps seven or eight, the boy might have been allowed an old gun or pistol just for the fun of taking a pot shot at birds. Right the way through the winter, from November until about May, every day, including Sundays, he would be stuck out in the fields doing nothing much at all, in theory guarding the seeds and sprouting crops from avian predation.

There was always the good old-fashioned scarecrow, of course, and even before 1900 someone had invented one of those irritatingly loud and repetitive automatic

Left : Scaring the birds, many a farm labourer's first job as a young boy.

SHOUTING FOR A LIVING

George Brann claimed to be the last of the Kentish bird scarers: he had been 'shouting for his living' for 73 years when he was interviewed in his Pepperbox Cottage at Fairbourne Heath, Headcorn, on the edge of the Weald. He had started at the age of nine, when his job was to patrol the boundaries of a 20-acre cornfield (which must have looked pretty big to a nine-year-old) by swinging a clapper, blowing a penny whistle (with a pea in it), turning a policeman's rattle or ringing a ship's bell. He also shouted out bird charms that had been passed down in his family for generations, such as:

Away, birds, away,
You eat too much,
You drink too much,
You carry too much away.

If that didn't work, he would try:

Run, birds, run!
The master's coming with a gun.
You must fly and I must run.
Away, birds, away!

Finally, if the rooks, pigeons and starlings failed to take notice, he'd holler:

Back, birds, back!
You're on the wrong track.
Back to Headcorn.

By the time he was 16, his hollering voice was so powerful that he was the most sought-after bird scarer south of the Thames. But he loved birds, or at least birdsong – especially if their music was mixed with the sound of two or three hundred bird-scaring lads mocking each other from hill to hill.

Above: The rat-catchers' gibbet, 1935, Hampshire. Vermin catchers were paid by the tail for each rat killed. One or two gamekeepers were skilled at being paid more than once for the same carcass.

bangers for scaring off rooks, going off all day long and probably all night as well, and which still drive country-dwellers crazy today.

Rats, cats, sparrows and rabbits

Rats were an inevitable part of farm life, especially in among the ricks and barns. The Reverend John Coker Egerton, who died in Burwash, Sussex, in 1888 at the age of 58, was told by one of his parishioners: 'I be a miller, and I've got rats, and I keep cats, and one day I looks into a place under my mill, and there I sees cats and rats all feeding together out of one trough at my expense!'

During World War I, many a rural parish council was insulted to be told by higher powers how the local farmers should behave. The tiny rural parish of Chithurst in Sussex was one of many that received a circular (contents unknown)

in 1915 that infuriated all its farmers: the minutes at the time stated that 'the farmers of the parish have done, are doing, and will continue to do their best to farm the land in the most suitable manner'. How dare people – especially people in cities like Chichester – tell them how to farm! In the following year the county War Agriculture Committee sent all its parishes a circular on the subject of 'Rats and Sparrows', which were pests that country people had been dealing with all their lives. Chithurst responded: 'Considering the geographical configuration of the Parish of Chithurst and the neighbouring parishes, the problem … should be dealt with by the District Council.' There was a bounty on rats' tails at the time.

Warwickshire farmer Aubrey Seymour was permanently at war with rabbits, and other nuisances. The north side of his farm was 'one big warren' and poaching was lucrative:

> *A particular gang of gypsies frequently camped in the middle of my farm … and as far as I could see, they lived on the proceeds of poaching my rabbits and the sale of clothes-pegs made from ash cut from my fences. … I tolerated them for a long time, but when I found they had turned their horses at night into my best fields and had milked three of my cows in the early hours one morning, it seemed high time to do something.*

So Seymour decided to profit from his rabbits himself. Between the wars, in the depressed years, he was shooting up to 200 rabbits a day during the winter and selling them for pelts and meat. He did have another good thing to say about rabbits: they were useful for those who wanted to produce turf for golfing greens and lawns, as they nibbled out all the coarser weeds and grasses. He also noted that crows were usually after wireworm and leather jackets rather than seed, and thus the seed would be safe if it was planted deep enough not to be pulled up accidentally by the birds when they were kindly removing these root-attacking pests. Seymour had long since decided that employing small boys to frighten birds off the corn with noisy contraptions was pointless: 'it only sent the pillagers from one part of the field to another'. He could remember a time when gangs of local youths used to catch roosting sparrows by means of bat-fowling nets: half the gang would go down one side of a big hedge and the rest walked along the other side with a lantern held behind the long, folded, raised net. When the hedge was tapped, the sleepy birds fluttered towards the light and were trapped. Seymour was all for the balance of nature and pointed out a few handy equations: sparrows down = caterpillars up; cats down = mice up = bumblebee nests destroyed = clover not fertilised; squirrels down = wood pigeons up (because their eggs were not being raided). One man's pest is another man's ally.

In the early years of the 20th century, and right through to World War II, rabbit trapping was a good source of income for many, as well as providing meat for the family table. In some parts of the country, rabbiting was a serious part of the local economy: there were the men who trapped, snared, ferreted or shot them; there were those who collected them and took them to a central depot; and of course there were those who bought them, either as butcher's meat or for their pelts. Then there were those who provided the rabbiters with traps, snares, knives, bicycles and suitable clothing: stout waterproof boots against the dew; baggy corduroy trousers so that the knee could bend easily to its tasks, with a leather strap below the knee, or breeches and leggings; leather knee caps made by the local saddler; a sleeved weskit, probably of corduroy and maybe with a 'turnip' watch in its pocket; at least two heavy brown gaberdine coats or ones of bluish Melton to absorb the rain; and a sturdy cloth cap.

Alphaeus Ball was a rabbit trapper, until the myxomatosis epidemic of 1954 killed off some 95 per cent of Britain's wild rabbits. Alphaeus's daughter, Hilda Harvey (born in 1920), recorded her memories of her father's rabbit-trapping days in a local history book, *Life Stories of Bygone Days*: 'He used to sell them to Tonkins in Kingsbridge and he also used to cycle to Plymouth on an old Post Office bike, with them hanging from the carrier on the front and over the cross bar.'

ROOK SCARER

Aubrey Seymour did not have much good to say about rooks, and his deterrent methods were macabre: he would shoot one or two, cut off their heads and fix them with beaks pointing skywards as if the bodies were buried. Assorted corvids would soon gather and fly round and round above them, cawing, but would not settle in that part of the field.

Left: Rabbit trapper Alf Ball, with his donkey.

Alphaeus also had a donkey, laden with wooden panniers containing his traps, and the pair would potter down the traffic-free lanes to the fields so that he could set the traps one day and then pick up the rabbits the next morning.

During World War I, Walter Johnson, one of those erudite ramblers who had been wandering all over Britain for many years observing rural life, found himself somewhere near Eastbourne. He was actually trying to record conversations with shepherds, but on one sultry August afternoon he was loitering at the head of a coomb to watch the reapers clearing the last patch of wheat:

The narrow strip was steadily getting smaller and smaller, until, from our rather elevated position, it looked little larger than a kitchen table. What chiefly attracted our notice was the eager attitude of three or four men in khaki who belonged to a tiny camp near the farm, and who were evidently on the watch for any stray rabbits which might be still vainly hiding in the corn. When the strip had shrunk to about two or three swathes, out sprang a terrified rabbit, and a chase began. The men had no guns, but being well on the alert, lost not a second. Then one realised what systematic training will do for the lungs and muscles of young men. The rabbit fled wildly, turned in fear from one man only to be waylaid by another, then frantically doubled on its tracks, while all the time the soldiers whooped as they ran. The course, however, mainly tended uphill, and, despite elastic muscles and sound hearts, the pursuers had to confess themselves beaten. Nor could one really feel sorry. The shouting died down, as soon the last breadth of corn was levelled.

That rabbit was lucky. Usually men would have been waiting with dogs and shotguns – it was one of the sports of harvesting.

The Harvest

Farmers are on edge as harvest time approaches: it just needs a mocking spell of bad weather to change their mood from optimism to frustration and despair as they watch winds and rain battering down the grain fields, lodging the heads and shedding the corn before it comes anywhere near the combine. And, bang, a whole year's work has been sabotaged at the whim of the weather, however advanced the machinery. On today's farm, just as on yesterday's, farmers rely on the weather for swelling and ripening the crop and for giving the right conditions in which it can be cut.

But at least today's farmers, when the weather does briefly relent, can leap into action instantly, switch on an engine or two and race out to gather the crop at top speed – before the rains have a chance to return and spoil the party.

From Manual Labour to Machine

Gertrude Jekyll, writing in 1904, could remember the days of manual labour, when a man would mow an acre and a half of barley in a day (two if he was a first-rate mower), or an acre of hay for half-a-crown, toiling 'the long day through with all the strength of his body – every muscle in full play' and definitely earning his refreshments under the shade of a hedgerow oak.

He would start at daylight and some farmers offered the incentive of a pint of ale to the first man to arrive on the job, as well as giving each man a bottle of beer or cider for the day. The regular meals were breakfast at six, lunch at half-past nine, dinner at noon, afternoon lunch at four and supper at seven.

Jekyll noted that nearly the whole of the change from hand to machine work by horses in agriculture had taken place within her recollection. With haymaking, for example, in the old days all the necessary tools – scythe, fork and wooden rake – could be hung on one nail in the labourer's back-kitchen or outhouse. But at the time of her writing, mechanised haymaking demanded a pair of horses, a mechanical mower and a

Left: Perfectly bound handmade sheaves proudly displayed at Pitstone Green Farm in Buckinghamshire.

wide range of horse-drawn equipment for tossing and turning the hay: kickers, tedders, swathe-turners and horse-rakes, all of which needed maintenance and housing in a large building. 'And all these cumbersome things,' as Jekyll said, 'are for use within perhaps four weeks of the year!'

As for the corn harvest, what would Jekyll have made of combine harvesters, costing a fortune but sitting idle for ten or eleven months of the year? She had delighted in wielding a rip-hook (or reaping hook, like a sickle) herself as a child in the early 1850s and she recalled what very dirty work it was. 'Honest sweat and dry dust combine into a mixture not unlike mud. Hay-making is drawing-room work in comparison.' Times had changed since her childhood and most wheat was now harvested by horse-drawn machines.

Above: The family harvest.

Right: Family lunch break during harvest. The stone 'harvest bottles' probably contain cider or beer, or possibly cold tea.

Above: Harvesting with a reaping hook in Herefordshire, about 1900. The hooked stick in the reaper's left hand was used to secure the stems while hooking.

Sickle wielders competed with steam as well as with horses. Louis J Jenning (sometime MP for Stockport) liked to ramble the field paths and green lanes of Surrey and Sussex in the 1870s and he recalled the following scene on the chalky road from Beeding.

It is a long and steep road, and near the top I could distinguish a steam-plough at work, and could hear its noise and fuss while still afar off. A man was cutting oats in a field which I passed, and 'after compliments' I said to him, 'So you have got the steam-plough even here.'

'Ay, it be steam everywhere now,' said he, wiping his forehead; 'a poor fellow don't get no chance.'

'Well, you see, it saves the farmer money.'

'No, it doänt; it ain't cheaper in the end. The reaping machine do gather up all the stoäns, and mucks the carn all over the plaäce. It wastes a sight, I can tell ye.'

'But it does the work quickly.'

'Not much quicker on these hills than we can. And look how clean it is done;' he pointed down to his little sheaves with some pride. They were all tied up carefully, and laid by in rows

as if for an agricultural exhibition. 'You can't get ne'er a machine to do that. I sometimes think I will emigrate.'

'You will have to go a long way if you want to get out of the way of steam.'

'Well, it be hard to get a living here, and yet this be the best way of doing the work after all,' going on with his reaping; 'you don't gather up no stoäns with this.'

The competitors, man and machine, were both left doing their best ...

Harvesting

Even in Jekyll's childhood the old-fashioned sickle was rarely used for harvesting grain: it was too much of a back-breaker. Instead, where harvesting was still done by hand, men with scythes moved forward across the field in a diagonal line, swinging their implements in harmony. Each man cut a strip about 6 feet wide, and at a signal each man stopped to whet his blade. A sharp blade was essential to efficient scything.

Reapers and binders

In the Autumn 1945 issue of *The Countryman*, E-H wrote:

Working in threes, two women and one man, they start to open up the field. The man scythes, swinging wide-apart arms from left to right, each stroke a little shock of sound. As the first woman stoops to gather the loose corn into her breast the second bends to make a band of straw to bind it with. In a while they overtake the next three and have a rendezvous, something in the manner of a country dance – set and turn single – a tale shared, a joke, a bit of life's philosophy such as you hear only from poets and those who fix the braces of their dungarees up with a nail. The adjoining threes part and in the same rhythm take up the dance again.

It all seems very romantic. But:

Then come the binders, whirring machinery, thudding of horses' feet. They mow the corn down in great reaches, throwing out sheaves remorselessly – the dance has turned to a marche militaire. Everyone available is sent to set up sheaves; not only the people on the place, but a busload of townsfolk 'holidaying'. An oddly assorted flock, they spread over the headriggs of the field like birds and finally settle into pairs.

'Noo play your pavie,' the gaffer says; 'lift up twae sheaves – hud them weel ablow your oxters – bash their heids thegither as ye set them doon.' ... All set to work to join in this new eurhythmic ... There were typists with sensitive fingers who felt every jag of thistle and thorn; town romancers who had always thought of corn in pastorale, as smooth and clean; mothers of families in garden hats and sun-bonnets; slightly stiffening fathers, and youngsters who found some of the long sheaves so heavy they had to lift one and support it against their little, slim posteriors while stooping to pick up its mate.

The first patent on a reaping machine had been taken out in 1800 and it simply imitated the action of the scythe. In 1822, schoolmaster Henry Ogle in Northumberland had invented a reaper that also laid the corn in sheaves but it never caught on. In 1851 a couple of horse-powered reaping machines were on show at the Great Exhibition – the launching pad for so much of the innovation for which the Victorian period would be famous.

Top: Edward Cooper scything a path for the binder.

Above: Sharpening scythes during haymaking.

Above: Taking a break from scything.

Below: A McCormick reaper/binder drawn by an International Farmall Regulator tractor reaper on the fenland Coldham Estate between the wars.

Mechanical reapers were here to stay, and soon they would also do the binding.

In September, 1880, the following report appeared in *Deanery Magazine – Castlemartin and Bosherston*:

A very sad accident occurred at Pen-y-holt Farm in the parish of Castlemartin. A young man named Tom Hall was reaping a field of barley with the machine, and whilst driving it down one side of the field next the hedge, the fan rake caught a branch and broke short off. This frightened the horses and made them start off at a considerable pace, causing the young man to lose his seat and fall in front of the knives. He, however, for a little while held on by the reins and was dragged along some distance until they broke. He then managed to lay hold of the box on the pole which contains the tools necessary for the adjustment of the machine, and was dragged for a short distance further until this also gave way, and he at once came in contact with the knives. He was frightfully cut about the arms, one of which was severed in two places, and was otherwise cut and bruised. He managed, nevertheless, in spite of his fearful condition, to throw himself clear of the machine and standing up called for help which was then close at hand. The arm which was so badly hurt was bound up, so that the loss of blood was not very great. He was taken to the Pembroke Infirmary where the mutilated limb was properly removed under the influence of chloroform, and the other wounds dressed. But so great had been the shock that he rapidly sank and died the same night.

By the early years of the 20th century the mechanical reaper-binder, or self-binding reaper, which could cut as much as an acre an hour, every hour, without having to pause for frequent refreshment and tool sharpening, had driven most of the acre-a-day men with their reaping hooks and scythes and the women binding by hand off the cornfields, though the machine-bound sheaves were still set up in stooks in the field and later taken to the rickyard or to the barn for threshing.

Flailing and threshing

In September 1874, Francis Kilvert in Wiltshire heard 'the old familiar sound once so common, the sound of the flail on the barn floor. I had not heard it for years. I looked in at the barn door and found a man threshing out his barley.' Gertrude Jekyll could remember when flail-threshing was common; in Surrey this hand-wielded implement was known as a frail and was made of ash and raw hide and she described it in some detail.

A flail was basically a long wooden handle with a beater, or swiple (in Surrey, a swingel) at the end – a rod a yard or more long and perhaps an inch and a half thick, bound to the handle by a system of thongs that allowed the swiple considerable freedom of movement. You swung the contraption above your head to give it impetus and then smashed it down on the ears of corn to beat the grain free from the chaff and straw – which took a fair bit of skill, dexterity and strength. Flailing usually took place in the central part of the barn, with a good through draft from the open doors to blow away the chaff. It was extremely hard, dusty, sweaty and noisy yet it was handy employment on wet days when other work might not be available.

In 1920 Walter Johnson came across an old man on the Isle of Wight; he was in his seventies, short in stature, and 'gnarled and crippled by work and weather'. He remembered flail work in his early days:

It was 'ard wurrk, dreshing carn that way, but it kept us goin' ahl the winter. I used to loike winter-time 'cäase the hours were short. We ploughed till one 'clack, then we'd nawthen to do as you med saäy, but feed the 'arses and clean 'em. One farmer, 'e started us worken Scotch fashion; we ploughed till eleven 'clack, then we stapped, an' started again at two and went an till five. But I didn't bide lang wi' 'un.

Top: A fleet of WLA girls harvesting a bumper wartime crop on a vast 400-acre field, believed to be Britain's largest wheatfield at the time.

Inset: Hot dusty work, using a flail to thresh the crop by hand.

RACKETING JACK

Among the many splendid character photographs taken in the 1920s and 1930s by George Garland in Sussex is one of old Jackie Baxter (below), perched on a sack beside a wooden rake and telling stories to a couple of schoolboys. He was often known as 'racketing Jack': his job was 'racketing' or 'caving', which is not as exciting as it sounds. Cavings were the dust and fine material left once threshing was over, and it was Jackie's job to clear them up. A contemporary said that he had seen Jack 'absolutely smothered so that I couldn't see either his eyes or his bowler for racketings'. One dreads to think about the state of his lungs.

The old man had used the local pronunciation 'dreshing' for 'threshing', and well within living memory farm-workers in many parts of the country called it 'thrashing' – a word that echoes the repetitive and vigorous nature of the task.

Men had been inventing threshing machines since Roman times but it was not until the later part of the 19th century that flails were at last ousted for good by implements powered other than by human muscles. In between there were various hand-turned threshers but it was much easier to use wind, water or a horse (or a donkey or a dog on a treadmill). The horse-gear sheds that can still be seen in some old farmyards were often the

heart of the power that drove a threshing machine. But horse-gears, watermills and windmills were fixed; they couldn't go out into the field and so all the grain had to be brought to the fixed engine. The next step was to devise portable threshing machines, for use on your own farm and to hire out to your neighbours. One splendid invention had a pair of horses running on a treadmill of the type that would not look out of place in a modern gym but placed inside a cart (with access up a ramp from the back), its gearing driving a portable thresher that ejected grain from one spout and straw and chaff from another.

As threshing machines became increasingly complicated, they also became increasingly expensive, which naturally led to men setting up as threshing contractors and travelling around the countryside. The culmination of these travelling machines was the mighty steam-powered threshing engine, which brought excitement into rural areas – all that energy and noise and colour! It was as good as going to the fairground.

Dorinda Jeynes, recalling her childhood in Devon in the 1920s, remembered how she and her sister Lavinia:

> ... were always scared of meeting 'the dresher' on its way from another farm to ours. It was so big – and we were so small and the road was so narrow! We did not know it was controlled by men – it seemed a monster with a mind of its own. We flattened ourselves against the hedges to let it pass ... The 'steam tackle' would be driven to where the ricks had been made ...

Below: A typical travelling steam-threshing gang.

Above: Lunch break for a steam-threshing gang at Cholsey Five Ways, Oxfordshire, in the early 1920s.

Opposite: The Rector's family making hay in 1892. The white-bearded Revd Joseph Henry Hutton of West Heslerton, Yorkshire, summoned not only his family but also his groom and the village bootmaker to help with the harvest. The Rector's son Jack (seven years old in this picture) later recalled that the parson had three cows and two or three pigs, and grew enough hay and oats to feed his livestock and the essential horse (for his trap).

There was always a peculiar smell with the equipment in use and it was due to the burning of the steam coal, the lubricating oils and the sheaves of corn, whether wheat, barley or oats … Underneath the 'boneshaker' part where the residue of the shaken corn collected there was a 'fowl heaven', a bonanza which kept the birds scratching for days and little food need to be given to them.

In Wiltshire, Avice Wilson described travelling threshing machines during World War II, when she was an agricultural trainee at Cocklebury:

Sometime during the autumn months of the war years came the threshing machine with its crew of two men and four landgirls. From the taking of the sheaves off the ricks to be pitchforked into the whirling maw of the machine to the wheeling away of the heavy sacks of grain (especially if the grain was

wheat), this was a dusty job and hard work for everyone. As the rick became low, a chicken-wire fence was unrolled and placed around it. Everyone in the area who had a dog stood by, and as the bottom two or three layers of sheaves began to be moved, the rats and mice left the rick. The place became bedlam, men shouting and dogs barking. Not until the last rat was killed by the dogs or clubbed to death did the noise stop.

In Lancashire during the same war, Rachel Knappett also remembered the threshing gangs, whose arrival brought bedlam and entertainment to the farmyard for a week or so:

The thresher men are a kind of news agency. Moving as they do from farm to farm, they pick up and embroider all sorts of tit-bits. They are always shrouded from head to foot in thick dust … There is the driver, the bale carrier, the wirer, the bant cutter, the chaff carrier and a numerous collection of men who work on the 'moo' (thresherman's word for stack). The machine arrives draped with bicycles strung on to it with rope, and men jolting along on top, sitting on every part of the machine where it is possible to sit.

It is a modern thresher, power-driven by a huge tractor, which is also used to pull it from one place to another. In old days … the threshers were driven by engines rather like steamrollers. They burnt coal, and two people had to carry buckets of water to throw over the engine to keep it cool. Then there was smoke to add to all the other turmoil of threshing.

Harry Gambrill came from a family of agricultural contractors. He was born in about 1890 at Petham in Kent, not far from where a gang of labourers in 1830

TRAVELLING

Harry Gambrill's memories continued at length with detailed information about the machines and the seasonal routine of travelling round the farms: sometimes they would visit eight or nine small farms in a day, or they might spend six weeks on one large farm. Very often Harry would make his way to the farms by bicycle, though his father insisted that cycling would ruin his legs and always walked instead: it might take several hours to walk home from Thanet and he'd arrive about midnight on the Saturday for his weekend break and leave again in the early hours of Monday. Someone would have to go off as early as 3.30 in the morning to get the steam up – a job that would take a couple of hours on a Monday as the coal was 'dead'. It was not an easy life, and by the end of World War I it was extremely difficult to find men prepared to do such hard work.

The Gambrills' family business also carried out general repairs on all types of farm machinery and provided a comfortable living – until tractors came along. Tractors were less specialised (they could carry out a wide range of farm operations) and they were more affordable to farmers than traction engines had been. In 1948 Harry sold his last traction engine, 'for a song'.

had destroyed a 'thrashing' machine at Lower Hardres, south of Canterbury. His grandfather had started the business before emigrating to Australia in the 1880s. Harry's father had once owned 17 self-binders, eight grass mowers, two Aveling plough engines, and three threshing machines (two Marshalls and one Ransome) for hiring out. It was the threshing machines that provided continuous employment and a regular income for at least eight months in the year, and by the early years of the 20th century virtually every farm in Kent used firms like the Gambrills to do their threshing. Harry recorded his memories as part of Michael Winstanley's oral history project at the University of Kent in the 1970s:

When I were quite young they still had a threshing machine that was driven by what they called a horse gear. That was a crocodile. It was a stump down to the ground and it had got two pinions. There was a round set of gear and it had got a casting at the top and a four inch pole about ten foot long and they used to attach a horse to that. He'd got a small bar of iron come from his mouth to the pole so that he couldn't get out of the way and he couldn't go the other way, so he used to keep going round and round. The horses got used to it. They didn't want no handling. They used to put them in and they walked round and round for hours.

Well, no doubt the horses were pleased when steam-threshing machines took their place. It could also be a dangerous business. Dorinda Jeynes described the use of the winnowing machine in a big barn in the 1920s, worked by horses in the round house next door 'attached to special wooden yokes'. On one memorable day a young man got his scarf caught in the moving part of the machine and

… before they could stop the horses every bit of his clothing had been torn off him. He was as naked as he was born, very very shocked and cold. Someone called Grandma out and she put her apron over him and carried him indoors to the comfort of the open fire. They found him clothes of sorts and gave him hot drinks before returning him to his own home.

Ned Lethbridge was born in 1934 and spent a lot of his boyhood days with his father on the farm. One of his jobs was to lead the horse to pick up the sheaves of corn and take them to the rick builders.

Below: Bundling straw for thatching in 1929.

Later on we would take all the wheat sheaves to the barn to make reed and I used to go in the barn with them. We would pick up a sheaf and knock out the corn on a reed maker, a curved slatted bench, and then tie up a bundle of reed to a beam, all ear ends together and comb out all the grass from the stubble. After harvest we would take a horse and cart or wagon and go around to the hedges and cut spear sticks. On a wet day we would go in the barn and Father would use a little hook to split the sticks down into spears and twist them. The spears were all ready for thatching the ricks. Father would take up the bundles of reed; I wasn't big enough to do that. He would spread out the reed and I would be on the ladder passing the spears to him to hold it in place.

The combine harvester

The tractor-drawn harvester that was widely used until the 1940s was a combination of reaper, collector and binder. The next step was to add threshing and in fact the first 'combine harvester' had been invented way back in the 1820s in the United States, drawn by horses. It was not widely used, even when the power was provided by steam and later by oil-driven tractors, and when a self-powered combine harvester came to England in 1928 farmers largely ignored it. But Reg Sampson remembered seeing combine harvesters in 1938 being hauled across Salisbury Plain by caterpillar tractors, and he and his brother were impressed at the prospect of how much time and effort could be saved on their own family's farm by using these new machines instead of the team of six horses that did all their ploughing, cultivating and harvesting (they did not buy their first Fordson tractor until 1942, when Reg was 17). Other farmers were being converted and it was not too long before the miracle of the mighty self-powered,

THE GLEANERS

Gleaning has connotations of scavenging, scrabbling around in the dust for the leftovers, but it was an important contribution to the family's income. It was possible to gather enough ears of corn from the field to keep the family in bread for the winter: they took the corn to the local miller for grinding and he kept part as his payment and returned the rest as flour for home baking. Edwin Grey of Hertfordshire recalled how each gleaner tied an 'earbag' round his waist, like a small apron that was 'nearly all pocket'. Gleaning often turned into quite a village party and in the 1860s a Lincolnshire doctor thoroughly disapproved, huffing that it was 'one of the greatest sources of evil ... Young and old are congregated together in one field, and the greatest immorality results'.

Above: Early combine harvester in 1940. As well as the driver up front, two men were needed on the trailer that carried assorted traditional equipment to form this makeshift 'combine'.

Right: A team of self-propelled Massey-Harris combines at work in Norfolk in 1943. On smaller farms it was still more common to see tractor-drawn combines at the time.

high-seated combine harvester, which in one whirring motion and with the help of a single driver would cut the standing crop, separate and collect the grain and spit out the straw, was a common sight. The biggest problem was how to store this sudden deluge of ready-threshed grain and what to do with all that straw if you did not have livestock in need of bedding.

When I lived in my tiny Sussex cottage in the 1970s, the local farmer's combine was so huge that the driver was at eye-level with the bedroom windows. The first day of the harvest was always an exciting one, with the monstrous machine manoeuvring into place and its warning pinwheel accelerating into life like the eye of an awakening dragon. It would usually start on the previous eve, opening up a swathe around the headland in preparation for the continuous work of the following day, when in due course its lone driver would be joined at intervals by a tractor driving its trailer in parallel with the beast to catch a stream of golden grain from its tall delivery chute. There was no need for binding, sheaves, stooks, stacks or ricks: the grain was taken straight to the farmyard grain dryer and stored in huge bins, waiting for the price to be right for its sale to the merchants.

Balers

Meanwhile the straw was left in its long rows to wait for the ker-clunking mechanical straw-baler, which packed the straw tightly into handy-sized brick-shaped bales and wrapped the two strings or wires around them and tied the knots before ejecting them into convenient groups for collection and carting back to the barn. When it worked. If the ker-clunk changed its tune and rhythm, it was a sign that the string was snarling somewhere in the baler's innards and a cue for extensive sweating and swearing. Somewhere in the field were the ghosts of all those big cheerful groups of men, women and children of the past harvests, the reapers and binders, the carters and stackers and thatchers and threshers, now as redundant as the horses, all replaced by one man in his huge combine harvester and another with his tractor and trailer, who would later be alone in the field cursing at his recalcitrant baling machine.

Below: World War I landgirls help with the baling with the aid of steam power.

Haymaking

In the agricultural year, haymaking comes well before harvest and is even more of a nail-biter. At least three clear days of guaranteed good weather are needed for haymaking – dry, breezy and preferably sunny.

Haymaking by hand

There is something beautiful about the action of an expert with the scythe. It is a large, potentially unwieldy implement and, as with many other tools, needs to fit its user and was usually handmade by a village craftsman. The blade of a harvesting or reaping scythe is up to a fearsome 48 inches long and it differed from a haymaking scythe in that there was a 'cradle' near the heel of the blade to let the cut corn fall neatly, making much easier the job of the following gatherers, whose role was to draw the cut stems into sheaves. A mowing scythe for haymaking was a simpler implement but on a similar scale, with a sinuous wooden handle called the snead or sneath (sometimes steamed into shape) just the right length for its operator. It was fitted with short wooden handholds, adjusted to the user, and a simple scythe blade set at an angle that was personal to the user's height and to the type of crop he was mowing. The blade might be as much as 5ft 6in long, which made it quite a weapon.

After it had been scythed, the grass was left to dry in the sun and wind, helped on its way by being fluffed up and turned by hand from time to time by gangs with long wooden peg-toothed hay rakes. At a certain stage it was ready to be piled up into haycocks, which would then be hand-loaded on to carts and taken off to be made into hayricks. The business of getting the hay into the cart, and from the cart up on to the stack, by means of pitchforks was a strenuous one and required a certain amount of skill as well as brawn.

Left: Scythe and harvest bottle, essential equipment in a Westmoreland hayfield around 1900.

Mowing machines, haymakers and tedders

Haymaking was labour-intensive and, with such a short weather window of opportunity to make good hay, mechanisation had to be welcomed. First came horse-drawn mowing machines, combined with horse-drawn haymakers that turned the hay and left it in long, straight windrows that could easily be picked up by a mechanical hay loader. There were also many and various horse-drawn hay sweeps to draw scattered or windrowed hay to the side of the cart or field rick, and horse-drawn hay sledges to transport the hay to the stack or the barn.

Dorinda Jeynes remembered how, in the 1920s, her grandfather in Devon always seemed to make very good hay:

On the appointed day, he would tap the barometer, study the sky, and learn about the phases of the moon from a diary somewhere. One of the men … would set off with a scythe and cut a swathe all round the outside of a field of standing grass. … The two horses would be harnessed to the mowing machine, which had been overhauled and oiled. The sharp blade would soon bite into the standing grass and it would fall backwards over the knife, row after row. The person who probably felt a bit shaken up at hay harvest time was the man sitting on the mowing machine seat. There were no springs, and there certainly were no cushions, only a hessian bag folded and laid in the big metal 'pan'. The continual jolting could not have been very good for his spine! He had to keep his wits about him, too, and his horses on the move at the right pace. At the corners there was a particular manoeuvre to keep the corner as a corner. This involved 'reining back' and when the right position was reached the sharp click of the tongue, a slight slap of the reins and a few commands to Farmer or Violet and they'd be rattling along again.

Horse-drawn mowers had a pair of iron wheels with a seat above them and a row

Above: Warm work:
a Leicestershire man
rests on his hay rake.

of spikes on a bed with the blade behind them. With the machine in gear, the blade went back and forth at high speed and it was wise not to be in front of it when the horses started pulling and set it in motion. The horses walked abreast of each other on either side of a long pole. Unfortunately, many a baby hare would be cut to shreds: leverets 'lie up' in long grass and won't move, pretending they are not there, paralysed with fright. The screaming of a lacerated leveret is appalling. Nestfuls of young mice would also become victims, and the occasional lark sitting tight on her eggs. And hedgehogs. And frogs. And fawns – they too, like leverets, lie utterly still in the long grass, hiding and hoping. A man with a scythe would have noticed them in time.

Turning the hay by hand during the field-drying process was laborious, albeit satisfying. Tedders were implements that meant the horse could do the work instead, but at first they tended to scatter the hay wildly into the wind. Horse-drawn side-rakes were devised to do the job rather more tidily. Swath turners, in the early 20th century, also helped with

Above: Evacuees help out by raking hay in the Lake District, near Keswick.

Right: A horse-drawn tedder, or 'shaker', used for fluffing out the hay to encourage the drying process, at Side Farm, Patterdale.

the important business of ensuring that all parts of the windrowed hay dried out to the right degree to avoid later pockets of mould, mustiness and moisture in the stack or bale.

Haycocks and stacks

Then, of course, the weather would threaten to change just as the hay was beginning to ripen nicely. That was when pitchforks, or pikes or pikels, came to hand and the hay was piled into 'cocks', the theory being that the weather would only affect the outside of the cock. In some parts of the country these were known as pooks, and the lumps or locks of still-green grass within them would be scattered as soon as there was a settled sunny day. When at last the hay was ripe, the single-horse hay-rake would return to put the hay back into 'dram-rows' (my, how the language changed, depending on local dialect – we are now in Cornwall) and at last the wagons could come in and the pitchers and loaders could set to work

in filling them, taking the whole load back to the 'mowhay' next to the farmyard if they were not building a rick in the corner of the hayfield.

Once the hay was deemed ready, the men would not let up: first of all, the farmer would turn patches here and there to check that the hay really was ripe for carting; meanwhile the hayrick site was being prepared, with faggots of brushwood and 'browst' being laid in an oblong on the ground to prevent damp seeping up into the stack. Next came the hay sweep, looking something like a buckrake but made of wood, with two wheelbarrow-like handles in the middle: the horse would be fastened by long ropes from the hame of his collar to a fitting at each end of the row of teeth. The joy of the sweep was that it literally swept all the hay into a heap on to its long tines; when it had a full load, the horse headed for the rick area and the load was tipped

Above: Ever adaptable, a farmer has converted his car to help with haymaking.

Inset: Horse-drawn haymaking combination of side-rake (to draw hay into windrows), swath-turner (gently turning the row over and placing it on the dry area between the rows to speed the drying process) and tedder (fluffing up the crop to ensure that air reaches all parts of the row) in 1940.

Above: More ingenuity with an old car, here with a hay-sweep attached to the front to gather field hay for stacking.

off. Then the men set to with pitchforks to make the rick by tossing the hay, working up a fair old sweat to match that of the horse and in both cases attracting clouds of flies.

Throughout all this labour, nobody had time to stop for a meal indoors and so cider and tea would be brought out to them, along with farmhouse cakes and sandwiches. The men would clamber down from the rick and find some shade by the hedge while they refreshed themselves, wiping away the sweat with their big colourful handkerchiefs. But however hot they were, they never removed their shirts and they always wore a hat of some kind – a straw boater, a flat cap, an old trilby or a four-knotted kerchief. As soon as the rick was finished, with its top shaped to throw off the rain, it would be thatched. And then everyone hoped that the hay had been stacked in perfect condition and that

it would not all go up in smoke later in the year from spontaneous combustion.

On Rachel Knappett's Lancashire farm, once the hay was deemed to be perfect for stacking the really hard work began. Each person had a specific job: some were reachers, lifting great pikefuls of hay up to the loaders on the wagons. Reaching pikels were six feet long and like a pitchfork except that their two prongs were very large. The reacher thrust the prongs into a big pile of hay and then, legs set well apart and body braced, he swung the pikel and lifted the pile high above his head, pausing there for a moment before gently lowering the hay on to the top of the wagonload. Then he relaxed all those braced muscles and walked to the next haycock to start the fluid motion of lifting the hay all over again.

On top of the wagon, the loaders took the hay from the reachers in their arms and built it skilfully into a square load on the unrailed wagon, making sure that the load did not 'wart' (bulge on one side) – a sure ticket to everything tumbling off the wagon when they geed up the horse to pull it back to the yard. In the yard, each man threw his own wagonload up on to the haystack and rode back to the field for more.

Stacks required very careful building, even when the hay was simply piled into a Dutch barn. Generally there would be timbers at the base and the stacker's job was to keep the stacking firm, using a pikel to adjust everything so that he kept a straight line. First the sides were built, and then the middle was filled in.

THE ELEVATOR

Rachel Knappett's wartime farm had a huge old wooden elevator, worked by a pony going round and round underneath. The elevator was shaped like an enormous chute and the hay was thrown into the lower end and rode up the chute on iron spikes and dropped on to the stack. Most farms of the period would have had a small engine to work the elevator, not a pony like Lassie, who found the work tiresome and certainly beneath her dignity.

She would express her feelings by stopping dead and refusing to continue, knowing full well that nobody could get at her without clambering down off the stack. As soon as anybody did make a move to come and deal with her, she would set off again at a terrific pace and the hay would shoot up the elevator at such a rate that the stackers could not keep up with it.

Above: Using a 'donkey' as an elevator to transfer hay from wagon to rick. Mrs Wadey is persuading the horse to move back and forth to operate the donkey mechanism. Out of sight behind the wagon, a man is working a grab to claw the hay from the wagon. The forward movement of the horse pulls the rope taut, swinging the grab's high crossbar so that the claw-load of hay is suspended over the rick. At the appropriate moment, the man opens the grab to release the hay.

Feeders took pikefuls of hay as it was
thrown off the wagons and passed them
to the stackers. When the stack was high
enough, an elevator was brought in to
keep up with the rising level. As in so
many other aspects of farming, every
region had its own style and shape of
rick or stack building, as well as local
thatching styles.

Hay bales

All of this was dealing with loose hay, of
course. The next step was to compact the
hay into bales, which were so much easier
to handle and stack, and by the end of
the 19th century there were all sorts of
hay balers, usually steam-powered. Philip
Wright, later to become chairman of the
National Traction Engine Club, recalled
staying with his grandparents at Rivetts
Hall Farm, Hartest, in Suffolk, when he
was a lad of seven in 1915 and having his
first glimpse of a hay baler at work:

> It was a Ruston Proctor baler driven
> by a traction engine. The British
> Army of that day had commandeered
> over a million horses that required
> a colossal tonnage of hay and stover.
> Rustons having produced the baler,
> the government took over the entire
> output. A year after this incident a
> baling outfit visited our own farm,
> Bryers Farm, Hawstead. The baler
> was staffed by a team of landgirls,
> the engine was a 17-ton Fowler which
> proceeded to bury itself by its sheer

*Above: Threshed
barley straw being
compressed into wired
bales and then carried
up by elevator for
stacking.*

*Right: A farmer and
his wife (near the
ricks) celebrate 'harvest
home' somewhere in
northern England in
about 1900. Note the
pair of oxen at the
back of the line of
horses.*

weight in our stackyard. Crowds came to see her resting on her 'tender behind' and it took another engine, plus a lot of jacking-up and a load of faggots to extricate the engine again.

By the 1950s the bale heap had arrived – nothing like as elegant and well crafted as a hayrick, albeit sometimes in rick-like pyramidal shape, propped up by hunks of timber and heavy branches. By then string or baler twine was being used more than wire to bind the bales, but string-tied bales were not as dense as wire-bound ones and this made tidy stacking more difficult. Tractors, when they took over from steam and horses, were ideally suited to baling work.

Silage

In the meantime, a new way of preserving the grass crop for winter feeding was emerging: the making of silage. The following report appeared in the *Deanery Magazine – Castlemartin* in 1883:

> *On Wednesday, December 19th, a large number of those who take great interest in agricultural improvements assembled at Brownslade by invitation of Colonel Lambton to witness the opening of a Silo-shed. No other attempt has been made in this neighbourhood to produce this winter food for cattle, which, for the past two years has been much talked about. The experiment was looked upon with the greatest interest by the farmers and others present, some of whom had come from the other side of the Haven. The shed, which had been converted into a Silo pit, was part of the old farm buildings at the back of Brownslade. When it was opened the ensilage was found to be in excellent order giving out a fine aromatic smell.*

Well, the Pembrokeshire Colonel was a go-ahead man for his time. Silage making

THE CHEMISTRY OF SILAGE

To make good silage, a farmer needs to be a bit of a chemist – it is not that different to brewing beer or making wine, as it is based on fermentation. The whole process is the antithesis of hay making: hay needs to be dried, whereas silage needs to retain moisture, and is preserved in a succulent condition. The result should be nice green-coloured silage with a sharp acid flavour and a rather delicious aroma, full of protein and exactly what a cow fancies in mid-winter when she's fed up with dry hay. But how was an early silage maker, experienced in the art of hay making, meant to get to grips with the science of the silo?

Above: A tower silo in the early 1940s.

had only been introduced into Britain a year earlier, largely as a result of a series of wet haymaking seasons that drove livestock farmers to despair. The joy of silage is that, in theory, you can cut it and cart it on the very same day. But on the whole the science was not well enough understood for any practical farmer to succeed with the process in those early years. In 1901 a new type of American wooden silo was introduced but it was far too expensive for most, and by the 1930s there were even fewer silos than there had been in the Colonel's time. In 1939, nearly all the grass was still preserved as hay; the very little silage that was being made was cured in tall tower-silos. In the 1940s most farmers had abandoned towers and, like the Colonel, made their own silage pits or built above-ground clamps.

Above-ground silage clamps had the advantage that the cattle could feed directly from the clamp. Part of the face of the heap would be made accessible to them and they simply helped themselves, which did away with all the heavy work of cutting the stuff out and carting it to the feed areas.

Other Crops

Those evocative summery scenes of haymaking
and the corn harvest were only part of the picture.
Many other crops needed harvesting, often in far less
pleasant weather. Potatoes and roots were among the
worst when it was a matter of harvesting by hand, and
before they could be stored roots such as swedes and
wurzels also had to be trimmed by hand, sometimes
in frosty weather that made the job even worse.

*Above: Hop pickers from London cooking up a meal in 1890, still
wearing fancy town-style hats.*

Richard Jefferies (1848–1887), the well
known young chronicler of rural life,
described in *Hodge and His Masters* how
a woman sat all day long alone out in the
open arable fields trimming roots:

> *She has a stool or log of wood to sit
> on, and arranges a couple of sacks or
> something of the kind, so as to form
> a screen and keep off the bitter winds
> which are then so common – colder
> than those of the winter proper. With
> the screen on one side, the heap of roots
> the other, and the hedge on the third
> she is in some sense sheltered …*

Mechanisation eventually came to the
rescue of the root diggers and by the
1920s mechanical potato planters and
diggers were popular, to the relief of
manual tater gatherers. But those bulky
roots still had to be carted, and that was
heavy work.

Hops

In some parts of the country, a major crop was hops for brewing. The crop has very specific requirements in terms of soil and climate (hops love the sun) and the whole business of hop growing has always been highly specialised. It used to be heavily dependent on plenty of cheap labour, especially at harvest, when whole families would descend in large gangs on the hop gardens, pouring out of the towns and cities to enjoy a working holiday in the open air. They came in trainloads and were often met at the station by farm wagons; they then camped or were given living space in huts, sheds, barns and so on, and it was all one big party, though also a lot of hard work. Many families returned year after year and hugely looked forward to this rural break.

Freda Vidgen remembered her childhood on a farm at Chainhurst, near Marden, before World War I. Her father was the bailiff there and she recorded her

Above A gang of fenland potato pickers in 1930.

Right: Farmer McClure and his family bagging up export seed potatoes in Ulster in the 1940s.

Taking a pipe-smoking break from hop-pole wiring on stilts.

memories for Michael Winstanley's oral history project in the 1970s:

> *The London hop pickers had from January on been writing postcards to book hopper huts and bins for the coming year, so we children in the winter evenings used to address the postcards and put 'Hop picking will commence …' and leave it until my father had been in the hop garden in the autumn. Then we had to get these couple of hundred postcards out and send them off to London and book the hopping train. Then the farm wagons used to be got out, the horses were dressed over all with catis, which is coloured coarse ribbon, and brasses, and they went three miles to Marden station with us country children running behind them all the way. Two vans went for luggage, and a dung cart went for old people. They had a sieve basket, which is a bushel basket, a wickerwork basket that they used to pick apples in and they would throw it up in. Most of the old ladies weighed about twelve, fourteen, sixteen stone for the porter they used to drink in London made them so stout. So the waggoner would put the basket down, put his shoulder under their bottom and heave them up into the dung cart. All the children would sit up on top of the luggage. Then coming down Pattenden Lane, the horses would stop and the families would undo bags and tip out two or three children. They had put children into sacks so that they shouldn't pay the fare down, taken them out on the train and then put them back into the sacks to get off. Then they had their huts, and they all renewed acquaintanceships with children from last year.*

The hop harvest usually lasted for three to five weeks, starting at the end of August. Pickers were paid by the bushel, or by the tally (an agreed number of bushels at an agreed rate), so every child's contribution helped the family. The pickers tended to work in families and the hops were picked into bins or cribs made of canvas covering a wooden frame. After the pick had been measured, the hops would be carted in large sacks, usually known as pokes, to the oasthouse for drying.

Even in the early 1940s the picking season was still bringing crowds of Londoners and other townsfolk into the country, but on not such a big scale; brewers only needed a pound of hops to every 20 gallons of beer, and they were anyway importing their hops from Bavaria.

It was not only the harvest: there was always work to be done in the hopfields and always a demand for labour to do it. For example, from late April to early June women and children would help with tying the hop bines to the poles: they fastened rushes carefully around selected young and tender shoots on the bine (not so tight as to restrict them, but not so loose that they could slip out). As the bines grew up the poles, further tying was needed. Mrs L Gilbert recorded her early memories of hop work in the West Kent Federation of Women's Institutes' *Old Days in the Kent Hop Gardens*. She first went into the hopfields at the age of three back in 1887:

> *At hop-tying time we would get our rushes from the oast and put them to soak all night in water and then take as many as we thought we would need for the day to the farm in a sack. … When there were only two poles to a hill we tied four bines round each pole clockwise, with the rushes in our 'lap bags'.*

The actual poling (putting the poles into the ground) and pole-pulling were done by the men. Fred Grover, who died in 1905, lived in a hopping area and, among many other jobs, was a pole-puller for many years. The pullers worked in gangs at harvest and their job was to cut off the

bines close to ground in early September and then lift the entire pole, weighed down by the whole season's growth, and carry it to the pickers' baskets. After the hop-pickers had started their weary walk back to their accommodation at the end of the day, the pole-pullers still laboured. All the newly picked hops, emptied from the baskets into coarse open bags, known locally as sarpliers, had to be carried out of the hop-ground to the wagon (the farmer would not let horses trample over the hop-ground). Each sarplier held 15 or 16 bushels, and when they were full of wet hops each load weighed 1½cwt. It took two men to lift the bag on to the back of a third, who then had to trudge over the slippery, sticky clay with water oozing from his load down his back. Each man might have to carry as many as nine of these hefty, soaking bags in a day, and in Fred's case it meant carrying them 120 yards across the sticky hop-ground and then across two acres of a wet-haulmed potato crop to reach the wagon. By the time Fred began to walk the two miles home he had worked for 15 hours, from dawn to dusk.

Above: Hop pole-pullers in Sussex take a break after loading full sarpliers.

HOPPING TIME

There used to be an old song, sung lustily in the hop gardens, about the marvellous power of hops in drawing the old, the young, the sick and the well to the 'bins' at hopping time. It began:

Old Mother Nincompoop had nigh twelve months been dead She heard the hops were pretty good, and just popped out her head …

Jobbing About

In his Victorian diaries in the mid 1860s, farmer William Hodkin on the Chatsworth estate often recorded that he had been 'jobbing about' during his working day – or 'jobing about', as he tended to write it. This catch-all phrase covered all those incidental jobs about the farm, of which there were many.

Hedging

Ken Ainsworth, born in 1915 in Leicestershire, was still laying hedges well into his eighties, until one day a particularly vicious stab in the arm from a piece of blackthorn led to muscle weakness and joint stiffness that meant he could no longer raise his arm above shoulder height, severely curtailing his hedging ability. So, reluctantly, he hung up his hedging tools and then watched with growing grumpiness as other men started cutting 'his' hedges with flail machines that ripped at the hedging plants, flaying their stems and leaving the hedges looking mangled and beaten, the gashed stems wide open to infection and the thorny brash left scattered all over the lanes. Ken had taken a pride in the neatness of his own work and often despaired of modern farming methods: it grieved him (a favourite phrase) to see the results. Leicestershire was particularly well known for its careful hedging.

The purpose of hedge-laying was to thicken the hedge properly so that it was stock-proof; after all, hedges were intended to keep the animals in the field long before barbed-wire and sheep-netting were invented. They were laid from about January to March and were cut in the

---

WINTER WORK

In the old days, hedge-cutting was a winter job to fill in idle hours when nothing much else could be done on the farm and meant a good excuse for a warming bonfire: all the cuttings, particularly the blackthorn with its vicious spikes, were carefully raked up and burnt, especially along the lanes – bearing in mind that most of the workers travelled by bike.

Above: A mole drainer, cable-drawn across the field by a pair of steam plough engines. The 'mole' was a bullet-shaped snout making a four-inch drainage tunnel through the soil about two feet below the surface.

Opposite: Old hedger and ditcher in Victorian times. The long leather leggings would have been essential protection in his daily work.

Right: Hedger, well protected by leather gauntlets and knee pads, laying a hawthorn hedge between the wars.

autumn and winter. Hedge-cutting was yet another of the skills that many of the older farmworkers learned over the years. It was also hard physical work in the days when hand-tools did the job, rather than chainsaws and tractor-driven hedge-cutters and flails.

Ditching

Ainsworth also used to complain about how farmers no longer cleaned out their ditches at the base of the hedges or along other field boundaries. Ditching by hand is a most laborious job, but not as laborious as laying piped drainage systems across a whole field. At the end of the 18th century, drainage gangs must have cheered the invention of the mole plough: a device that drags a torpedo-like bar through the soil beneath the surface, creating something very similar to a mole run and, in clay soils, holding its shape and drainage abilities without the need for pipes. The early machines were hefty wooden things, sometimes dragged by a chain and winch turned (apparently) by eight women, or drawn by horses. Life became easier when mole ploughs could be drawn by tractor.

Talking of digging, the inhabitants of a parish in Essex in the 19th century sank a deep well at public expense during a period of severe drought. Once the well had been dug, there was inevitably a large heap of the earth that had been removed from the shaft. They all agreed that the heap was an eyesore and should be removed, and they called a parish meeting to decide how to deal with it. Many suggestions were made and at last it was proposed (carried unanimously) that they should dig a large hole and bury the heap in it. This saga could run and run…

Farmworkers

The Oxfordshire labourer is very slow, stated an enormous Ministry of Agriculture report on agricultural wages and conditions of employment in England in 1919. In contrast, there was an unsourced and much earlier but undated quote in Gerald Hagan's book *Dry Docking* (which has nothing to do with ships but is about the Norfolk village of Docking that used to be always short of water) claiming that the agricultural labourer of Norfolk was 'second to none in the kingdom'.

No doubt many another county boasted that its agricultural labourers were second to none, just as they all boasted that their local breeds of livestock were not only the best but also the oldest in Britain. But in Docking the writing was on the wall: machines were already replacing large numbers of labourers on the land. Between 1851 and 1901, the population of Docking dropped from 1,640 to 1,185, mainly because many agricultural workers decided to emigrate to North America or Australia. They had seen the future, though surely in the mid-19th century nobody could ever have imagined that within a hundred years the work of ten, a dozen or even a score of men and their horses would be done by one man and his machine and the fields would no longer be full of busy people – just a driver alone in his cab.

Farm Servants

There was a time when it was customary for unmarried agricultural workers, often still only children, to live in the farmhouse itself, or in yard buildings, in the system by which they were known as farm servants. This could mean that they were well fed, relieving their own parents of the burden of that extra mouth at the table, and in many cases the farmer's wife mothered them and even made sure they had decent clothes and went to night school.

Sometimes, as can be imagined, a group of lads living away from home could get up to a bit of mischief, and worse. In 1884 the *South Wales Echo* reported on a court case in which 20-year-old farm boy John Phillips had been charged with the manslaughter of 15-year-old Charles Eynon, a fellow farm servant at Prickiston. It was a case of mischief getting out of hand. Nine farm boys slept in a cowhouse loft above the calves and they had a foolish custom, when the master was away, of firing a blank charge at the boy who came in after nine o'clock at night. Phillips had previously been seen to load the gun with powder and 'reddening', to frighten the others into believing that he was spattered with blood. On the night in question, Phillips took the gun and went out to the steps. The others heard the gun being fired and saw young Eynon coming into the loft, followed by Phillips, who put Eynon on the bed and held him in his arms while the other lads pulled down his trousers and washed a wound on his leg. The district nurse was summoned the following day and dressed the wound, using an oil suitable for a burn, but the boy became feverish and the doctor was called out. The doctor found 'a circular wound midway between the hip and the knee joint, the fleshy part having been blown off, leaving the muscles exposed'. He also noticed a 'peculiar red colour' that came off with the nurse's dressing. Unfortunately the boy died.

Many farmers felt an almost paternal sense of responsibility for their farm servants. The term servant instantly suggests a master, and indeed many farmworkers would call their employer Master, even up to World War II. But by the time JH Barwick entered plough service near Eastry in Kent in 1902, very few farmers were still willing to share the family home with farm servants. That meant Barwick had to lodge with a married waggoner, whose wife was

Left:Employees on the Titsey estate of the Leveson Gower family in 1861. Left to right: John Richards in his smock frock; Dame Hook; James Linsey (a stable helper); an unnamed labourer in high hat; Mrs Sarah Wood (keeper of the lodge); Dame Argent; and roadman Benjamin Hook, husband of Dame Hook.

Opposite: Farm-workers in the late 19th century, typically attired.

paid by the farmer for taking him in. He recorded his youthful memories for Michael Winstanley's oral history project in the 1970s:

I lived on fat pork for twelve months. That's all we had, bar Sundays, we had a beef pudding. Course I used to be allowed to come home one Sunday in a month and I used to get different then. But that's all I had for breakfast, dinner and tea – fat pork. Cor blimey! And sometimes it wasn't done properly and when the knife went through it you could hear it sort of crunch. Pork not done properly is awful too. The waggoner used to go down to the stable at four, come home at five, have his breakfast and back again at five-thirty. Well, when he went back he used to call me, but because his breakfast was all cleared away there was no telling what he had. No! We used to have to be out at the stable at six with the horses to go out in the field ploughing and stay there till two. That was eight hours. Do you know we didn't have a bit to eat or drink in between that time. She wouldn't lay anything out. She used to get nine shillings a week for my board

and lodging and she had the lot. But it was only for one year because that waggoner left and another one came and I boarded with him. His wife used to bring us tea and a piece of bread and cheese out if we were down at the farm. I was in clover!

Farm servants were girls as well as boys. In the 1960s an old woman in Devon, around the Okehampton area, recorded her memories back into the 1880s for EW Martin's study of rural life. She had been only too thankful when, at the age of 14, she managed to persuade her parents to let her go into farm service. It was hard work from morning to night, she said, but at least she did not have to 'bow and scrape' and she did get a bellyful of potatoes, turnips and greens. She had first gone out to service when she was only 12, but not in farming: her 'missus' was a parson's wife, 'a bitch' who made her tie her hair up 'in a bun like a little old woman' which made the young girl cry.

She'd begrudge us maids even an extra piece of bread. Our food was the leftovers from their meals. When they had visitors our food was a bit better;

and then the missus would count every potato to make sure us didn't help ourselves to any. I've gone to bed hungry many a time.

The girl's father was a farmworker and his master would complain if the girls failed to curtsey to him or his wife.

Some of the big farmers were as bad as the bettermost folk. The farmer would tell father that he didn't mind for himself. What he wanted was to make sure us poor children were brought up to respect their betters.

THE BENEVOLENT MASTER

In The Kentish Gazette in 1850, a 'Rural Rector' offered advice to local farmers who were thinking of hiring farm servants. He told them to 'be very careful to choose one who bears a good character' and that the potential servant should be informed that the farmer hoped he would go to church regularly – 'not that you mean to make him go, but that you will feel disappointed if he does not go.' It should be made clear that the employer expected that 'nothing like bad language will ever be heard from his lips' but it should be shown by the farmer's manner that he took an interest in his servants, by asking them about their homes and their parents and trying to show them that he was their friend. Above all, 'If there should be any fair going on in the neighbourhood, warn them of the harm they may get by going to it. A kind word of sober advice may just serve to check them in time when they are rushing into danger ...'

This old lady recalled that 'touching of the forelock' to social superiors was 'part of a natural law' for farmworkers in their fustian jackets and worn corduroy trousers. Most of those labourers' wives and daughters never questioned the necessity of 'making their curtsey' and it was common to see them – poor bonneted women in shawls and trailing skirts, or small girls in their heavy hobnailed boots – making a little bob of the knees whenever they met or passed a yeoman, parson or squire or their ladies.

A vicar in the Fen country related in 1921 how he had come across a self-made small farmer who had always been poor. At his first place as a farm servant he worked for a year for £2 10s and his keep, and when he got £5 for his second year's work he thought he was 'a man'. They were never allowed out, never went off the farm, never had a holiday. 'When you'd done your day's work, you came in and took off your boots, and then you had your supper and was locked in for the night.' On Sunday mornings they had to feed the livestock; on Sunday evenings they went to church or chapel but had to be back at the farm by 8.30 and with the long sermons of the period that did not leave much free time.

If you was home in time there was a bit o' cake and a glass of wine for ye, if you was late they showed ye the whip and shoosh'd ye off to bed. If we'd had too much liberty we might ha' gone roamin' all over the place and mebbe got into mischief. The only time you was off the place was at the Statutes, when you hired yourself out for another year.

The Statutes were the annual hiring fairs. Yet he said he had a good 'missus', and he even liked the brimstone and treacle all the lads had to take every Saturday night. This was in the 1860s and since then the man had 'struck out for himself' and become relatively wealthy.

Above: Farmhouse domestic servant cleaning fish under the pump.

Hiring Fairs

Michaelmas: today the instant connotation might be with daisies, but in rural areas the strongest association was with the farming year. Many agricultural labourers were engaged for a year at a time, beginning at Michaelmas – the Feast of St Michael on 29 September, or, on older calendars, 11 October.

Old Michaelmas Day was traditionally the day that marked the start of the new farming year and the end of the old one; it was the day on which farms changed hands, debts were settled and men changed their masters. At midday on 11 October, all work ceased and did not start again until the morning of 16 October. It was an uncertain few days for many, moving from one employer and one home to another. Many of them would find a

new master at the big hiring fairs and mop fairs, where each person seeking work would wear an emblem of their expertise: a shepherd might carry his crook, or put bunches of wool on his cap, while a farm labourer usually carried a short pole, known as a shining stick. George Dew, in his diaries in the 1870s, noted that male farm servants had a whiplash fastened to the band of their hat by way of identification, carters a piece of horse hair, cowmen a piece of cow hair (presumably their prospective employers had good enough eyesight to tell the difference) and shepherds a piece of wool. Jack Larkin told the University of Kent oral history project in the 1970s about waggoners:

If a chap wanted to go to the hiring fair, he used to take his whip and what they called a war-line, that was a very long lead, all done up nice and neat, and he'd attach that to his belt and carry his whip over his shoulder. As soon as he'd been hired, he'd carry his whip like that – straight up. That was to say he'd been hired, and then he'd go and have a drink with his new boss then go and find out where he'd got to bed-in like for the twelve month.

In Scotland and northern England, it was customary for married farmworkers to commit themselves to a farmer for 12 months (single men usually contracted for only six). Sometimes a farmer felt unable to keep a married man on for a further term because his family did not include the type of additional workers the farmer needed. It was up to the farmer to speak, and a man who was not asked by the farmer to re-engage knew that he was not going to be hired for the next term and started to look for a new job. If a worker intended to leave, he would rarely inform his master of his intention unless the master himself brought up the matter of staying on. This he might do six weeks before the hiring fair, in what was known as speaking time – a time when the workers could also air any grievances they might have.

Looking back, it seems demeaning that men and women (and children) had to stand around like so many cattle in the market-place while farmers weighed them up as potential workers, outdoors or indoors, but it was more two-way than it

Left: Burford Hiring Fair. Most hiring or mop fairs waned in the 1880s but Burford was still busy in the early 1900s.

INDOOR HIRING FAIRS

When the old street hiring fairs had degenerated to being held more in the pubs than in the street, the Scottish Farmers' Union and the Scottish Farm Servants' Union combined to conduct their own indoor hiring fairs.

seemed. The workers were there to negotiate and bargain with the farmers and it was generally turned into a festive occasion – and very often a bawdy one.

Hiring fairs, mop fairs, statute fairs, call them what you will, but they were a good excuse for entertainment for all. There would be stalls and sideshows, fairground rides, food and drink aplenty, so much so that the chattering classes of the time condemned them for encouraging frivolity and immorality, especially as the traditional 'earnest money' shilling or half-a-crown that was given to a labourer once

Below: Roasting an ox at the Stratford-on-Avon Mop Fair in 1913; by then it was no longer a true hiring fair.

the deal was struck with his new employer would promptly be spent at the fair or in the local ale house.

By the early years of the 20th century the hiring fairs were losing their importance. Whether at a hiring fair or in some other context, by the 1920s terms of engagement were generally by word of mouth rather than in writing. By this period, hiring fairs survived mainly only in the north, one of the few parts of Britain in which men tended to be hired by the year and actually would quite often have a written contract. Elsewhere engagement by the week was more common if there was a sufficient supply of labour, and the usual way of finding labour was to ask about in the neighbourhood and on market-days, or to put an ad in the local paper. Farmworkers in need of employment no longer went to look for it at hiring fairs.

FUN OF THE FAIR

In Oxfordshire in the 1870s, George Dew regularly attended Bicester Fair but was shocked to find young and old, married and single, male and female 'of the lower classes' making good use of a dancing booth in the square. He also noted that in recent years the servant girls attending the fair had 'so altered in their style of dress that it is in some cases most difficult to judge as to which is the mistress & which is the servant'. Tiddly-tut and fie upon them!

Bothies, hinds and bondagers

In the 19th century, the old system of unmarried farm servants living with the farmer's family was already breaking down and many had become mere agricultural labourers, living separately in cottages and bothies or chaumers. The bothy, a dwelling for unmarried men, might be a single-storey cottage, or even a room in an outbuilding, whereas a chaumer (chamber) was a roughly furnished room, usually in an outbuilding or as a separate one-room building.

In Scotland and northern England the farm servants included 'hinds' (married ploughmen) living in farm cottages. The cottages were usually of the old 'but and ben' sort, with a kitchen (the but) and an inner room or parlour (the ben), with a windowless closet or scullery at the back. A hind not only gave his own labour to the farmer, but, in return for his cottage, he also often pledged to provide someone, usually his wife or daughter, to help at harvest for a fixed number of

Above: Group of men working at the water-powered Iping Mill which, at various stages over the centuries, was a fulling mill, a corn mill, a malt mill, a paper mill and a timber mill, offering alternative employment to farm labourers. The men seen here, wearing typical clothing for rural workers of the period, include the grandfathers of villagers still alive today.

Right: Bothy men in Angus. The bothy was accommodation for single men on the farm, especially in Scotland.

days – anything up to a month a year. In addition a hind would contract to supply labour for the farmer for longer periods and this was the bondage system. Again the bondager was usually a woman – perhaps his daughter or his sister or, if he had neither, a woman whom he had to hire and for whom he would provide board and lodging, with the farmer paying him an allowance in cash for each day that the woman was employed on the farm as an outworker. Thus the farmer had a ready supply of labour but only had to pay for it when the outworker actually worked, which might

Above: Taking a break after a lifetime of work to watch the harvest at the outbreak of World War II.

unlike the slave markets of olden days, with the hinds standing about on the cobbles, waiting to be spoken to by a farmer trying to spot a likely man. 'Are ye gannen or are ye stoppen?' was a common greeting during the week before hiring day. And the 'arrl' money was responsible for not a few 'sair heeds' the 'morn's morn'. Also a few 'forced marriages' and some 'love bairns' were heard of afterwards. I also remember the 'Kirn supper', the 'guizers' on Hogmanay night, the first-footing, old Mrs Parker who milked in record time and then sat down on the kitchen fender to 'heve a draaw at me pipe, hinny', the 'gordle cayeks' with currants galore, and butter oozing down one's chin, and old Mrs Smith, who did our washing and 'ploated' our geese, describing her first place at the age of ten when all the servants at the hall, after returning from church on Sunday, donned their working clothes after a meagre supper and lay down until Monday morning, when they were roused and had to do the enormous family washing before

be for about 180 days during the year. For the rest of the time the hind was supporting the bondager.

The bondager system persisted right into the 20th century, and you could tell a bondager by her distinctive clothing: a 'drugget' skirt made from a coarse, felted fabric, blouse, side-buttoning boots and wide-brimmed straw hat. In a letter to *The Countryman* published in the summer of 1945, M-R wrote on the subject of 'North Country Bondagers':

I am well under sixty but remember their sonsie faces, practical though not very picturesque dress, and sturdy build. Hiring days were great days then in the Alnwick and Morpeth districts, and I remember thinking as a small girl, when walking along Bondgate Within, that the scene couldn't be very

breakfast! Never did I see 'Pace eggs' to equal her dyeing of them, or more gaily patterned 'clouty hearthrugs'. A very old relative told me, as he pointed to a peel tower north-west of Alnwick, that he remembered watching there as a laddie so that he could warn his brothers when the press-gang was out, and yet another – scornful of the early railway trains – boasted of what he had won by riding his horse from near Wooler to Alnwick in less time than the new-fangled trains!

Workers all

You had to be tough to work in farming. Fred Brooking, born in 1906, remembered that his father, working on a Devon farm, had only one day off a year – and that was Good Friday 'and we always had to go gardening'. Perhaps that is where the rural tradition of planting your potatoes on Good Friday (regardless of the date) arose; it was the only day when a labourer had time for such work.

Many remained loyal to their farms

and there are countless examples of men working on the same farm for 60 years or more, some of them still alive today. My neighbour Ken Ainsworth, born in 1915, had only two employers in the whole of his working life, starting on a Leicestershire farm when he left school at the age of 14 and moving to his second job, in Sussex, in 1956.

POTATO PLOT

In 1875, Benjamin Hawkins had told Francis Kilvert that sometimes, when a rick in a field was threshed or brought into the barn, the shepherd or carter was given the privilege of planting a few potatoes on the rick site 'and he was so overjoyed with his good fortune that he thought he had got a small farm'. In those days of Benjamin's youth, it seems, there was no such thing as planting potatoes in the field and so every inch of space in a cottage garden was precious for growing vegetables, especially potatoes.

Below: The smallholders' harvest: the Holloway family at Ashwell, near Baldock, in the early 1900s.

LOYALTY

Jimmy Puttock (pictured below) worked on the same Sussex farm in Balls Cross for almost 64 years (he died at the age of 84) and his photograph appeared in the Daily Mirror and in the News Chronicle in 1936 under the caption 'Sunny Jim – over 60 years on one farm'. Puttock, who almost made a career out of winning long-service prizes at ploughing matches and agricultural meetings, was an accomplished accordion player, and many of his vintage were more than adequate musicians in the days when you made your own entertainment and when most villages, even in southern England, had their own brass band.

Puttock was among several characters photographed by George Garland in the 1920s and 1930s, most of them sporting a set of whiskers. Others included Jimmy Ifold ('still going strong at the age of 90') and William Slaughter, aged 65 in 1933 and still unmarried: he had started his working life scaring rooks at the age of nine for three shillings a week and had entered the service of Lord Leconfield on a farm at Steyning when he was 20, moving six years later to a farm at Byworth, where he was still working four decades later when Garland found him 'ministering to the hungry demands of a promising batch of Middle White pigs'.

Top left: Henry 'Pickle' Hammond lighting his pipe with a magnifying glass.
Centre left: Successful one-handed poultry farmer Walter Alfred Edwards.
Bottom left: One of George Garland's unnamed 'rustic characters'.

Above: Carter Edward Cooper of Coultershaw.

COUNTRY CHARACTERS

Among the winners of long-service prizes were several of the bewhiskered characters photographed by George Garland in the 1920s and 1930s. It is surprising that most of Garland's characters had straightforward names. In my own parish, nicknames were rife at that period: off the top of my head I have been told of Squibby, Major, Purty, Captain, Goody, Timber, Pusser, Thumper, Bugle, Piggy ... In the 1870s, Richard Heath was walking in the Yorkshire Dales and found that most people were known by their nickname, to such an extent that their real names were often forgotten. A woman asked the local minister: 'Who has joined the church?' 'Mary Alderson,' he replied. She looked puzzled, though she had probably known the girl since she was a baby. Then it dawned on her: 'Oh, I know who 'tis you mean; it's Bessie Billywidow.' In court at Richmond one day they called out for John Metcalf; there was no response. Somebody suggested that they should shout Sandy John Jock, and he immediately stood up. Quite often the nickname was the addition of a father's and grandfather's Christian name to the person's own, such as Simon's Dick's Maggie. I prefer the more colourful ones in my own village, even when nobody has any idea of their meaning or origin.

Gangs

In many parts of the country, it was the custom for farmworkers to get together in a gang and make a contract with their employer at harvest time. Instead of the usual weekly wage, the farmer would agree to pay a lump sum based on an agreed price per acre. At this crucial time of year, the workers usually managed to earn about double a month's normal wages – and the faster they could get the harvest in, the better off they were.

Harvest contracts

The contract was a formal one, in writing, drawn up in negotiation with the nominated Lord of the Harvest (usually the farm foreman). It listed what the gang had undertaken to do and who its members were, and it gave details of their payments, whether in cash or in kind. For example, in the mid 19th century a farmer at Blaxhall in East Suffolk drew up an agreement for six workers for a lump sum of £30, based on 92 acres at 6s 6d (£29 18s), plus 2s, for which the men agreed to cut the corn, stack it, provide a gaveller each (a woman with a short hand rake to gather the corn for the men to pitch up to the wagon) and also hoe the turnips twice and turn the pease once. There were penalties: 'Should any man lose time through sickness, he is to throw back two shillings per day to the company. Should any man lose any time through drunkenness he is to forfeit five shillings a day to the company.' But there were also rewards: the contract allowed each man one coomb (four bushels) of wheat at 20 shillings, three bushels of malt (for home brewing of beer) as a gift, one pound of mutton per man 'instead of dinner' and 2½ pounds of mutton at fourpence a pound every Friday. The shepherd on the farm would kill a sheep every Friday night during harvest month to supply these meat allowances.

Before the corn was ripe, this Suffolk farmer would have held a dinner (locally known as a frolic) for all the workers at the farmhouse. After the harvest came the traditional harvest supper, or 'Largesse

Left: Somerset harvesters at Henstridge pause to refresh themselves with farm cider at the turn of the century.

Opposite: Village women in Suffolk helping with the potato harvest in the 1920s. The crop had been loosened but the women spent many back-breaking hours picking up the potatoes by hand.

Spending' – named for the largesse that the Lord and Lady of the Harvest had collected as gifts of money around the village and neighbouring towns, where they sought money from traders and townspeople who did business with the farmer. All the rabbits caught during harvest would be auctioned and the income added to the Largesse. The dinner itself was essentially roast beef, plum pudding, beer ... and gin.

Fenland gangs

Ah, the fenlands! King George III dismissed them with: 'What, what! Lincolnshire? All flats, fogs, and fens – eh, eh?' The huge tracts of fenland soil were so prolific that they needed plenty of labour to cultivate them, especially to keep in check the weeds that grew so vigorously. The farms were large and, on the whole, there were no farm cottages, the farmers relying on labour from the villages that lay along the highways. For about eight months of the year every available woman and child, as well as all local men, had to be pressed into service in the fields and a system of gang labour arose, whereby a gang-master contracted to supply the farmer with labour when and where it was wanted. To quote Richard Heath, writing in 1873 but harking back to 1864:

> Up at earliest dawn, for they must start work at half-past five or six, breakfast is scrambled through, and the children hurry out into the street, to meet like a company of factory hands at a given rendezvous. Boys and girls, big and little, corrupt and innocent, they flock together; and there in the pure morning light the more depraved give the tone to the assemblage, by commencing some disgusting badinage.

The gangs might have to trudge anything up to six miles into the fen, where they would divide into companies to begin the tasks of pulling weeds, lifting potatoes, topping beets, peeling osiers or whatever the

GANG-MASTERS

Gang-masters were said to be mostly men who could find no other employment because their character made them unemployable on a full-time basis.

The Children's Employment Commission described them in an 1867 report as 'catchwork labourers', 'men of indolent and drinking habits' and in some cases 'of notorious depravity'. These men were paid on a piecework basis and wrung as much work as possible out of their gangs of children (some as young as six), paying them so much a day and pocketing the rest for themselves.

Above: Farmworker's wife and child at the cottage door.

Above: Taking a break from preparing the land for potato planting.

season demanded. Most of the work involved continual stooping, or kneeling on the damp soil, or little children getting soaked up to the waist when hand-weeding a standing crop of corn. They would work like this, children as well as adults, for ten to twelve hours a day, leaving home in the dark and returning in the dark in winter, six days a week.

Illegitimate babies were common among those who worked in the gang systems and rarely survived. Even the legitimate ones had a hard time, with their mothers spending such long hours in the fields. A quarter of them died before reaching their first birthday, very often from sheer neglect.

Among the women and girls, the biggest complaint was about getting their clothing so damp from weeding in wet corn that they had to yank off their petticoats, wring them out and hang them up to dry. Their footwear would be so wet that their feet were soaking all day, and many subsequently suffered badly from rheumatism. Another problem, not usually mentioned, was how a woman was supposed to answer, with any modesty, a call of nature while she was out in a big open fenland field.

Richard Jefferies described a wide range of women's work in the fields – hoeing, stone picking, clod beating, tedding and turning hay, reaping with a sickle and fagging-stick from early summer dawn to moonlight, even though they may be suckling their babies, 'sheening' (feeding the threshing machine) and, as well as endless days of hard physical labour, running a home in which they would rise before their labouring husbands to prepare meals and see to the children, clean the cottage and do the washing before setting out for work in the fields.

Gang women, and girls who had done general agricultural labour as children, were despised by many employers. Many of the girls aspired to better things and the peak of their aspiration was to be a domestic servant in the farmhouse, or perhaps a dairymaid (dairymaids usually had greater respect than mere field workers). An indoor servant had the benefit of living in, with better accommodation and food than she could ever find at home. She might help the farmer's wife with basic domestic chores and might help in the dairy, making butter and cheese, or with planting and harvesting when extra hands were needed. Ruth Carey, interviewed by Jennie Kitteringham in her History Workshop pamphlet, *Country Girls in 19th Century England*, had been a 'general girl' in a farmhouse and explained that you had to be able to 'dip your hand in everything'. With a good employer, a farm domestic servant would learn a great deal that would stand her in good stead for her next job, or indeed as a wife. Many a farmer's wife complained that as soon as she had trained up good girls they would leave her and the next employer (or a new husband) would be the one to benefit from all that careful training.

Above: Minding the babies; evacuee mothers planting cabbages at Peckham Health Centre's Home Farm, Bromley Common.

MIND THE BABY

Older women were usually given the role of child-minding during the day, and the mother might be tempted to dose the infant with a mixture based on opium, treacle and sassafras before she left for the fields to keep it quiet for the sake of the child-minder, who might have as many as 35 little ones in her one-woman baby school.

Cottages

In the 1870s, the Hon EB Portman and his fellow Commissioners spent two or three years travelling the country, meeting landowners and farmers, corresponding with hundreds of clergymen and so on while they investigated the 'cottage question'. On the whole the cottages improved as they travelled northwards through the Midlands, but there were many exceptions.

They found an unusual situation in Warwickshire, where apparently field work was confined to married women, the men expecting their wives to help towards the support of the family in this way. A medical officer of the Warwick Union said:

I have known at least eight cases in which children left at home have been burned or scalded – three or four of these have resulted in death. I have occasionally known an opiate in the shape of Godfrey's Cordial, or Duffy's Elixir, given by the mother to the children to keep them quiet.

A report in the same period about the cottages of Northamptonshire attributed the 'very defective' level of education to the 'indifference and want of affection' on the part of parents, which in turn was attributed to 'the demoralisation resulting from bad cottages, and to the poverty of the people and consequent want of hope'. The report referred frequently to overcrowding in the houses.

The 1881 census showed that the small 18th century stone farm cottage attached to my own was home to farm labourer James Dawtery and his wife, along with seven other family members who ranged in age from a one-year-old infant to its 25-year-old father who also worked on the farm. The cottage had but two rooms upstairs, the larger about ten foot square. Yet in the main farmhouse just up the track, the only occupants were shepherd William Messingham, his wife and three toddlers in a house two or three times as spacious. The same pattern of crowded cottages was repeated in other parts of the parish for that year, and some still living today can remember sleeping several to the bed as children. They can also remember when that little stone cottage was almost derelict in the 1960s, though still inhabited, with its broken windowpanes stuffed with rags and newspaper to keep out the weather.

In the 1920s the agricultural labourers' union ran a competition in which women were invited to write essays under the title 'My Cottage as It Is'. Some 160 women in Scotland who were the wives of farm servants seized the opportunity. One woman, typical of many, wrote:

My cottage stands by itself at the top of a very steep brae. The house consists of two rooms. Some of the stones of the walls project so far that the furniture cannot be placed close. The roof is just the trees as they grew, but cut in two; the bark has never been peeled off. The flooring of the garret has shrunk until there are good openings between the boards. A former tenant has laid bags of sand on, to stop the draught we suppose, and now the bags have moved and the sand trickles down on our faces when we are in bed. The grate is four ribs between a lot of loose bricks. They require to be built up every day or two.

Now for the parlour. At the door there is a hole in the wooden floor that would let in a man's foot. There is no fireplace. There are two windows – a small one in front and a smaller one at the back, which the cattle in the field come and lick with their tongues.

The water we have to carry about a hundred yards from a hole scooped out of the ditch where a drain comes out of a field. Sometimes when we go the rats have been sporting in it, so we just have to wait till it clears again. My husband put a barrel at the spout at the end of the house to get the rain water to help on washing-day, but the horses in the field drink it as far as they can reach down. The closet is just a wood hut, which blows over every windy day.

There is no road to our place – just a cart track, so rough that our furniture was pitched off and some of it badly smashed.

These essays were written only a dozen or so years before World War II, well within living memory. In virtually every village in Britain, you will even now find people who can remember a childhood in such circumstances. Some elderly friends of mine, he a farmworker all his life, raised half a dozen children in half a cottage in the 1930s where the rats were so bold that they were almost family pets.

Above: The old type of Shetland crofter's cottage, still in use in the 1930s.

Opposite: Many cottagers kept wild songbirds in a cage by the back door.

Below: Home for a Somerset villager, who lived in the same cottage from birth until her death at the age of 92.

Clothes

A whole book could be written on the subject of country clothing, and many writers have described in great detail what was worn by those who worked in the fields and farmyards and out on the hills and in the woods in days gone by. But you would need an old dictionary to understand some of their descriptions a century or so ago.

Above: Gleaners in Warwickshire going home.

In more recent times, the clothes were more recognisable. For example, in 1947 WP Livingstone published a detailed book about life in the Shetland Islands – real life, away from the eyes of tourists, at a time when the population was about 20,000 and many of its young men were serving in the Mercantile Marine but there were also a number of farmers and stockbreeders and 3,214 smallholders. Much of the work on the crofts was done by the women and very hard work it was, too. The many vivid descriptions in his book included this one:

The community lived in the open. More women than men. Those trundled the manure in barrows over the rough ground, tipped it out, and forked it lightly on the surface, performing the task vigorously and more deftly than the men. These landgirls of the North wear short skirts and long gum boots that are indispensable for outdoor work all the year round. The elderly prefer dark dress, sometimes with a hap on head and shoulders: the younger adopt lighter shades and wear berets.

A hap is a cloak. He watched a group lifting potatoes from wet, sticky soil with their light spades 'displaying the same

LONDON

As a young man, Merry Todman of Sussex had been offered good pay by a cousin on a milk-walk in London, 'but I didn't seem to take to it,' he said. ''Twas a place called Kilburn. I left home and I got there one evening and next morning I couldn't see nothing, 'twas all thick yaller. So I'm off, I says, and away I comes home.' That was his only visit to London in all his life.

unity of movement which characterised all their team-work'. There was a man wearing a yellow pullover, a woman in a red jumper, another in blue and a third in grey. They were throwing the potatoes into a 'kishie', which one of the younger women then slung on her back and carried the load to the barn. Livingstone could barely raise the basket from the ground.

Dorinda Jeynes remembered that, in the 1920s, all the farmers' wives seemed to wear ulsters (long loose overcoats, usually with a hood and belt) when they went to town, partly to look decent and partly to keep out the rain. Without exception, on these outings, every woman wore a proper hat of some kind, never a headscarf and never bareheaded.

Bessie Todman, who died in 1937 at the age of 98 and whose memories were recorded soon after World War I by Maude Egerton King, talked about her second 'situation' in her young days in which she was required to manage most of the housework and all of the dairy work for £8 a year. She really longed for a hoop around her skirt, 'for it was all the fashion in the village', but her mistress, though kindly, was 'wonderfully set against vain show' and would not hear of it. One day Bessie found a cart rope in the road so she took it home and, late on a Saturday night, carefully stitched it into her skirt hem so that, just for once, it would 'stand out nice as anyone's in church next day'. But the mistress noticed that her light was burning so late and came into her room. Shocked at Bessie's vanity, she ripped the rope from the hem and ordered the young maid to kneel and pray against such temptations of the devil. A few years later Bessie was married from the same house, to a farm labourer known as Merry. 'And we did look nice, I promise you, Merry and me, and me in my Tuscan bonnet and fringed shawl give me by my poor old mistress … and six groomsmen, all Merry's friends, in round-frocks and red ties and tall hats.'

BONNETS AND CLOGS

Cottagers always took great pride in their black satin Sunday bonnets, worn over close-fitting muslin caps that were their usual indoor headwear and kept their hair in place and protected from dust. Only a few used a cotton headscarf (or, more properly, kerchief, from couvre chef, meaning a head-covering). The cotton bonnet was usually lilac in colour and homemade, with rows of plain cording and pleated frilling. Footwear in the mid 19th century included wooden clogs, or pattens, with a leather toe-piece and bands of leather over the instep tied with a short lace. The main feature of pattens was an oval iron hoop fixed to the sole to lift the wearer's foot above the inevitable mud if they were nipping out to fetch water from the well or to go down the lane. But most women (and girls) wore hobnail boots for working.

Sacks, smocks and frocks

At work, nobody cared about appearances. Aprons made from old hessian sacks were ideal for messy jobs like plucking poultry. In 1946, JC Pochin was part of a potato-picking gang around the Solway Firth area. There was a strong wind driving the rain at their backs as they laboured and the horse kept moving – he didn't like standing around in a gale while the potatoes were put into the cart:

Above: Walter Boniface in his round-frock, checking the orchard in his cottage garden at Borden village, West Sussex. Boniface, born in 1855, recorded his vivid memories shortly before he died in 1940.

At tea-time I attained the supreme agricultural dignity of a sack round my shoulders. This looked well with my gaiters – an old pair of Wellingtons with the soles and heels cut off. I have worn them in the stubble-fields and for picking brambles, and they have been a great success.

In 1861, photographs taken on the Titsey estate of Mr Leveson Gower showed many of the farmworkers wearing smock-frocks, and on Sundays they would don ancient beavers or tall hats, while their wives dressed up in print frocks and poke-

bonnets or frilled caps. In my own village's scrapbook there is a photograph of Walter Boniface (born in about 1860) dressed proudly in his round-frock in the 1930s. John Coker Egerton, writing in the 1880s, said that the round-frocks that had been the pride and glory of Sussex labourers 50 years earlier were rarely seen:

> *Never more shall we see 'Tom Cladpole' start for London, arrayed in one of these frocks; in leather leggings, the special production of native talent; in a hat made in his own parish; in half-boots which could have been made nowhere else; and with an umbrella which, if not made at home, had been made after a strictly home pattern … In short, the change produced by the last fifty years in Master Cladpole's outward appearance, in his manner of speech, in his methods of locomotion, and, in some respects, in the man himself, has been so complete that it is even now difficult to realise it. He probably started in life fully impressed with the wisdom of the advice which a Sussex man has told me that he used to receive, almost word for word, from one of his seniors – 'Mind,' the old man would say to his young friend, 'mind you don't never have nothing in no way to do with none of their new-fangled schemes.'*

Children, Gertrude Jekyll recalled, were very simply dressed. The girls had short-sleeved cotton or 'stuff' frocks and always long pinafores. Up to the age of eight or nine, their hair was cut short like a boy's and they wore the same round hats of coarse black felt as the boys. The boys wore short round-frocks like small smocks, sometimes called 'gaberdine', over corduroy suits. The adult version of the round-frock was the old carter's smock-frock, still in evidence when Jekyll was writing in 1904 but 'on its way to becoming extinct', though she believed

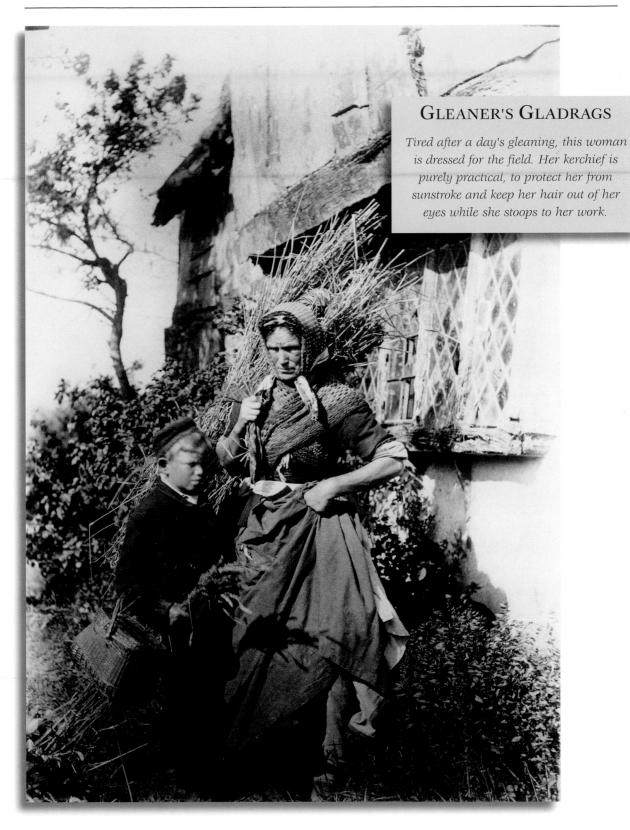

GLEANER'S GLADRAGS

Tired after a day's gleaning, this woman is dressed for the field. Her kerchief is purely practical, to protect her from sunstroke and keep her hair out of her eyes while she stoops to her work.

Above: Alf Townsend, a familiar sight at ploughing matches, dressing the part to inspect the furrows.

no better garment had ever been devised for any kind of outdoor wear.

It turns an astonishing amount of wet, especially when of the ordinary local pattern that has a wide turn-over collar, something like a sailor's, but coming square over the shoulders in front and behind. The frock is cut quite square; of two whole widths of the stuff, with side seams only. The shaping is made by the close gathering, either over the whole back and front, or in two panels on the breast and back near the buttons.

It can be worn either way about; back and front are alike. It sits just as well either way. The sleeves are put in very low; not on the shoulder, but some inches down the arm. There is a worked gathering at their insertion, and also at the wristband, to bring the greater width of the sleeve into the size of the wrist. The material is a strong, tough, closely-woven linen. It was in four colourings; light and dark grey, olive green and white.

Jekyll devoted an entire chapter of her book *Old West Surrey* to 'Old Country Folk – Their Clothing'. She could just remember when both men and women wore 'a real country dress', which, she said, went on until about 1860. In her youth most of the country women wore a print gown and apron, with either a cotton-print sun-bonnet with a deep 'curtain', or a plain straw bonnet tied in place by a narrow ribbon (you can see many examples in the somewhat romanticised paintings of cottagers by Helen Allingham). For haymaking and harvest they often wore an old bonnet tipped up almost vertically to shade their eyes from the sun.

In the 1870s, Francis Kilvert was told by old Sally Killing that, when she had been young, women never wore their gowns out haymaking and if a farmer saw one of his women working in her gown he would tell her to take it off. Sally said she herself had 'been weeks without putting on her gown from Monday morning till Saturday night, in the hay harvest'. She remembered that the women had loose sleeves, which they pinned to their 'shift sleeves' and which covered their arms down to the wrist to protect them from the sun. She said contemptuously that women now were 'all ladies. They wear *dresses* now, not *gowns*.'

Corduroy and slops

Even in the new century, Jekyll noted that farm labourers still wore the 'capital white slop jacket' in summer, though they no longer wore knee-britches; instead, they put a strap around their cord trousers just below the knee. Young Richard Jefferies, in a famously long letter to *The Times* in 1872 about the life of the Wiltshire agricultural labourer, included the following sartorial descriptions:

They are much better clothed now than formerly. Corduroy trousers and slops are the usual style. Smock-frocks are going out of use, except for milkers and faggers. Almost every labourer has his Sunday suit, very often really good clothes, sometimes glossy black, with the regulation 'chimney-pot'. His unfortunate walk betrays him, dress how he will. Since labour has become so expensive it has become a common remark among the farmers that the labourer will go to church in broadcloth and the masters in smock-frocks. The labourer never wears gloves – that has to come with the march of time; but he is particularly choice over his necktie.

OLD CLOTHES

So many of the old words for clothes are now unfamiliar, but here are some definitions culled from an early edition of Chambers' Twentieth Century Dictionary of the English Language, edited by the Revd Thomas Davidson.

beaver: *a hat made of the beaver's fur; a hat*

billycock: *a man's low-crowned felt hat (from bully-cocked, cocked like the bullies)*

broadcloth: *a fine kind of woollen fulled cloth, used for men's garments*

chimney-pot hat: *familiar name for the ordinary cylindrical hat of gentlemen*

corduroy: *a ribbed kind of fustian*

drab: *thick strong grey cloth; a grey or dull-brown colour (perhaps from the muddy colour of undyed wool)*

drabbet: *coarse linen fabric used for smocks*

frock: *a wide-sleeved garment worn by monks; a loose upper garment worn by men*

fustian: *a kind of coarse, twilled cotton fabric, including moleskin, velveteen, corduroy, etc.*

gaberdine: *loose upper garment formerly worn by Jews*

gown: *a woman's upper garment*

moleskin: *a superior kind of fustian, double-twilled, cropped before dyeing*

poke-bonnet: *a bonnet with a projecting front, like the Salvation Army woman's*

pork-pie hat: *a hat somewhat like a pie in shape worn by men and women about 1850*

print: *a printed cloth; calico stamped with figures*

slops: *any loose lower garment that slips on easily, esp. trousers; cheap ready-made clothing, etc*

smock: *a woman's shift; a smock-frock*

smock-frock: *an outer garment of coarse white linen worn over the other clothes in the south of England*

stuff: *textile fabrics, cloth, esp. when woollen*

twill: *a woven fabric in which the warp is raised one thread and depressed two or more threads for the passage of the weft, thus giving a curious appearance of diagonal lines; a fabric with a twill*

Oddly, this useful early 20th century dictionary does not include a definition for round-frock.

Emigration

Time and time again, those who trawl through local history records notice that whole farming families suddenly vanish. They emigrated, looking literally for pastures new overseas, especially in some of the major agricultural depressions of the 19th and 20th centuries. The examples are numerous and often in those useful minutes of church vestry meetings you will see mention of emigration.

Above: The Kennard family of Loddiswell, Devon, in the 19th century.

TRANSPORTATION

Emigration was not always voluntary. In the 1840s John West was found guilty of stealing two sheep and was transported to Van Diemen's Land for 15 years along with his young brother. He managed to escape during the upheaval of the Australian goldrush, returning to his faithful wife and their five children after a nine-year exile. He became a successful smallholder and fathered three more children, living the rest of his life close to where he was born and reaching the ripe old age of 96.

The Loddiswell family of Kennard is a good example. John Kennard was a blacksmith, as were several of his seven sons. His eldest son, Frederick, remained in Loddiswell to carry on the family business and to manage the local animal pound, and two or three of his brothers also continued as blacksmiths in various parts of Devon. But the third son, William, emigrated to the United States in 1870; the fourth son, James, emigrated to New Zealand in 1863 and was quickly followed by his younger brother, Richard. Another branch of the family were of farming stock and five of them emigrated to Canada, though a generation later than their cousins; and one or two of them returned to farming in Devon after some years.

In the Cotswolds, George Garne was known as a fair and just employer and usually his men remained with him for many years. One of them did heed the lure of emigration and went out to New Zealand but he did not like it, so Garne and the local squire sent him enough money for his passage home and gave him his old job back. He repaid the loan in full by instalments over a long period. And it was not just the labourers who emigrated; it was also the offspring of farmers hit by the depression. Ann Garne, born in 1870, went to New Zealand and married out there, remaining near Auckland until she died in 1928. Her elder brother Fred joined her but then moved on to Western Australia to take part in the Kalgoorlie gold rush and stayed in Australia for the rest of his life – a life of great hardship and hard manual work. He settled at Benjaberring, 120 miles northeast of Perth, and had a government contract to supply timber sleepers for the new railway. In due course he acquired 1500 acres of land that he ring-fenced and on which he built his own timber house and gradually cleared his dry, scrub-covered land, using horses to cultivate it for wheat. It was very

different from the life he had lived back in the English Cotswolds.

In the 1870s, the agricultural labourers of East Anglia were building up a head of steam about their working conditions and were becoming much involved in creating a trade union. Many farms were overstocked with labour, which meant that farmers could always find another man to do the job if someone became too demanding. Thus it was the policy of the National Agricultural Labourers Union to encourage both migration of labour within the country and emigration away from it; in fact the union set up a string of emigration agencies throughout the country to move surplus labour. Emigration agents from various colonial

governments would appear at most union meetings, dangling the carrot of promised lands abroad. The unionists saw these agents as allies in the crucial battles of 1872–4 and their comparisons of a working life in England with what life could be like in the colonies helped to stir the brewing discontent and probably to prolong it. Sometimes it was farmers themselves who became emigration agents.

It was not only emigration; many farmworkers simply migrated into other, better paid jobs that had nothing to do with agriculture. Between 1871 and 1921, rather strangely, the number of farmers in Britain *rose* from 269,200 to 295,900 but the number of male farmworkers dropped dramatically from 1,028,200 to 734,600.

Above: The Luff family at Robins Farm, Iping, shortly before emigrating to Canada in about 1909. Two of the grandsons returned to England during World War II and enlisted to fight for their mother country.

Effects of War

Bessie Todman was born in about 1839. During World War I she saw most of the able-bodied men leaving the village to enlist right from the start, and several of her own grandsons became soldiers. Always a charitable soul, whatever she could make or give for the sake of soldiers, she made or gave.

Above: Trimming sugar beet near Gilbert White's Selborne, Hampshire, in 1916, soon after the crop was first introduced into Britain.

In 1916, she recalled the time when the young son of a shepherd 'come back all of a sudden out of those trenches and the mud all over him, hair and all, and walks straight into the cottage and kiss his mother and out and away again without sleeping or nothing': he had simply been homesick, and he was killed in action almost immediately after returning to the trenches. She remembered also a young 'gentleman' officer convalescing from a wound and several operations, and she wrote in her diary:

> *I do think it mean of the farmers all round here shooting nigh every day and the Park have had big Partys shooting hundreds of Phesients and not one of them sent to my dear Lootennant, it ought to be put in the newspaper, selfish things they are, they don't show little Acks of kindness neither do they sow little Grains of sand that makes the boundless Occian and the beautifull land; but there, what is not in them cant come out of them, Poor unhappy Grabs, but see what he has got to suffer poor young man trying to keep them in Peace and Safty – and what do they care, O I do feel cross.*

Wars sucked men out of the villages and into the armed forces, depleting the local agricultural labour pool. With world wars the scale of depletion was even greater, even though agriculture was a protected occupation and its workforce was generally encouraged to remain on the land, since feeding the nation to save it from starvation was almost as important as protecting it from being bombed and invaded. A major source of reinforcement on the land in both world wars was the army of women who volunteered for agricultural and forestry work, many of them with no experience of the work or even of living in rural areas. During World War II another source of extra manpower was the many prisoners of war, largely Italian and German, who found themselves working in the fields and barns of the countryside.

Landgirls

Writing just after World War I, Peter Ditchfield (rector of Barkham in Berkshire) remarked:

The advance of civilisation and the late war have brought to our villages the neat-handed and masculine-clad landgirls, some of whom are of gentle birth and education, who have devoted themselves to agriculture. When men were scarce on the farms during the war, desiring to be useful and to help their country in that grievous time of emergency, they left their comfortable homes, took lessons in farming, and performed with much assiduity and hard work the lighter duties of an agricultural labourer. All honour to them for their patriotic toil! Nor is their task yet over. The war has dealt hardly with ladies of limited means. They have discovered that they must do something to increase their incomes, so they have turned to their old Mother Earth, learnt the arts of milking and hoeing, if not ploughing and sowing, and are some of the most industrious labourers on the land. They lead a strenuous life, often rising at 4am to milk the cows in order to dispatch the milk by an early train to London or some large town, and then driving the cows to pasture, and all day long they are busy in the fields or farmstead. It is hard work, but healthy. There is no time for moping, and landgirls always seem very keen, and always in a hurry, as they march along in their breeches and gaiters covered with mud, their progress being somewhat different from the slow, deliberate tread of the masculine farm labourer. No time have they for reading or for the usual accomplishments of
their sisters. In the evenings they are dog-tired, and in order to rise with the lark they must seek their couch ere the clock strikes nine. A strange life surely for one who has been delicately nurtured, her own mistress, with refined tastes and accustomed to artistic pursuits.

During World War I, the village of Abthorpe in Northamptonshire (population about 300) had welcomed a French-speaking Belgian refugee, Maurice Thomas, and his invalid wife – two of several Belgians who had fled their homeland and had been found a new home in this and other nearby parishes by the War Refugees Committee in London. His appearance was unusual in such a village: he had a fine moustache and beard trimmed in the French style and wore a pinstriped London-style suit. He wrote a little story, later translated by Tricia Holmes and printed under the title *Do you remember what Granny told you about the Women's Land Army?*, in which he called himself Oscar Mathieu, remembering in particular the day that the Women's Land Army arrived in Abthorpe. It was June 1914, and about 20 young ladies were dropped off at Towcester station and then walked the three or four miles to Abthorpe, in two well-disciplined columns

Above: Women's Land Army at work during World War I. Some are wearing bonnets that would have been a familiar sight in rural areas in the 19th century.

and marching in step into the village square. Here they dispersed and went to search for their various lodgings. Their imminent arrival had been announced several days in advance and the whole village rushed to their doors and windows as soon as they heard the ringing of the boots on the pebbled road surface. They were amazed and indignant to see women wearing trousers – brown velvet trousers, leather gaiters, heavy boots, short overcoats and soft felt hats. Most of the villagers were shocked, though some pointed out that the work the women had to do (in this case in the woods) could hardly be done in a skirt. 'If this work can't be done by women in skirts,' was the retort, 'then let it be done by men!' And when the women turned up at church on Sunday still in their uniform trousers, it was even worse.

Above: Landgirls unloading grain sacks in about 1917.

In 1915, in the throes of World War I, the Board of Trade had begun to compile a register of women willing to undertake industrial, clerical or agricultural work as part of the war effort. The government was aware that it needed to replace 2.5 million men who were required for the army and another 600,000 or so for the navy and air corps. By 1916, a quarter of a million men had been called out of agriculture, and more were going, but only 50,000 village women had registered to fill the gap. But why worry? Most farmers and landowners had thought that the war would be over in 1915.

The government's Food Production Department began to issue weekly charts for each county, trying to predict where the demand for labour existed. Each county had a War Agricultural Committee by the autumn of 1915 and a special women's branch was formed as well. Soon some 40,000 women's names were on various county lists, mostly of middle-class women who expressed no desire for manual labour. Anyway, farmers seemed to be loath to employ women, describing them as the 'lilac sunbonnet brigade'; they simply did not believe that women could ever do horse-work and other kinds of general farm work.

Many of the city girls discovered that country life was not quite as romantic as they had imagined, and did not enjoy the reality of early morning milking or toiling in muddy fields. It was decided that they would work better in gangs or corps, managed by gangers or taking orders from farmers who would also oversee their work; thus, it was hoped, they would feel that they really were joining in the war effort, and would take their work more seriously. So it was that in January 1916 the Women's National Land Service Corps was formed.

In 1917 it was agreed that there should be a Women's Land Army, run by the government on military lines, and recruitment began in March. Unlike the Corps, it was not confined to educated women but its recruits had to sign up for the duration of the war and be prepared to work wherever they were sent. They had an agreed wage scale, a free uniform, free training and free transport to their place of employment. Out of 47,000 applicants, only 7,000 were accepted in those early days, because it was important to use only the best in order to counteract the farming community's general distrust.

Lloyd George described the Women's Land Army girl in World War I:

Breeched, booted and cropped, she broke with startling effect upon the sleepy traditions of the English Countryside. She was drawn from a wide range of classes of society … She brought with her enthusiasm and energy, an alert and unprejudiced mind that stimulated the activity of her fellow workers.

Breeches? Horrors! The WLA had even considered bloomers. But at least they had a proper uniform, and for free. The old Corps had no more than a bottle-green armband, embroidered with a crown, presented after the volunteer had attained 30 days of qualifying service; she also received a certificate stating: 'Every woman who helps in agriculture during the war is as truly serving her country as the man who is fighting in the trenches, on the sea, or in the air.' The women could purchase their own uniform: the Harrods Farm Outfit in 'good Genoa Corduroy, excellently cut jacket, button pockets, with convertible storm collar. The britches button at the side, with a buckle and strap at the waist. In dark brown only. All for thirty-five shillings and ninepence. Boots extra at thirty-seven and six.'

Well, now, how very nice. It took the down-to-earth WLA to change things, and real efforts were made to introduce a uniform that the women would like and that was practical for their work. Each recruit was measured for her outfit before she headed off for training. She was given two overalls, a hat, her breeches, boots, a pair of leggings, a jersey, a pair of clogs and a mac. After six months her wardrobe was boosted with another hat, another pair of breeches and boots and leggings. At first the girls were warned not to wear breeches unless they covered them with overalls, to avoid rude remarks on the farm. They certainly should not wear jewellery, and they must adhere to very strict standards of behaviour. The WLA *Handbook* said sternly:

You are doing a man's work and you are dressed rather like a man; but remember that just because you wear a smock and breeches you should take care to behave like an English girl who expects chivalry and respect from everyone she meets. Noisy or ugly behaviour brings discredit, not only upon yourself but upon the uniform,

and the whole Women's Land Army. When people see you pass ... show them that an English girl who is working for her Country on the land is the best sort of girl.

Isn't that just *too* delightful? Well, not always. Some of the girls complained about the lack of entertainment and asked for country house parties and tennis tournaments! In Wales, some farmers saw the girls as useful floor scrubbers and baby-minders and were surprised when they refused. A bigger problem was villagers saying these women had driven the local men into the army by taking their place on the land, which was particularly hurtful as the WLA girls were all unpaid volunteers.

In spite of all the prejudice and misunderstandings, there were some 23,000 Land Army girls working on farms between March 1917 and October 1919, about 15,000 of whom had actually been trained for the work.

In World War II, the Women's Land Army was even more important than it had been in the first. By 1943 there were more than 80,000 of its eager, willing but often unskilled members working on the land, many of them in need of careful instruction and close monitoring to ensure that they knew what they were trying to do. Sometimes they remained on the same farm for months or even years, perhaps working in pairs or threes; sometimes they worked in larger groups and stayed for a seasonal task, or travelled from farm to farm as the need arose. Some of them hated it; some of them loved it so much, in spite of the hard physical work and long hours (48-hour week in winter, 50

Below: Blinkered! Old-fashioned field bonnets still being worn in 1935 by potato pickers at Straiton, near Edinburgh. In the 19th century, most women working outdoors wore bonnets to protect their faces from unbecoming sun-tans.

in summer), that they wanted to carry on farming after the war was over.

Their jobs were as varied as agriculture itself: they might be hand-milking cows, lifting potatoes, helping with land reclamation and drainage, operating heavy earth-moving machinery, driving a tractor, mucking out pigs, thatching ricks, hedging, haymaking, harvesting, planting, weeding, muck-spreading – whatever needed to be done on the farm.

Quite apart from the hard work of farming, the girls in some parts of the country had to dodge the danger of shells landing from guns on the French coast and, worse, machine-gun fire from German aircraft, or the occasional bomb casually unloaded after a city air raid as the aircraft made its way home. In Hampshire, some of the landgirls were issued with tin hats as they were so often in danger of injury from shrapnel when they were bringing in the cows for milking. Many farm animals were destroyed during the war by shrapnel, machine-gun bullets, stray bombs and the like.

Below: Italian prisoners-of-war helping with the harvest while a corporal keeps an eye on their work.

Prisoners of war

During World War II there were, eventually, hundreds of thousands of prisoners of war in Britain and many of them were in camps in rural areas. In the middle and later years of the war they became an important part of the agricultural labour force. Here and there they married local girls and made a permanent home in Britain after the war. Others kept up long-lasting friendships with the families they had met during their farming work.

Those who went out in groups to help on the farms wore dark blue overalls with distinctive large green patches sewn on to them. Most were Italians, many from farming stock themselves who did their work with a mixture of enthusiasm (some had no desire to be sent back into the war) and often happy-go-lucky carelessness, but usually with such charm that they won over the locals – especially the children and the women but also the farmers. The atmosphere was so relaxed that you might see a party of 30 or 40 Italians working out in the fields with only a single British soldier overseeing them. They often spent as much time as possible enjoying their outdoor meals and making little woven baskets and wooden toys for the local children and young women. There are women now in their sixties and seventies who still cherish a little basket made for them by a prisoner of war.

Mr J Powis described how one of his local women helpers, a grandmother, remarked of one of his Italian prisoners that he was 'very beautiful – wavy hair, beautiful eyes and teeth; but oh! look at his nose; I could slide down it; it's so long'. Powis was quite sorry when the Italians went home: he'd had two of them living with him for 2½ years, and others as day-workers, and he thoroughly enjoyed their company, even though 'they seemed to love you one minute and the next not to like to look at you'. One of them, however, went a little too far in his attempts to overcome his lack of good looks: he used scented soap and hair oil and also (way before his time) skin cream and face powder. Another arrived one day with 'a wire arrangement fastened on his head to keep his wonderful waves in place' – and vivid red-painted fingernails. His first words, on arrival, were: 'Do you think me very beautiful?' Powis, not impressed, set him to top-dressing potatoes with sulphate of ammonia. 'Boss!' came the cry, 'you are no good; you ruin my beautiful hands.'

The German prisoners tended to be less carefree than the Italians and less likely to relax with the locals, but they were usually more productive and efficient – and not only with farm labour. An inspector of prisoner-of-war labour visited a farm one day and noticed that the number of men working in the field was one less than it should have been. The old farmer eventually explained why: 'Willy' was indoors where there was a long spike, hanging from the fireplace, on which many, many papers of various sizes and colours had been stuck. On the other side of the fireplace many neat bundles of paper had been carefully clipped together by the German. The farmer could neither read nor write and he had been deluged with letters and paperwork since the start of the war – from Ministries, from the local War Agricultural Committee, from the tax inspector and so on – and he had simply stuck them on the spike. Willy had arrived six months ago, a banker before the war and fluent in English, and ever since had been answering all the farmer's letters.

In Hampshire, Peter Lambert of Manor Farm, Langrish, remembers that his father employed Italian and German POWs from 1940 until 1946. He was a threshing contractor for the War Agricultural Committee as well as being a farmer, so he always wanted staff. The POWs stayed in Stroud village hall and the Italians arrived first. Farmer Lambert would catch them asleep under the corn

Above: Harvest time in the summer of 1942: the Army and the RAF help to feed the threshing machine.

ricks but some of them were very keen to learn about farming. Many of the Italians were moved elsewhere and more Germans arrived, who seemed to love working on the farms. Many did not want to go home and some settled in the area, two of them marrying local farmers' daughters. The POWs made toy tractors for young Peter out of ration cans and wood and he still has them.

When the war came to an end, it was some time before the prisoners went home. Late in 1946, German prisoners could still qualify for a 'good work' bonus of nine shillings a week, which would be paid to them in Reichsmarks on their return to their own country. Some felt that they should have gone home sooner to help in the rebuilding of Germany and especially in the feeding of their countrymen, for whom Britain was sending over food, but more than 400,000 German prisoners of war were still detained in Britain after the end of the war and the last of them did not go home until the summer of 1948.

Above: Men from the Royal Air Force and women from the WAAF picking potatoes at Aston Down airfield.

Returning soldiers

Maude Egerton King, writing just after World War I, thought that demobilisation was a golden chance to replant a peasantry. Instead, she complained, the soldiers were being welcomed home with miles of bunting, thanksgiving services, jazz balls and cheap beer but the government had no scheme to nurture their desire to plant their roots and live on the land they had been protecting on the nation's behalf. So, having hankered 'wistfully or bitterly' for the chance to be smallholders, they gave up and sailed off to the colonies. Those that did succeed in becoming involved in farming in Britain would soon learn to regret it, because of the agricultural depression that saw many made bankrupt and driven off the land.

After World War II, many returning soldiers also wanted to take to the land and advice came in an endless stream. For example, *The Countryman* ran a series of columns, 'Advice to Returning Soldiers', from the summer of 1945, investigating the possibilities of fruit growing, forestry training, smallholding, market gardening, farm machinery repair and beekeeping. The Ministry of Agriculture had already instructed that the training of ex-servicemen was to supersede, temporarily, the teaching of farm students. After World War I, very few of the ex-servicemen who had received agricultural training at government centres had actually settled on the land, and fewer still had survived the stresses of the between-wars depression and the endless hard work of farming. This time, it was hoped, it would be different and there would be many more opportunities for training in skilled agricultural jobs for wage earners, though perhaps rather less for those who wanted to farm on their own account. The government's training schemes began with an assessment of whether the applicant was suitable for farm work and also, sensibly, whether a man and his wife would both be able to settle happily in rural surroundings.

One of the problems faced by some of the trainees was antagonism from regular farmworkers, especially where the trainee was a townsman whom they felt had no business to be handling horses, bulls or the men's own pet tractors, or to be trying a callow hand at specialist work such as rick-building and thatching. There was also the sheer hard work. On a dairy farm, for example, the trainee's working day might start at five in the morning and not finish until six in the evening, much of the day being spent on his feet and involving lifting hefty weights and dealing with much muck and dirt.

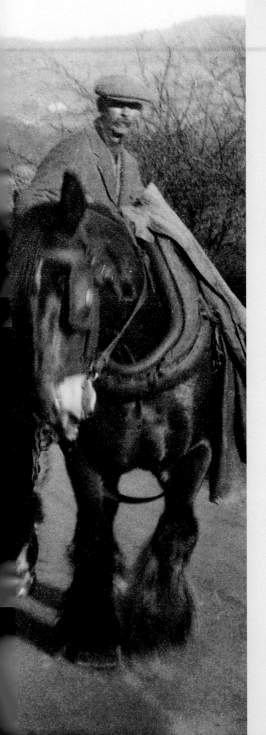

Horses and Horsemen

Horses were the engines of farming for a long time, though not as long as you might think. Men who could handle horses were top of the labour tree in arable areas and on mixed farms, where horse muscle power was so important both on the land and in the yard.

In 1988, with heavy horses reduced almost to playthings, the Shire Horse Society commissioned an investigation into reviving their use for work. The report, edited by Keith Chivers, pointed out that tractors consume large quantities of non-renewable energy, whereas horses are fuelled by renewable resources; that horses can reproduce themselves, which tractors cannot; that horses respond to verbal commands, which (so far) tractors cannot; that horses drive themselves; that horses can learn routine and repetitive tasks and do them without bidding, stopping and starting as a matter of habit, but also having sufficient intelligence to avoid or work their way around difficulties and obstacles; and that horses are manoeuvrable in tight spaces. Chivers did not mention the other, less tangible advantages of working horses: that they can sense your mood, respond when you converse with them, recognise you from a distance and greet you, appreciate your singing, have fun when they are turned loose in the field and kick up their heels and bring the onlooker a sense of joy ... oh, and so much more.

Breeds and Breeding

In 1910, a manual on *Heavy Horses, Breeds and Management* described in detail the three main British heavy horse breeds of the time: the Shire, the Suffolk and the Clydesdale. Each of these three breeds had had its own breed society since the late 1870s and during World War I a society would be formed for the British Percheron, a breed originally from the Perche region of northern France that was best suited to draught work.

HORSE POWER

Horse power is a phrase used even now as a measure of working strength. In general, on a mixed farm it was suggested in 1919 that you needed three horses for 100 acres, five for up to 200 acres, ten for 500 and 17 for 800 acres. It was calculated that each team of horses would be able to plough and cultivate 50–60 acres annually. The mixed farm would need one ploughman for every 100 acres.

Above: Clydesdale stallion, 1894

Right: Carter wearing a shallow-crowned felt hat and carrying a whip as the sign of his calling. This is probably how he would have presented himself at a hiring fair.

the most popular breed as a dray horse in the cities and large towns but it was also a useful farm horse. The Clydesdale was the general farm horse in Scotland; it was less massive and was a faster walker than the rather sluggish Shire, and stood at 16 to 16.5 hands. The Suffolk Punch, standing at 15 to 16 hands, had small feet and was good for working on clay soils; it was very docile, a willing puller and its popularity was on the up.

By the mid 1920s the four societies, which had traditionally treated each other with great suspicion and jealousy,

The creation of a Shire stud book had given 'great impetus' to carthorse breeding in general, to the huge benefit of tenant farmers, but the authors of the 1910 manual warned that the large studs established by 'noblemen and gentlemen', while undoubtedly bringing the breeding of Shires to almost a science, had indirectly ignored the 'user of the Shire in the labour for which he is bred'. That is to say, they bred for show, not for work.

Just after World War I the massive, broad-chested, big-footed Shire was the most widely distributed workhorse in England. The typical Shire of the time stood about 17 hands high; it was by far

realised that they faced a much more serious threat than each other in the form of the internal combustion engine, particularly tractors and lorries. By the 1960s the heavy horses had almost disappeared, except where they were preserved by a few loyal breeders. After more than a century and a half of being essential, the farm horse simply was not needed any more.

Travelling stallions

A regular sight on the lanes, even well into the 20th century, was the travelling stallion, being led to another farm to cover some mares and decked out to look his best and impress passers-by.

Only breeders who kept large numbers of mares would have their own stallion; small farmers certainly could not afford to keep one and had to send their mares to another man's stallion and pay the breeder a fee. The railway companies began to offer improved facilities for transporting brood mares to distant studs, which meant that in theory the best horses were within reach of almost everyone – if they could afford the expense. There was a high stud fee, plus the cost of keeping the mare at the stud farm for several weeks and the cost of railway freight. On top of those outlays were the inevitable risks associated with travelling and the disadvantage of the job being done without the farmer's personal supervision and observation, and the possibility of a negative result after all that. Very often, a stallion that won prizes in the ring was disappointing at stud.

During the later years of the 19th century, farmers who bred Clydesdales decided to unite in local groups and form themselves into a society, which would appoint some of the best judges among their members to select a good stallion to travel their district for the season. Over a certain number of weeks the horse would serve a specified number of mares

Above: A travelling stallion outside an inn at Lechlade.

belonging to the members, with the society paying an agreed amount, or so much per mare covered, or a combination of both. If the society's judges could not find the animals they wanted at the Glasgow Show (the great market for Clydesdale breeders), they would visit the owners of principal studs and select what they thought the most suitable for their mares. The Shire breeders quickly latched on to the same idea, the main difference being that their major market was the London Show. Such stallion societies were formed in many districts and were very convenient for farmers, as they no longer had to send their mares over long distances to a suitable stallion, and also, if they were not too sure of their own ability to select a sire, they could rely on the judgement of the experts.

During the winter, posters were put up to advertise the stallion and invite owners of mares to book a place on his itinerary. It needed careful planning. The stallion and his

HORSE COUNT

At the beginning of the 20th century there were about 3.3 million horses in Britain, and about 2.6 million of these worked in agriculture or in trade. Just after World War I, the number of farm horses in the UK was estimated at just over 2 million. At the end of the 20th century the number of farm horses was almost uncountably low.

Left: Rock II, a locally famous travelling stallion accompanied by his groom, 'Old' Bill Tull, and bred by Edward Lamb, MP, of Borden Wood in West Sussex. This Shire was a regular prize-winner at the Smithfield Show.

handler would work on a 21-day cycle, which meant perhaps 16 or 17 days out on the circuit and then home for a few days' rest before setting out on the next cycle. A very good stallion might cover up to 120 mares in one season. The mare owners paid a service fee of up to 30 shillings in the 19th century, plus half-a-crown for the groom, but exceptional stallions could command 30 times as much. The fee included two return visits if they were needed, and the groom's half-a-crown was paid on every visit.

The stallion's handler would groom his animal to perfection, polish his hooves and plait his mane, and the pair would set off with pride. Both stallion and groom kept pretty fit with all that walking from farm to farm and they would strut into the yard with a flourish, generally with the horse eagerly ahead, whinnying to the mares, pulling his handler along behind him on the short lead.

The groom would also look his best and he could cause almost as much of a stir with the locals as his horse – especially with the girls. He stayed overnight at the farm or in the local inn, sleeping in the hayloft above his stabled horse to keep an eye on him, and generally would have arranged a collection point to which local owners brought their mares. Innkeepers welcomed travelling stallions: they brought in good business and most innkeepers were more than willing to offer their own stables, yards and paddocks as the collection point. Most of the photographs you see of bedecked, arch-necked travelling stallions have them standing outside an inn.

The Working Horse

The mare had been covered, the foal had been born, the colt had been reared and now it was time for farm work. Some colts began to work at two years but usually they were broken in after harvest and just did a little work over their first winter, so that as a three-year-old next spring they were ready to take their place in a team.

The head wagoner or ploughman did the breaking and might start with stubble ploughing in the autumn. Even before that stage he would have got the young colt used to being led in a halter, then to having a bit in its mouth and to answering to its own name.

In Scotland, farmers liked to yoke a colt abreast with a steady old horse as its teacher. In England they tended to put the colt between two old horses working in a single line, with a steady leader ahead of him and a quiet stager behind. The colt would probably jerk and plunge for a bit but would soon settle into the work, with the two older horses keeping him straight and pulling him along, and also buffering him from hurting himself in his excitement. After a week or two he would be quiet and tractable enough to be hooked abreast or put into the shafts (though quite a few horses decided very early in their lives that nothing would induce them to go into shafts, ever) to do some rolling. After a few days with the roller, he would be ready for a cart or wagon, and by the time harvest came he could take his place and do his share of the mowing and reaping as well as the carting.

In the north, ploughing and cultivations were generally carried out by two horses abreast and so usually a colt would be put alongside a strong old horse. In the Midlands and southern England much of the heavy land was worked by horses in single file (two, three or four in a team, depending on the weight of the implement and the state of the soil). In a three-horse team, the one at the front was known as the fore-horse, the middle as the body and the one at the rear was the thiller, and some claimed that in most cases three horses were only doing the work of two.

A colt could do his full share of the work when he was four years old, and at five he was 'fit for anything' – but only if care had been taken in his earlier years. Most manuals of instruction about the breaking-in of colts stressed

how important it was for the breaker to be patient, firm and even-tempered. As the 1910 *Heavy Horses* manual put it: 'Whether actuated by the dictates of reasoning or instinctive powers the horse is not slow to resent unkind treatment bordering on cruelty.' It also said firmly:

It was formerly said that a pair of Suffolks could plough more land … than any other breed. They used to do so. Much of this kind of thing depends more on what follows than on what leads the plough. A horse's pace greatly depends on the man behind. Although no horseman can get through a great day's work with a pair of lazy drones, the most active, the best walkers, readily lose their pace if the ploughman is allowed to tie both, or even one, back to the whippletree.

Below: RL Fox of Wingham (left), Champion Ploughman of East Kent in 1950, and the Reserve Champion, LA Johnson of Adisham. Pride in winning trophies at ploughing matches continued when tractors replaced horses.

PLOUGHMAN'S PRIDE

Any ploughman would take a pride in his everyday work in the field, and even more so when it came to ploughing matches. These great social occasions, with beer aplenty, were the highlight of the year and the men would often keep a special set of polished steel hames (as opposed to everyday wooden ones) and well-oiled harness just for the matches. Of course the brasses would be polished to perfection: the turn-out was just as important as the ploughing itself.

Caring for the Horses

Many a country lad in Victorian times had an ambition to work with horses, especially in areas where ploughmen, carters and wagoners were able to earn more than most other farmworkers. The wagoner was also guaranteed his level of pay every week, regardless of the weather, as his horses still had to be cared for, whereas labourers lost an average of 85 days a year because of bad weather preventing them from working.

Below: Five pairs and an orra ('unpaired' or 'extra') beast at Ingilston Farm, Essie, in Perthshire. The Clydesdale was a popular heavy-horse breed in Scotland, and a pair of Clydesdales combined with the invention of lighter ploughs could do the work of up to a dozen oxen working the old heavy Scotch plough.

Usually horses were worked in pairs, with each ploughman having his own pair to feed and groom as well as work. In some districts, a wagoner would have four horses to feed and groom, with the help of a boy or labourer for working them in the field, especially where the local custom was to use long single-file teams. But for most farms, the pair system was the most economical and two horses were quite enough work for one man to look after in the morning and evening on top of a day's work in the field. By the early 20th century most of the farm implements were designed for two horses.

There was a hierarchy among the men. For example, on a farm with three teams, there would be a first, second and third wagoner, each with his own mate, and so a lad wanting to train as a horseman could see a career ladder ahead of him, starting as ploughboy. His problem was that wagoners tended to carry on in the job for many years, and they jealously guarded their hard-won knowledge and expertise. In the 1920s JW Robertson Scott was north of the border talking to a Mr Duncan, who explained:

Any ploughman would refuse to allow any other ploughman to work his pair of horses. He grooms, feeds, and stables them. Most ploughmen

Makeshift snowshoes fashioned from old sacks for a timber-hauling horse in northern England.

*Above: The pride of
Suffolk.*

for bran and another for oats. There was
an art in feeding according to the amount
of work, which in turn depended on the
season and the weather. On a farm, a
horse might be idle for days if the weather
was frosty, snowy or wet, and might then
have to do extra work once it was fine.
The peak work periods for a horse were
sowing wheat or turnips, carting mangels
and harvest time. On most farms the
horses would be able to run out on pasture
during the summer, but on some of the
arable farms there was no pasture and
the horses spent their time in the stable
or were turned loose into a yard and had
green food carted to them, such as vetches,
clovers, meadow grass or green oats.

Wheat straw, green rye grass and the
like were run through the chaff-cutter,
which was a wheel with curved blades
fixed to its spokes to cut the hay as it was
automatically fed through a trough by a
horse-engine (it could also be worked by
hand). In Kent an old-fashioned chaff-
cutter known as a monkey-box had a
treadle system: you pushed the hay along
the trough with a short fork in your left
hand and compressed it by pressing the
lever with your left foot; it was cut by
a knife hinged on another lever, with a
sawing movement.

Each horseman had his own views on
feeding, and whole manuals were written
on the subject. In Scotland, the horses
often had a sort of porridge of boiled food
(chaff, turnips, beans, inferior barley and
oats) but this sometimes led to colic and
constipation. It needs to be remembered
that horses have quite a small stomach
and do better on little and often, well
chewed: they are simply not designed for
long fasting and tummy rumbling.

The working day

The day was a very long one for those who
worked with horses. In Kent, for example,
a wagoner would be up at four in the
morning to feed his horses and prepare

*would refuse to do any byre work.
When a number of ploughmen turn out
to plough together or to do any other
work as a team, they are punctilious
to keep their due order, from the first
ploughman, who leads, to the haflin'
or callant, who has been promoted to
his first pair, who brings up the rear. A
ploughman will not remain in a place
where he has not a pair of horses in
which he can take a reasonable pride.
His drills must bear the criticism of
his fellows. His stacks must stand wind
and weather. He must be able to handle
his horses yoked to any implement.*

Robertson Scott said that those in charge
of horses included horsemen, horse-
keepers, wagoners, carters, teamsmen
and hinds and it was not always
possible to differentiate
between these terms.
They included 'men
of widely different
standing and degrees of
responsibility'.

In the stables, each
man usually had an
oak chest (often known
as an ark) big enough
to hold a week's
supply of corn and
divided into a section

them for work; he would have his own breakfast at about five thirty and make sure his mate was out of bed, so that they and the horses could be out of the stables by six, even if this meant ploughing in the dark. They would work in the fields until two or so, with a quick beever (mid-morning snack) if they were lucky and a nosebag and drink for the horses. Back at the stable in the afternoon, the horses would be hot, sweaty and probably caked in mud up to their knees. The horseman, however exhausted after a day in the fields, would have let his charges paddle in a stream or farm pond on the way to loosen the dirt and now took off his jacket, rolled up his shirt-sleeves, grabbed a wisp of straw and vigorously rubbed each leg clean and dry. Not until the horses had also been fed could the wagoner finish his day's work, by six in the evening, leaving his mate to carry on in the stables for another couple of hours with more grooming and bedding the horses down for the night.

Grooming was hard work but could be immensely satisfying and was the best way of sealing the bond between man and horse. It was not just a matter of currycombing and brushing. Tails might need special attention: sometimes, if they were allowed to grow long, they would be plaited with ribbons and straw. Old hairs would be pulled from time to time and could be made into strong rope for use about the farm. The 1910 *Heavy Horses* manual said that draught horses should be as carefully 'dressed' twice every day as the conditioned hunter; there was no excuse for a horse coming out to work in the morning with a staring coat full of dust and the hair matted with sweat from previous days. The anonymous author of the chapter on farm management of the heavy horse wrote:

In my boyish days the Clydesdale farm horses on Carrick Shore were a sight that would well repay a long journey. To see the men in their white moleskin trousers and waistcoats; their horses as sleek and fine in their coats as the best carriage horses, with every chain and buckle shining like silver, afforded great pleasure.

Top: Taking a break on the job. A team of horses tucking into their nosebags during a day of harrowing in 1933.

Above: Carters coming home at the end of the day on Lord Woollavington's estate.

Above: Watering the horses at a farm pond.

The horseman also had to take care of the harness and tack, and the stable itself. Perhaps it is not surprising that some horsemen claimed that if cobwebs were removed from the stables, the horses would catch cold.

Carting

A cart is a versatile two-wheeled runabout that can almost turn on a dime and is generally drawn by a single horse. A wagon is a heftier beast with four wheels, usually rising to about six feet high at the back and measuring perhaps eleven to fourteen feet in length, and needing at

least a pair of horses or oxen to pull it. You could compare a cart to a van and a wagon to a lorry.

A wagon's front wheels were often smaller than the rear wheels, the latter being perhaps five feet in diameter and the former four feet, and the big size was more than necessary in the days when the road ruts might be axle-deep. There was a design of cart or wagon for every conceivable purpose, and there were also recognisably regional designs.

Oak was generally used for the framework, elm for the boards, elm logs for the wheel naves, ash for the spokes and shafts. Wheelwrights were much

SHOEING

Mary French, a farmer's wife, and a lot more besides, wrote a detailed study of the rural Cornish parish of Quethiock at the end of the 19th century and in the early years of the 20th. She described a St Ives man who was a small boy in the days when the farm horses used to queue outside his father's smithy to be shod. If the wait was likely to be a long one, the carters would leave their horses and get back to work. Later, after they had been shod, the boy would lead these massive animals down the road to the end of the farm track, let them go, give them a little tap on their huge rears and they would find their own way home.

George Wren was born in Wheathampstead in 1847 and left school at eight to start as an 'oss boy' (horse boy) on a large farm, helping to care for the horses and leading them at plough. He lived with other boys and men on the farm, visiting his parents from time to time to take his wages home. Like many others, he also went home on the night of the census return in 1861, when he was 14: his occupation was described as horsekeeper. By the time he was married and had three young children in the 1870s, he decided to work for himself and bought a donkey and cart, with the help of which he did a wide range of jobs locally, eventually selling the donkey and buying a horse. During his lifetime, George had three horses and his last and favourite was Old Vic. George would say to the horse, 'Goo and git yerself some new shoes,' and Vic would take himself down to the smithy. The smith would say, 'Want some new shoes, Vic?' and Vic would hold up a foot in reply. He would then make for what he considered his rightful place, edging out any other horse that might happen to be waiting there.

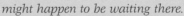

more than makers of wheels: they could make the entire cart or wagon as well, though often with the help of the village carpenter.

The name mufferer is a slurring of the word hermaphrodite. Unsure of whether to call itself a cart or a wagon, the mufferer was cobbled together by taking the shafts off a two-wheeled cart and fixing the front wheels from an old wagon to it with a simple frame. It was used around the Norfolk Broads and north Lincolnshire.

Long though the hours were for all horsemen, they still found time for more work. Bessie Todman, born in the 1830s,

COLOUR-CODED CARTS

You could often recognise the county of origin of a cart by the colours of the paintwork. In many counties the colour was blue, often with red wheels, but in Kent it was cream or stone, in Oxfordshire and Buckinghamshire ochre brown, in Dorset blue-black, in Lincolnshire and Cambridgeshire orange fading to terracotta, while in Yorkshire's West Riding there was a positive rainbow of choice – red, orange, brown, black, blue, white ...

mentioned in her calendar for March (the spelling is all her own):

This is the month I go Wooding in the Copice, gather wood, tye it in bundles, stack it in heaps, and at end of Month give the Carter 1s, bread, cheese and drink of wine to fetch it home, after he have done his day's work for the Master, with the Master's concent.

And they could still find time for fun. Fred Grover, in the 1850s, used to take wagon-loads of hops down to Weyhill Fair, near Andover, and had the thrill of 'driving for ribbons' that were awarded to the carter who brought the first load of hops on to the hill:

I've drove all night, purty near a trot, purpose for to git the ribbons. There's four bunches o' ribbons for your 'orses ... Who gives 'm ye? Ooh – I dunno ... They up there. I s'pose it comes out o' the fair ... You should see our old Miss laugh when we come 'ome with the ribbons.

Fred remarked that, in Sussex, farmers did not stable their horses at night: they simply shut them up loose in the farmyard, with a crib in the middle of the yard for self-help feeding. One night, when he was part of a travelling harvest gang of 30 or 40 men in Sussex, they were all sleeping in a barn and the last man in was always supposed to check that the yard gate had been fastened properly. Well, one night the last man forgot, and the horses escaped:

Oh, we could hear 'em as we laid there in the barn, gallopin' for miles! 'Cause everything was so still, ye know – 'twas in the dead o' the night – miles an' miles along the roads we could hear they horses gallopin'. They was so pleased to be out. The carter he got up in a hurry, an' the shepherd too ...

John Coker Egerton, writing in the 1890s, recalled a young carter's mate talking about an accident to one of his horses, a team of animals 'so lean and poor that they looked more like skeletons than working animals, and their heads, as in skeletons, seemed large and heavy, and out of proportion to their bodies'. It seems that

his amazement was greeted as he did so with a faint 'Holloa!'. He immediately stopped, and under the hat, to his still greater astonishment, he found a man's head. He asked at once what was the matter, and the reply was: 'I am on horseback, and my horse has sunk in the mud; for mercy's sake help me out! I am sinking deeper every minute.' Men were collected and the horse and his rider were dug out. The horse, to the intense surprise of all present, came up with his mouth full of hay, which on further search was found to have been taken from a load that had sunk with a waggon and four horses before the man got there.

Left: A Victorian carter.

Opposite: Drawing stream water for animals at Elmstone Hardwicke, Gloucestershire, 1935.

Below: A carter with a sense of humour dresses himself, his horse and his wagon for a village festival.

one of the horses kicked another in the stable, and the carter-boy was asked how it had happened. 'Well, you see, somehow he's head fell out of the manger, and that overbalanced his body, so he's hind leg flew up and het agen t'other horse, and that's jus' how t'was.' Another lad was working with his father with their team of four horses, of which three refused to draw and the wagon was 'stood'. The carter began to use his whip on the three unwilling horses, to no effect. The boy, after watching for a while, advised: 'Lash into him, father, as will draw; what's the good of lashing into them as won't?'

Sometimes carter boys were condemned as dull, slow and stupid, but quite often their responses to intrusive questions were a wind-up, deliberately aimed at discomforting the questioner, especially where the latter was on his high horse. Bear that in mind when you are told tales of local yokels. Coker Egerton tells another tall story:

> A man walking along the road between Burwash and Ticehurst was surprised to see a hat in the middle of the track. As he passed he gave it a kick, and to

On the Road

When a wagon was taken on the roads the wagoner or carter, dressed in a smock and with his breeches tied up with whipcord, walked on the near (left) side and carried a whip with a brass-ringed handle. He would be accompanied by a boy or under-carter, who might help to adjust the nearside drag-shoe (to brake the hind wheel) and drop-chain (to brake the front) when they met a hill. In really hilly country, the big heavy wagons were useless and farmers tended to use sledges; and in Radnorshire, even in the 1930s, they compromised by using a gambo, or ground-cart, with two large cartwheels for drawing it uphill and two heavy bosses or slides at the back so that it could sledge its way downhill with the wheels locked.

Horse Talk

Talking to your horse was a vital part of a horseman's work. Like a shepherd working his collie, a horseman largely directed his horses with his voice and what might have sounded like rough shouts to a layman were specific terms instantly understood by the horses but depended very much on what part of the country they were in.

Although in most counties the command to start would be something like go on, gee up or come on, and to stop would be a local variation of whoa, there were all sorts of phrases telling a horse to turn right or left, which means it was no good talking to a Kentish horse using a Herefordshire phrase book. In Sussex, the command to turn right would be 'gee wut', or in Berkshire 'wug off', in Scotland 'hupp' or 'weesh', in Yorkshire perhaps 'gee-back', in Suffolk 'cuppy-whee' and in Hampshire 'woag'. The command to turn left varied locally between 'cop y holt', 'cup yere', 'come here', 'ga' wut', 'hie', 'vane', 'woa-beck', 'come-agin', 'haw', 'gee', 'woi' or simply 'come-hither'. Just try telling a tractor to come hither.

Sometimes the horseman's accent or dialect is so thick that the words themselves become no more than an unintelligible sound – not so much pronounced as rumbled through the throat from the depths of the stomach.

GOOD FRIENDS

Alan Rutter, born in 1911 in Buriton, started with horses at the age of 14. His long working day began at five in the morning and ended at eight in the evening. In summer he would start a little earlier to fetch the horses from the meadows. 'In the dark of an August morning,' he said, 'you could not see them, but if you stood by the gate and called their names they would come galloping in, ready for a feed of corn and a grooming. They were true friends, worth looking after, never letting you down, and always trying their hardest; just working horses.'

with envy and, if the traces did not burst, that tree had got to move!

Bramble was firm with his team but never used his whip to thrash a horse. The last time Seymour saw this superb horse-handler he was driving an enormous steam tractor and Seymour was very sure that this was not by choice.

Henry Hooker was carter on the same estate at Upperton in Sussex for more than half a century. He had started his working life as a carter boy when he was 13 and finally retired when he was 82.

You just might be able to pick out something like 'gee-whut-ah' (usually with the first syllable a tone or two higher than the others), or perhaps 'mither-wee' (come to me, or turn round), with the 'ther' syllable jumping up an octave between the other two, something like a yodel. A horseman communicating with his team can be very like singing.

Between the wars, Aubrey Seymour sold his hedgerow elms to a big, burly, good-tempered man known as Bramble, who used six horses to drag the big butts out to the road.

What secret words of command he used I never could make out, but the horses knew what he meant and obeyed instantly. At one word the thiller, that is the one nearest the load, would lean into the collar, just enough to tighten the traces; at another word the next horse would do the same, and so on till the leader's traces were taut. Bramble would talk to them till every one of the six had got its legs well under it and, that done, he would let out such a yell as would have made John Peel green

FL Wadey wrote about his grandfather in the *Petworth Society Bulletin* in 1982:

He was a carter on the Mitford Estate … and he had three Shire horses to look after. He was always up between 4 and 4.30 to go up and clean out the horses, groom and feed them before coming back for breakfast. He'd prepare them for whatever they had to do on that day, harness them up and have them out in the field by 7.00. … Grandfather was a very amiable man and I never heard him swear all the time I knew him. In the summer when we'd take his tea out to him in the harvest fields, he'd let us come back home on the horses with him when he'd finished. … He was always gentle with animals and birds and never ever rough. He never shouted at the horses. 'Whoa,' he'd say and stroke the horses' nose, or 'Over, boy'. Horses always came first with him.

Horse sense

Horses, once they were into a routine, were often left to get on with their work. They also knew their way back to their stable. There are many tales, often highly embroidered, of horses so used to their farmers' drinking habits that they would find their own way home from the pub, with a very drunken farmer lolling and snoring in the back of the cart. You'd never trust a tractor to do that for you!

Joe Boniface was working on the Leconfield estate in 1937, a moment in time when horses were on their way out and the farm where Joe worked as a horseman no longer bred its own heavy horses. They were still using horses: one called Venter seemed to be particularly good at the tedious job of trudging in endless circles to work the horse-gear, wearing a track into the ground with his hooves. This was the sort of job in which the horse was generally left to get on with it by himself, plodding and plodding and plodding, with the occasional encouraging shout or even a quick whack if he was a bit 'lacky'. In my own village, horses were used to work the pugmill that softened clay for the brickworks, and the one that pulled a cart to collect sand and clay from a pit at the top of the hill was so accustomed to its job that it was simply given a slap on the rump and off it would go, finding its own way up to the pit and back down to the brickworks.

Below: A Lincolnshire carrier's cart calling at a farm in Wootton.

Opposite: Cider from the harvest-bottle on a Kentish farm.

CARRIERS

The carrier, trundling the country lanes in his cart laden with goods or a covered van that could also take passengers, has long since been displaced by the country bus and couriers. The old carrier's horse knew just where to go and when to stop, so regular was the route, and when it reached a market town you might see a surprising number of chattering country women with their country produce tumbling out of the dusty tilt-cart or curtain-covered van.

By the end of World War I, the carrier's cart might still be seen in country areas but it was changing: even before that war, it was more likely to be petrol-driven than horse-drawn and might be a motorised van or, increasingly, a bus. The reign of the horse, on the roads as in the fields, had been remarkably brief.

And with the horse went more than you might think. For example, the red-backed shrike, or butcher-bird, likes dung beetles. Dung beetles like dung. No farm horses on the roads, no dung; no dung, no beetles, no shrikes. Dung from horses is also manure for gardens, more highly prized than cattle manure, especially for roses ...

Ada Mary Luckins, who was born in 1901, remembered her father's brother, Uncle Reuben Marriner, a great character. He was one of a family of 14 but Ada only knew Uncle Reuben, Uncle Ben and Uncle Tim. Uncle Tim was 'a most lovable but drunken old reprobate'; he had a large family who got on well in spite of him and all had small farms. Uncle Reuben was a dealer and travelled a lot in his cart and horse; he was a carrier too. His carthorses were always males and they were all noted for hating women. Men and boys could handle them, but girls or women would get a nip or a kick. One of Ada's most vivid childhood memories was

CIDER NIGHTS

Dorinda Jeynes's grandfather, born in 1860, was younger than 20 when his father told him to take a wagon-load of the farm's apples to the cider mills in Taunton some 28 miles away. He had no idea of the route, but his father said, 'Put the black horse in front, he knows the way.' It was an uneventful journey to Taunton and the apples were duly unloaded, but by the time grandpa was ready to turn for home he was utterly drunk on cider. The men at the mill harnessed his team for the return journey, hoisted the lad up, put the reins in his hands, tapped the rump of the black horse and off they went. Despite it being a cold night in late autumn and despite the tremendous jolting of the wagon on the poor roads, grandpa slept all the way home.

hearing Uncle's mare come along after everyone had gone to bed, steadily trotting on her way to the stable. She would bring Uncle safely home at any time of the night through all weathers and he was probably stretched out and asleep in the cart after taking one, or more, over the eight. She needed no guidance and neither would she stop for anyone until she got home.

War Horses

After World War I many of the horses that had survived the dreadful life on the field of battle were returned to work the fields of Britain's farms. Rachel Knappett, working as a landgirl on a Lancashire farm in World War II, talked lovingly and with admiration about 'old faithful' Kitty, the farm pony, who was by then 31 years old and 'as round and plump and sometimes just as foolish as a colt'.

Above: Land Army women leading horses over Metropolitan Railway wasteland designated for potato crops during World War I.

Kitty was not really a pony, more the size of a hack, but was always known as 't'owd pony' or 't'owd mare'. She was brown, with a large white star, and had been born on a wild Canadian prairie. When she was about four, World War I had broken out and she had been bought by the British government and shipped to England to serve in the army. At Liverpool, she and many other half-wild horses had been taken to a big remount depot not far from the farm: locals would often see strings of fractious animals being led along the roads, breaking loose and stampeding over the countryside, to be rounded up by angry men on galloping horses.

Kitty had been shipped from the remount depot to the mud and turmoil of Flanders and eventually came back to England with a bullet wound in her neck and an army brand on her quarters. At the age of nine, instead of carrying a soldier on her back, she had to learn to pull a plough and a wagon on the farms of the firm of merchants who had bought her after the war. Many horses found this demotion unbearably humiliating, but Kitty accepted her new role with dignity. She was eventually bought by Rachel's boss for £20 and served him faithfully for more than 20 years. She knew every job on the farm inside out and when she reached the age of 30 she decided that she herself should be the judge of the length of her working day. When she was tired she simply stopped, shook her head and asked to be allowed to go home for a drink and a rest – a request that was always granted and she was set free to walk slowly home by herself, have her drink and wander into her stall until somebody came in to unyoke her. If nobody came, she would wander round the yard until she found someone who had time to do the job: she would make her request by pushing her head into their chest and whickering or blowing warm breath down their neck. It

Left: Gas mask for a working horse in 1939, a dress rehearsal shortly before the outbreak of war.

was Kitty who taught Rachel how to do a multitude of farm jobs.

Bill Tull, born in 1920, started working on my local farm while he was still at school, helping out with the early-morning milking. As soon as he left school at 14, he took over his grandfather's heavy horses and quickly learnt how to plough the hilly fields – work that he described as 'beautiful'. He would also take a horse and cart, or two horses and wagon, to the railway station to collect coal, 'half a ton on the cart, two ton in the wagon', for the big boilers at the big house. This journey involved a steep hill on a narrow lane. The schoolboy (as he still was) would stand up in front of the double shaft wagon and drive the two horses all the way to the station along mud-and-dust roads. There was a big rut down the side of the hill lane in the bank and 'they used to tie the wheels and the wagon used to stay in the rut so horses could hold it back. It was easy. But soon as the council filled the rut up, when they tied both wheels the wagon used to slide around on the road and try to overtake the horses!' Many other locals tell alarming tales of horses and wheeled vehicles on that hill.

One of Bill's early horses was Prince; the other, Colonel, was an old army horse that had been right through World War I.

In the army they used to wear breast collars but on the farm we had a head collar went up his neck and made his shoulder all sore, so we had pads on the collars. I worked him on the ploughs and harrows, I used to work all the ground, plough all the ground, do the drilling. Then the poor old army horse I had, poor old feller, he'd had his chips; they had him done away and bought another one. But that poor old horse never lasted long, the other one, he came in the stable and died. He was old; they'd bought him from the knacker man. Then they bought a tractor.

Above: Wiltshire carter Charlie Gullis of Cocklebury and his horses observing the two-minute silence at the end of World War II. All six of the farm's horses were retired after the war and allowed to live out their natural lives at Cocklebury.

It was a 1917 petrol-driven Fordson and farmer Giles said to Bill, 'I shall learn you to drive tractors.' Bill told me:

I got on pretty fair with it. No mudguards or anything, dirt thrown in your lap as the wheels with the lugs went round. In the morning you'd wind and wind, nothing would start it, then next morning it'd be easy. Oh, she was an old thing! It was a smashing old thing! Father had a better old petrol one but I wouldn't go near that – it used to make such a noise. We had that old thing for quite a while and then went down to Tangmere one day; there was an air display down there, and there was a Rowes reconditioned tractor down there. He bought this iron-wheeled one of them for £75 and it was like driving a Rolls Royce – it had mudguards, gear stick and that. Those days you could buy a rubber-tyred standard Fordson for £120 and an iron-wheeled one for £90.

Bill's father, grandfather and great-grandfather had all worked horses and he knew very well that his would be last generation to do so. His father had worked on the same farm all his life, dying at the age of 83. His grandfather had worked on a farm all *his* life, dying at over 80, and Bill's great-grandfather, too, had been on the same farm all his life, at nearby Didling. Bill's father had been in World War I, during which his right elbow had been 'blowed apart': after seven operations it remained held together with copper wire for the rest of his life and he could only move his arm from the shoulder, not from the elbow. Yet he could use a shovel as well as the next man, he could drive the cart, manage a pair of horses and do everything he needed to do, except to button his collar.

Bill loved his horses, but he also loved his tractors and made the switch with surprising ease. (He reminds me of a cavalry officer I knew who found himself pushed into the Royal Flying Corps during World War I, the theory being that if you could ride a horse you could fly a plane and no tuition was needed.) But when the farm acquired a steam threshing machine, and had to strengthen the little bridge over the stream to take its weight, Bill hitched up a couple of horses (not a tractor) to barrel up 130 gallons of water at a time to feed the machine. Horses were in his blood.

BESS AND JAMES

James White started his trade as a carrier in 1900, buying himself a cob and a two-wheeled cart and then graduating to a covered van so that he and his mare Bess could take passengers as well as goods. In snowy weather he would take Bess out of the shafts, sling meat and other goods in sacks across her back, packhorse style, and lead her home, leaving the van and its other parcels until the weather improved. He often had to pull up at the side of the road in winter to put frost nails into her shoes so that she could get a grip on the icy surface. He had bought Bess as a five-year-old in 1914. 'During the War,' he said, 'when horses were being commandeered for War service, I often put Bess in a stable at Littlehampton or took her down a side turning to avoid the military authorities ... My mare was the exact stamp they were seeking but I could ill afford to lose her.'

TRAPPINGS AND HARNESS

Horse trappings belonged to the carter, not the master, and were often handed down from father to son. By the time of World War I, the sun still flashed on polished decorative metal crescents and discs as the heavy horses plodded along the highway but horse bells were by then chiefly for the show ring.

In earlier times, the large latten-bells had served a practical purpose: worn by the leading horse, in the lanes they warned of the approach of a team so that teams coming in the opposite direction could pause where the lane widened enough to give room to pass. Smaller bells that constantly jingled were known as head-bells; they were fixed to an upright ornament on the horse's head, or singly at the sides, tinkling gently.

For heavy horses on the farm, there were basically three types of harness: shaft or cart harness, for drawing a wagon or cart; trace harness, where the horses worked as a team in single file; and plough harness, similar to trace but where the horses worked abreast of each other. If the horses were also used for roadwork, they might need pair harness or pole harness to pull a trade vehicle or heavy dray.

Shaft harness and trace harness both comprised bridle, collar and hames. The bridle usually included blinkers to concentrate the horse's vision on the job in hand without distractions to the side or from above. Bridles had bits, which came in various designs but on the farm tended to be a simple straight metal bar. The well-padded collar went around the base of the neck, avoiding the windpipe and resting by the withers. The hames were two curved pieces of wood or iron rising above the collar to which the traces were attached. The traces were two side-straps, chains or ropes that connected the horse with whatever it was drawing.

Shaft harness had a cart 'saddle' or pad, whereas trace harness had a broad leather back-band with fittings through which the very long trace chains passed as they ran from the collar towards the implement. The cart saddle, anchored in place by a girth band under the belly and by a short strap from the front attached to the collar and a wide strap from the back attached to the breeching, took some of the weight of the vehicle by means of a chain passing from one shaft to another over the saddle's bridge. The breeching was a system of straps between the saddle and girth and the horse's back end: it included the crupper, which looped over the base of the tail, and the breech-band wrapped around the rump, and was basically a braking system to ensure that the vehicle did not run into the back of the horse on a steep downhill slope.

The trace harness was lighter and simpler: the back-band was held in place by a belly band around the girth, with a short strap along the withers to the collar and a crupper looped over the root of the tail, and there would be hip straps hanging down on either side of the crupper to catch the trace chains so that they did not interfere with the horse's legs.

Fully decked team at a ploughing match with ploughman AW Pearce of Cranleigh, Surrey, and his young son in 1934.

Mules and Donkeys

Many farm horses, and horsemen, took part in World War I battles; quite a few of those that survived came back to the farms after the war. Along with the horses came mules, which had been used by the army and for whom some of their handlers had developed a deep respect and fondness.

Above: Faithful donkey coming home to Selham, in Sussex, in the 1930s.

The splendid War Office manual, *Animal Management*, issued in 1923, gave detailed instructions on handling and caring for mules, donkeys, camels and oxen, as well as horses, including how to take a laden mule across a river (they are good swimmers), and praised their virtues highly, especially as the favourite of all pack animals.

Despite their reputation for stubbornness, mules were generally cheerful and intelligent but they deeply resented violence, tended to be shy with strangers, were touchy about the head and ears, and were known as free kickers. Mules, if you understood them, were good workers and not just as pack animals: they could be draught beasts as well and they, too, found jobs on the farms after both wars. They could be as big as 17 hands (almost as big as a Shire horse) and could go on working until they were 20 years old or more. Endurance was a mule's middle name and they were also good fast walkers, averaging three to four miles an hour, and quite happy to cover as much as 25 miles a day carrying a backpack of 160 pounds. You could ride them too (I know of a charming white mule that became a good fence-jumper). They had two major drawbacks: as army animals they tended to stampede under fire; and whether in the army or on the farm they could not reproduce themselves. Mules are hybrids, a cross between horse (mare) and ass (jack), and are sterile.

The mating of a jack and mare was not accomplished without some reticence on the part of the mare. Female offspring were deemed to be more tractable than male mules, which sometimes forgot they were incapable of procreation and would do their best to seduce nearby mares.

Asses, or donkeys, were far more numerous in Britain than mules and for many years were a common sight in country lanes and villages, though they were not really farm animals. They were much smaller than mules and quite a lot slower: their typical pace was two and a half miles an hour and they might walk up to 15 miles in a day, with a load of only 100 pounds.

Working with Cattle

Cattle, wrote Sidney Rogerson in 1949, were 'the axis on which the whole wheel of farming turns'. They supplied milk, meat and dung and, in days gone by, they had also supplied all the 'horse' power you could possibly need. Some of them were bred specifically as dairy animals, others for beef, but many were dual-purpose breeds giving both milk and meat. In 1945 a landgirl in Oxfordshire said of dual-purpose cattle that she did not like meat that had been milked to death.

She would have liked even less the meat from draught oxen, who were killed only after a long working life and might well have been as tough as old boots when they were turned into topside. But, by then, their meat was something of a bonus to a farming family after many years of faithful service and no one expected melt-in-the-mouth steak. Unlike dairy and beef cattle, they had been bred for muscle power, just like heavy horses. It seems strange, then, that the British were quite prepared to eat their placid, plodding, reliable working oxen but not their working horses.

Oxen

For several centuries before the horse became the general farmworker, the animals of choice for field cultivations and for pulling loads were oxen. In theory, the term oxen covers all cattle, male and female, but it is particularly applied to bullocks, which are castrated bulls.

By the mid 18th century, horses and oxen were more or less level in terms of their use on the farms, but from then on the improved breeding of horses and the development of lighter ploughs for them gradually edged oxen out of the picture, though they continued to be well used in parts of Wiltshire and Gloucestershire and certainly on the downs of Berkshire and in Sussex until into the 20th century. Sussex was the last true stronghold for working oxen and there were still a dozen or more teams working in the county up to World War I. In the 19th century many Sussex farms would have kept a score of oxen. Each team might comprise eight or even a dozen animals, especially for ploughing the heavy clay lands of the Weald. They were also used for pulling carts on the appalling Sussex roads.

Barclay Wills managed to watch what was said to be the last team of oxen at work in Sussex in 1927: they belonged to Mr EJ Gorringe of Exceat Farm in the Cuckmere valley and he first met them during a lunch break. The four oxen were wearing nose nets, rather than

Above: Teams of Sussex oxen. Their handler is holding a 'twitch', which was used gently to guide the animals into turning at the end of the furrow. Oxen were never switched, prodded or shouted at; they needed kind, gentle handling.

Right: Horse and ox join forces to help with the harrowing in a Banffshire field at Claymirres, Ordiquhill, in 1896 with Robert Thomson and his wife.

nosebags, to prevent them from grazing while ploughman WE Wooler, wearing a cowslip flower on his coat, rested and talked. The oxen had been fed first thing in the morning and would be fed again at four, having worked from seven to three. Normally the team would have been six – Lamb and Leader, Pilot and Pedler, Quick and Nimble (they were always paired) – but one ox was unfit and so his companion had the day off as well. The animals had brass knobs on the tips of their long, sharp horns to prevent accidents and they worked in yokes.

Young Wooler had a goad – a long hazel stick with a piece of wire at the tip that looked something like a blunt pencil. It was not for prodding; it was just laid lightly over the necks of the leaders to let them know it was time to turn at the headland of the field. All they needed otherwise was a quietly murmured 'ay' or 'gee' as they plodded methodically, steady and regular, up and down the field, hour after hour after hour.

In 1931 the only known team of oxen left in England belonged to the Earl of Bathurst at Cirencester. This team of six Hereford cattle were in constant work between eight in the morning and four in the afternoon, yet they always looked plump and well. At seven in the morning they were given hay – and this was an advantage over horses: cattle are ruminants, with considerable stomach space, and that early feed could last them for most of the day. The Earl's oxen would rest for a while at about nine and again at midday, to chew the cud. At four, the day's work done, they were watered and then simply turned out to grass; there was none of that business of chaff cutting and measuring out oats and they didn't even need grooming. And the natural grease from the animals kept the harness soft and supple, in contrast to the dry, cracked leather of a horse's harness. The oxman's life was a lot easier than the horseman's.

The Earl's oxen could plough an acre in their working day, no sweat. They were harnessed with collars rather than the traditional yoke, and instead of bits there was a chain under the jaw, with a rein on the left side only (a verbal command was used to turn them to the right). The hames and cart-saddles were of wood and as light as possible.

Oxen had several advantages over horses, according to those who worked with them. They pulled steadily, albeit more slowly than horses. They were cheaper to feed. They were much less nervous than horses and would work close under hedges and in places where horses

Above: Fancy headgear to fend off flies, modelled by a Jersey cow but equally appropriate for working oxen.

GIVE US OXEN ANY DAY

In 1919 three old Cotswold men told Walter Johnson, separately and without prompting, that they had preferred working with oxen. The teams were slow, but they worked more steadily and thoroughly than horses. They were easier to manage and cheaper to keep. One of the three, George, told a story of how a team of horses had failed to move a threshing machine from the middle of a field. In despair, the carter came to borrow the bullock team ploughing in the next field. One horse (the thiller, or shaft-horse) had to be left in place so that the traces could be properly attached (plough gears differed from those needed by the horse). The ploughman allowed his bullocks to be used on condition that the carter 'cleared out, and kept clear, and didn't start any holloaing'. So the ploughman yoked the bullocks and quietly spoke to his team, calling each by its name ('Blossom, Whitefoot, Smiler, or what not'). They lurched forward steadily and moved the machine with no problem. Who needed horses? George knew his oxen: he had been leading bullocks in the field from the age of six. He said that they used to say it took two bullocks to do the work of one horse, but bullocks were cheaper than horses and after a few years you could put him out to grass from August until the spring to get him 'what we call 'alf fat' and then sell him on to a dealer for further fattening. 'So you did get two benefits, and the meat was better. The mistake we makes nowadays is to kill all animals too young.'

would refuse to go. And after a few years they could be put out to grass and fattened for the butcher. Their worst problem was, as with all cattle, that they bolted at the sound of gadflies and did their best to high-tail it across the field at the first ominous buzz.

For road work, oxen were shod and the shoes were formed of two plates (cattle have cloven hooves). On long journeys a smith would go with them to mend or replace broken shoes along the way. It was not just working oxen that were shod: drovers of Aberdeen-Angus cattle might take them as much as 300 miles to London, on the roads for over three weeks, and these animals, too, were often shod.

The shoeing of an ox was quite a performance and it is not surprising that the animals soon became nervous when they had a sniff of a blacksmith. An ox would be 'thrown' before being shod, rather than standing patiently at the forge like a horse and offering its foot. There is a knack to throwing a bullock and he certainly would not have enjoyed the experience of being cast to the ground to lie on his side, his feet

Above: Dramatically horned oxen belonging to the Brown family of Aldbourne, Wiltshire, harrowing a field in 1911.

tied in a bunch and someone sitting on his neck to keep him still. The shoeing had to be carried out quickly to reduce the time that the poor old thing had to spend in such an undignified and uncomfortable position. It could also be painful and it was customary, during the shoeing, for a boy to stand close by with a lump of pork fat. If a driven nail happened to hurt the ox, the pain would immediately be counteracted by pork grease.

The working day

You needed to have a song in your heart to work with oxen: they worked at their best when their driver sang continually, but not just any old song. In Wales thousands of sing-along three-liners were composed for men who worked with oxen: the sound had to be soothing, with a prolonged note or two in each cadence; the words had to please the animals' intelligence and also appeal to their sense of humour. Anyone who has kept house cows will understand these criteria, and will also understand that the Welsh ploughman liked to confide in his team, telling the oxen about his love life, knowing that they would be on his side. The bards suggested that the ploughman should have a sense of his own importance and, to satisfy this, that the strength and beauty of the yoke should be expressed in his song. Most oxmen had a repertoire of perhaps three or four songs. If he stopped singing, the oxen stopped in their tracks – and that was just as true in England as in Wales.

In the 1970s, Percy Barnes told Michael Winstanley's oral history project about his memories of working with oxen when first employed by the Cheeseman brothers at Goddard's Green Farm, Cranbrook. He started as a carter boy:

I was set to work with two old oxen. I didn't know anything about them. I'd been used to bullocks and that all my life. I wasn't afraid of them, but I didn't know nothing what to say to them or do with them.

Mr Cheeseman said, 'You go round to George Head, he'll tell you how to get on.' He was stockman. He used to work them sometimes. Well, I went round the buildings and found him and we went out into the orchard, and as soon as we went in the gate the old bullocks, they began to saunter away up towards us. He put the yoke on one of them – that was old Winch, the one that worked the off-side – he held the end up and pulled the bow out and Winder, he come sauntering up under the yoke and he yoked him up.

'There,' he said, 'that's how you do that job! I never show anybody anything only once.'

I said, 'All right.'

So I had the old bullocks out, had them up to the cart, and the off-bullock stepped over the nib and they stood theirselves in position. He went up between them and lifted the old pole up and put the plug in.

'Now,' he said, 'there's one thing you want to remember when you put that plug in. Tie it in with that bit of thong because that might drop out.' ... They knew their names. You always worked two together, and the off-bullock never had only one syllable in his name, hence Winch and Winder, Pink and Piny, and such names as that. Always used to say

Above: Oxen were used to pull carts advertising Atora suet all over Britain from the 1890s. The last was pulled by two Herefords known as Dick and Sailor, who travelled to many parts of the country in the 1930s. Here they visit Fernhurst, in Sussex.

'yea' to them to come to you, and that off-bullock he'd always be the first one to come to you, and his mate, he knew, he might be back there amongst all the others, but he'd find his way up there. They was mates together and that was how they always worked.

... Sometimes we've had them sulk and lay down. We used to go down to a stream if we was anywhere near one and get a little old tin or a bottle, drop

Above: Shoeing an ox, Saddlescombe in Sussex.

of water in it, put a few drops in their ear. They soon jump up. They didn't like that. And when we used to break them in we used to have a stick, about five or six feet long, and have a little spike in the end of it. When you said 'yea' to them, you gave the old bullock a prick in the shoulder. Of course, that used to make him shoot forward. That's how they learnt that. They never forgot that either. I know when we've been harvesting sometimes we used to stick the whip in the back of the wagon and carry on picking up the sheaves, and if you wanted to start up just pull a straw out of the sheaf and you could guide them with that straw just as if you'd got a whip or a goad. They never forgot that spike.

Bulls

In the 1870s Francis Kilvert recorded that he had met a harnessed team of red oxen coming home from ploughing, 'with chains rattling and the old ploughman riding the fore ox'. It reminded him of the time when he himself used to ride the oxen home from plough at Lanhill.

I've wondered about this riding business. As a child I used to try riding heifers bareback and found their bony spines a most uncomfortable seat. Also, being heifers, they tended to bolt for freedom and leap the nearest fence. The amazing Yorkshire farmer Colin Newlove, who died in April 2005, actually trained his Ayrshire bull, William, to ride to hounds: the bull happily jumped hedges and gates with Newlove in the saddle. The farmer started the bull with three months of long-reining and lunging back in the 1960s and found that William loved being ridden – even through hoops of fire at the Yorkshire Show. Given the right approach, individual cattle are infinitely trainable and those centuries of working oxen prove the point. Mind you, Newlove also trained a fire-walking turkey called Trevor, who rode with him on his quad bike every day when he went to check the sheep.

Emma Griffiths, who had been in service from the age of 10 and married before she was 20, told Francis Kilvert an alarming tale. Her first place had been at Bron Ddu and one morning when all the men were away and the farmer's wife was still in bed, Emma had to fetch in the cows to be milked. There was a two-year-old bull with the cows. She left him in the field with one cow and brought in the others, but the bull came after her. She tried to get through the gate but he caught her and had her down on the ground for half an hour. No one knew, no one came to her rescue as he 'punned' her with his head and ran his horn into her side and into one of her legs.

Left: Colin Newlove jumping his Ayrshire bull William through a flaming hoop on his farm near Bugthorpe, Yorkshire.

Below: Tame Hereford bull helps with the lambs.

She was half-unconscious throughout the attack and felt no pain at the time. At last he pushed her through a newly laid hedge and left her. Eventually she came to and stumbled into the house, bruised all over, covered with blood, her eyes closed up and her body almost naked. She was at home for three months but then returned to Bron Ddu to finish her time, keeping well clear of that bull.

In 1883, the *Haverfordwest and Milford Haven Telegraph* reported another terrible tale:

On Tuesday last a butcher, named Benjamin Gwyther, known as 'Benny', who resided at Monkton, was so injured by a bull that he died from the effects. It appears that the bull was lying on the side of the road near Merrion Court, and could not be got up. Gwyther got out of his cart, and applied a whip to the animal, which at once got up, and catching Gwyther on its horns forced him against the hedge bank several times breaking the poor fellow's ribs and breast bone … He has since died.

Bert Walke was born in 1896 on a Devon farm where farmers used to bring their bulls to stop over for the night, bringing their own mangolds and hay for the animals, then they would catch the train at Gara Bridge the following morning to take men and beasts to the Totnes Bull Sale. One farmer stopped over with a cow and calf and Bert's father bought the calf, which grew into a fine bull. One day a boy had been teasing the bull, which turned on him and chased him into a drain. Fortunately for the lad, the brambles over the drain stopped the bull from kneeling him, but he was still badly injured: his arm was broken and the bull put a horn through his shoulder. You don't mess with bulls. As for Bert, he grew up to become a butcher in Loddiswell in 1927: he'd always had a good eye for beef cattle.

Beef Cattle

Britain was famous for its beef and it was also famous for creating breeds of beef cattle that have spread right round the world – superb breeds like the black hornless Aberdeen Angus, the white-faced red Hereford and the roan Shorthorn.

Above: A prize-winning Shorthorn steer with herdsman Robbins, who had worked on the Royal farms at Sandringham for more than 30 years at the time of this late 19th century photograph.

BULLOCK PITS

Tread gingerly when you are next crossing a farmyard, or you just might find the ground giving way beneath you and plunging you into a pit. Bullock pits were quite common in Victorian times and they were often close to the farmhouse. You dug out a straight-sided pit, say eight or ten feet deep and 15 or 20 feet across, in a sheltered corner of the yard. In the autumn you tipped in a load of straw and then you dumped your yearling bullocks into this nicely bedded new home. And there they stayed, being fed on all manner of odds and ends, even kitchen waste, and getting heavier and heavier as they had absolutely no exercise at all. Nor was their bedding mucked out; it simply built up over the months, and with good management it had raised the bullocks to about ground level just in time for them to saunter out and be taken to market. Then some poor souls had the exceedingly heavy job of literally cutting out all that lovely manured bedding, packed down into a dense mattress by the weight of the bullocks and their evacuations, and carting it away for spreading on the fields.

The problem with being a beef breed, however famous and however widespread, was that your role in life was to end up on the dinner plate. It was the quality of life between being born and ending up on the plate that varied considerably, according to the whims of the humans under whose care an animal happened to fall. With suckler herds, it could be a pretty good life: the calves ran with their mothers, usually out on the hills, and rarely had contact with humans until it was time for them to be weaned so that the cow could prepare for her next calf. Thereafter they had quite an easy life, certainly a leisurely one, as all their energy from feeding was supposed to be channelled into growing meat, not wasted on work or frolicking or any other distractions. The males might unfortunately find their 'tackle' being removed at an early stage but, hey, what they had never experienced they wouldn't miss. And life was all fine and dandy until the out-of-the-ordinary day when they found themselves heading for an unknown destination that they knew, in their bones, was not a good place to go.

Butchers

In 1938, just before the outbreak of another war, only 45 per cent of the beef and veal consumed in Britain was home produced, whereas in the 1890s it had been about 70 per cent. In the 1860s, the average consumption of meat of all kinds in Britain was 100 pounds per annum per person; by 1937 it had risen to 141 pounds per person, of which about 69 pounds was beef and veal. At the same time the Argentinians were each consuming 231 pounds of beef and veal and the Dutch only 31 pounds each a year. Tastes in beef had also changed: in the 19th century people wanted meat cut from large, well-flavoured fatty joints with a small proportion of bone. After World War I, they wanted small, lean, tender joints and were much less interested in boiling or stewing the meat: they wanted roasts and grilling steaks. These changes in demand meant that the farmers had to change their animals and concentrate on smaller beef breeds for smaller joints, selecting those that matured early for tender, lean meat; then they had to 'finish' their animals at a younger age for smaller and more tender joints, select animals that had higher proportions of best-quality cuts and lower proportions of second-quality cuts, and sell them to the butcher before they were excessively fat to give lean meat. A drawback to killing the animals at a younger age than had been traditional was that the meat, however small and tender the joints might be, usually had much less flavour.

The butcher, of course, only wanted to buy stock that produced the kind of meat he could most easily sell. In the late 1930s, that meant an animal weighing less than 10 hundredweight when it was alive and it also meant as little bone as possible. The butcher's ideal animal was well 'finished' – well covered with meat but without any excess blubber, because fatty meat no longer sold. (The term finished was certainly preferred to the old term, fattened.)

In about 1950, Bob Davis was training to be a sanitary inspector and the students had to spend many hours in slaughterhouses: all meat intended for human consumption had to be certified by inspectors. In those days the meat industry was not tightly controlled and many butchers' shops still had a small slaughterhouse at the rear where the butcher himself would slaughter the animals, flay the carcasses and prepare the joints for sale. Bob remembered:

They were dreadful places, often just a shed with a stone floor where the animals would be pole-axed and bled to death as they writhed around on

Above: Market for the sale of Hereford store cattle (animals to be fattened for beef) in the early 1940s. As lots were sold, the cattle were turned out to graze on the pasture in the background.

the floor. Pole-axing was not a certain procedure and it would often take several blows to the head of the tethered animal before it fell. A pithing rod would then be thrust into the wound, through to the medulla oblongata. This was done to reduce the reflex muscular contractions of the dying beast, and so reduce the risk of injury to the butcher from the kicking hooves. It was a gory and most unpleasant procedure.

He was glad that, half a century later, slaughtering was only carried out in purpose-built, licensed and controlled slaughterhouses where the animals were stunned by 'captive bolt' before being bled and where the beasts no longer writhed around in their death throes on messy, blood-covered floors. 'I don't suppose it makes a great deal of difference to the poor condemned animal,' said Bob, 'but it is certainly a better environment for the modern slaughterman.'

THE VILLAGE BUTCHER

Old-fashioned butchers often reared their own animals, or at least in the finishing stages. There was such a butcher in the Surrey village of Chobham right into the 1970s: old Ma Tanner (yes, a female butcher, and a small, slight one at that) had a few fields behind the shop and produced some of the best beef for miles around. Not only did she rear the animals; she also hung the carcasses properly.

The abattoir

In the 1970s I visited a long-standing family abattoir on the day they did no killing. George was to be my guide, dressed in white overalls and helmet, and I donned the same uniform. It was all a far cry from the backyard butchers of old, whose activities live on in streets named The Shambles in several market towns.

We skirted empty pens with a tractor mucking out and spreading fresh straw. 'We have three stockmen to look after 'em, see,' said George. 'Especially the cattle.

Above: Butcher Joseph Smith of Leicester demonstrating humane killing.

We're concerned for their peace of mind. Philanthropic? No, more like practical, really. A frightened animal shows in its carcass: the meat is dark on the butcher's slab. So we like the cattle to stay in the lairage overnight, to recover from their journeys, calm down. Remember, often they've come to us wild from the freedom of northern hills, their first close contact with humans, ever; their first enclosure, ever – and a moving one at that, travelling for hours. So we calm 'em here, rest 'em overnight, like, and kill in the morning. Unless one is really bad, really jumpy, then he goes straight off before he upsets the rest. A hundred and twenty cattle a day in here. Some of the cattle are tenderised, so it helps to keep them overnight anyway for that. Inject 'em with enzymes – extract of pawpaw, papaya.

Have to be alive for that, so it circulates all through the system and breaks down the tissues, so you couldn't tell brisket from fillet. We do a lot of that now.'

Cattle went in batches of five, up the ramp and along the race and through a raised metal door that looked like a guillotine. One animal would go through into the holding bay, almost as if it was going into the milking parlour but with the help of electric prods. The door shut behind it with a loud clanging of alien, heavy steel, and no escape ahead.

'The really jumpy ones might bash out sideways through the tilt trap before they're killed, and there are stories to be told on that,' said George, 'but usually they don't get out.'

'So,' he continued, 'a man stands above them here on the gallery, with a bolt gun. No electrocution for cattle. Chooses a precise spot – draws an imaginary line from ear to horn, horn to ear, cross. Fires. Bolt goes straight into the brain, instant death.' Cattle dropped straight down to the floor with a crash, and the bullock's own weight tilted the tilt door to the side so that he rolled through and dropped down a few feet to the next level.

'Then it's hooked up with chain and grapple and hung upside-down high in the air so it can go on thrashing about without hurting anyone. Then it's bled into the bath here – blood collected in a tank outside and later spread as fertiliser.'

From here on it was a production line, automated for the transport but most of the actual jobs were manual. Each man was a specialist. One gutted, another emptied the stomach contents, another chopped off hooves, another the heads, another the tails and tongues, another two skinned the carcass. Hides went down a chute to the hide-room for cleaning, hooves down another chute, head another, lights another and so on, but all in parallel with the animal itself so that they knew which bits belonged to which carcass. Offal was put aside for inspection for disease; the carcass was split into two sides, with inspectors along the line checking for disease and the animal still travelling along the production line all the while. Now it looked like meat: mountains of liver, kidney, tripe, tongue, cheek …

Upstairs there were loud metal doors, loud steam cleaners, loud steam-operated hydraulics to swing the carcasses high and keep 'em moving. We headed for the cold-rooms. There were many, many rows of fine sides of beef.

We visited the packing room where meat was being expertly butchered by the lads and then boxed and labelled.

Lots of the little slaughterhouses were closing because of all the regulations, said George, 'and all the little backyard butcheries are going and even some of the bigger abattoirs. They've a bad name, see, abattoirs. People love their meat but they don't like the thought of the killing. Funny, really. Nobody does much for themselves nowadays. Get other people to do the bits they don't like, then look down on us or accuse us of barbarity.'

Calves

Being young is a time of innocence and promise, even for cattle. Whatever their final destiny, calves have a pretty good life – at least for the first few days. They are with their mothers, suckling milk as nature intended, absorbing antibodies to protect them from this new world outside the womb, a whole exciting world just waiting to be explored. Calves born into suckler herds are free to enjoy life, secure in the protection of their mothers and the herd for months. But for calves born into a dairy herd, it all comes to an abrupt end before they are even a week old, when they are separated from their mothers and suddenly life becomes uncertain.

Bert Charman, living on the other side of the large area of woodland beyond my cottage in the 1970s, was my lifeline when I needed help with my own cows and

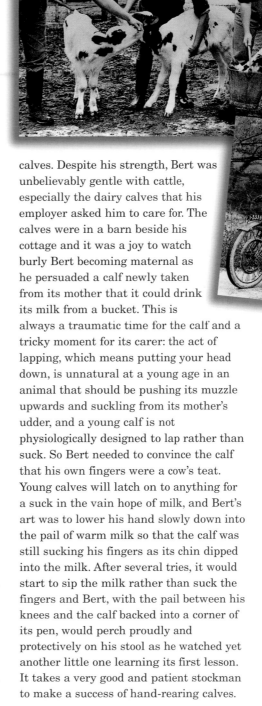

calves. Despite his strength, Bert was unbelievably gentle with cattle, especially the dairy calves that his employer asked him to care for. The calves were in a barn beside his cottage and it was a joy to watch burly Bert becoming maternal as he persuaded a calf newly taken from its mother that it could drink its milk from a bucket. This is always a traumatic time for the calf and a tricky moment for its carer: the act of lapping, which means putting your head down, is unnatural at a young age in an animal that should be pushing its muzzle upwards and suckling from its mother's udder, and a young calf is not physiologically designed to lap rather than suck. So Bert needed to convince the calf that his own fingers were a cow's teat. Young calves will latch on to anything for a suck in the vain hope of milk, and Bert's art was to lower his hand slowly down into the pail of warm milk so that the calf was still sucking his fingers as its chin dipped into the milk. After several tries, it would start to sip the milk rather than suck the fingers and Bert, with the pail between his knees and the calf backed into a corner of its pen, would perch proudly and protectively on his stool as he watched yet another little one learning its first lesson. It takes a very good and patient stockman to make a success of hand-rearing calves.

Top: Landgirls bucket-feeding calves.

Above: Breezy transport for an Easter veal calf.

Dairy Cows

There was at a time when most dairy farms were small. In my own valley, within living memory there were at least a dozen smallholders with a handful of cows each, of milking breeds like Guernsey, Jersey, Ayrshire and Red Poll, and some even grazed the road verges. Today there are no milking cows in the valley.

My personal experience is entirely with dairy cows: I worked on a family Jersey farm in the 1970s with a herd of a hundred characters – from the delightful Blossom to the difficult Teenager – and loved it so much that I also had my own Jersey house cows. Because dairy cows are handled twice a day every day for milking, they are on the whole very used to human company and you can get to know them as individuals, however big the herd. One could tell countless stories about why cows can enchant those who work with them, but I've always liked the tale told by Madeleine Day in the early 1950s. It was near the Buckinghamshire village of Chenies and the cows, a matronly bunch, were peacefully grazing and chewing the cud. Suddenly, from the village, came the strains of a brass band playing a lively tune. For a moment the cows paused in their chewing, and then the whole herd rose to its feet and started a rollicking dance round and round the meadow,

Above: Riding a Red Poll heifer.

Right: Herd of milking Jersey cows and their cowman.

romping in time to the music. When the music stopped, so did the cows – and my, didn't they look embarrassed!

❧

Bill Sweet was born in Dawlish in 1930. When he left school at 15 he became an errand boy, delivering groceries by pushbike, until he became a gardener. He had to do his National Service from 1948 to 1950, mainly in Egypt, but returned to gardening and general help on an estate where there were 40 South Devon milking cows.

We used a milking machine where the milk went through the jars direct to the churns but sometimes through a glass jar for recording. George Wakeham lived at Higher Hazelwood and looked after four or five cows up there and supplied the milk, cream and butter for Hazelwood House. ... We had a lovely lot of cows down here at Crannacombe and they grazed the fields all around here, that was a lovely job, I liked the cows. Most of them calved by themselves but sometimes we had one backwards and had to call the vet. If everything was all right I loved to see the calf struggle to get on its feet with the mother licking him all over.

Bill, when he was 73, decided that it had been running around after the cows and calves that had kept him fit. 'I loved going out early in the morning as it was getting light bringing the cows in for milking. The dew was rising down over the fields and over the river Avon.'

Milking by hand

Many older villagers remember hand milking about a dozen cows, and many more remember drinking the produce, sometimes with a shudder. Sidney Rogerson had lived in the Yorkshire Dales as a boy before World War I; after the next war he would write a book, illustrated by Charles Tunnicliffe, explaining to those who had always wondered as they drove through the countryside just exactly what farmers actually did and why. It had changed a lot, of course, since his boyhood days, when he could remember a taciturn Yorkshire farmer who was both his family's milkman and his father's churchwarden. On Sunday evenings the farmer would appear at the vicarage dressed in a sombre black overcoat and hard hat, but around his neck would be an old-fashioned yoke from which two cans of milk dangled. He would leave one of the cans for the family's weekend milk, and would prop the other can and the yoke by their back door and then walk over to the church with the vicar. His holding in the dales was 70 acres of small grass fields and he farmed in exactly the same way as had his father and grandfather before him. He had about five cows, which he turned out to graze on his hilly land and moor in summer; for their winter feeding he made hay, grew a patch of roots and bought a bit of concentrated cattle cake. His farmhouse kitchen was immaculately clean and shiny, but it never occurred to the farmer to keep his animals in clean conditions: the cowshed (or 'mistal') had but one tiny window covered with

Above: Hand-milking in an old cowhouse before World War I.

Below: A Leicestershire cowman, wearing a pair of typically heavy hobnail boots.

Above: Dorset dairymaid clutching her three-legged stool. All true milking stools had only three legs, enabling the milker to wheel quickly out of the way when a cow lifted her hoof to kick.

Opposite: Hand-milking. Dairy breeds included Jersey, Guernsey, Ayrshire and Shorthorns – the latter were ubiquitous before black-and-white Friesians displaced them in the milking parlour after World War II.

they would be standing waiting, sleepily, in their stalls. The boss's storm lantern provided the only lighting inside the whitewashed cowshed as he walked down the 'bing' (the passageway at the head of the stalls) pulling a big fodder-barrow and shovelling each cow's individual ration of corn into her manger.

Those who give most milk get the biggest share. As soon as the cows heard the rumble of the barrow and the clang of the shovel they would moo with delight; each would turn her great dark eyes on the boss in mute appeal, tossing her head and pawing the ground impatiently. The boss said he always hurried down the line as fast as he could as he couldn't bear to keep the poor things in suspense; the anguish of the last cow, still unfed, while all the rest guzzled rapturously, was dreadful.

Meanwhile the landgirl would be washing each cow with warm water and disinfectant and then squirting a little milk from each of a cow's four teats into a small can to check for any signs of mastitis or other problems that would mean keeping that cow's milk separate. The farm cats waited patiently, knowing that the contents of the little can would eventually be theirs.

On this farm the milking was still being done by hand even towards the end of the war, though many farms had machines by then. M-W generally enjoyed milking, but not when the neighbouring cow was a tail-lasher:

cobwebs, the wooden posts of the stalls shone from years of being rubbed by cows' flanks but were also caked with patches of dry dung, the walls were dung-splashed and the uneven stone floors were only brushed, never washed, after each milking. At milking time the farmer, who had probably just been mucking out the pigs, never thought to wash his hands before he pulled up his stool and started on the first cow, and he certainly never thought to wash her udder, or her dung-crusted tail or flanks. But at least he would have scalded out his milking pail since the previous milking session.

In 1945 the anonymous 'M-W' wrote a delightful article about being a 'cowgirl'. Like many another landgirl during the war, she had previously worked in an office and it was a rude shock to get up at half-past five on cold winter mornings, stumbling about to get dressed in the dark because there was only one candle and you couldn't find the matches. She would pile on as many clothes as she could find and top them with a thick milking-smock, grab a cup of tea and join the bearded farmer in the icy yard. As they opened the doors of the shippon they would hear the cows 'puffing and scrambling as we disturbed them from their slumbers' and

You will be sitting under cow number one, not thinking of anything in particular, when cow number two will find that you get on her nerves. She will then lift her long muscular tail and swish it vigorously from side to side. You will receive a stinging blow across the eyes. Before you have fully recovered from this, two more direct hits will

Above: Landgirls helping with the milking during World War II.

every few minutes I had to stop in order to rub her nose a bit. She received this courtesy with every sign of pleasure.'

In winter, the stars were still shining after the morning milking was over and the business of washing out everything that had been in contact with the milk began: first in cold water, then in hot and finally into the steam cabinet for sterilising. Then, at last, it was time for a farm-kitchen breakfast of home-cured bacon, eggs, toast and porridge. After that very welcome meal, M-W would be with her cows until dinnertime. She would open up a bale of oat straw and throw a great armful to each girl, and then she would get down to the warm work of cleaning out, with shovel and brush and a wheelbarrow to cart the old manured bedding to the midden. Then she would give her cows a fresh bedding of wheat straw, which they invariably ate.

So far the cows had been given a milking-time breakfast and an after-milking meal of straw but they were already ready for more food. M-W would harness old Charlie, put him between the shafts of the farm cart, load up with turnips from the clamp, put them through the root-chopper to cut them into small pieces and feed them by the shovelful to the cows. Then she would climb into the loft above the shippon and pitch hay down into the bing while the cows bellowed and stamped and stretched out their tongues in the hope of catching a floating wisp of hay. At last it was her own dinner-time, after which the cows had a 'light meal comprising a few hundredweight of potatoes mixed with a little corn. Lick, crunch, scrunch – gone! Second course, a little hay – delightful!' Then, while the landgirl went off to clean out the maternity loose-box or to nurse a sick cow, most of the animals would settle down for a rest to chew the cud and gossip, until it was time for the evening milking at four – and another meal, of turnips and corn. Such

have demolished your carefully erected coiffure and you will be blinded with pain and hair. The boss could tuck the offending tail under his arm and continue to milk in comfort, but this needs practice.

Fortunately the boss milked the most awkward individual cows himself and she would hear him crooning encouragement to them: 'Let it down now, little lady,' or 'Be good, my girlie,' or sometimes something rather stronger. She remembered one dearly loved cow in particular who always screwed her neck round to watch the milker intently. 'I could never milk her very fast because

TIME TO CALVE

Sometimes during the morning milking the boss would remark that a particular cow was looking 'thoughtful' and she would be removed to a separate loose-box known fondly as the maternity ward. (You can always tell when a cow is due to calve: ignore the textbooks that tell you to look for dropped pinbones and the like, and just go by her mood. My own Rosie would get an affectionate dreamy look in her eyes when her time was due and would wander away from the other animals, seeking a little privacy for her calving.)

anticipatory joy in all those brown eyes as she opened the shippon door! And there would be another meal at about six – hay to see them through the night. Then, at last, the cowgirl could close the doors on her ladies and let them sleep, 'their great heads tucked round and pressed against their sides', no doubt to dream of breakfast. What a relief it must have been to turn the cows out to pasture in the spring and let them forage for themselves!

Rachel Knappett remembered when she had to learn to milk by hand. She called it a fascinating, tantalising process:

The old hands can show the learner exactly how to sit on the low, three-legged stool, the exact position of the legs and the right way to balance the bucket between the knees. The learner can study the old hands, how they push their heads well into the flank of the cow, how they keep the left leg against the cow's leg, and how one arm is always ready to ward off a kick. The learner's hands can be fixed in the correct way round the teats, and the work of the fingers and wrists can be explained in every detail. But the actual power of being able to draw the milk has to come by itself and in its own good time. For days the milk refuses to flow and drips into the bucket in an uneasy, fretful dribble. For days the brow is damp with the sweat of frustration and the terror that the cow's dirty foot will come into unseemly contact with the bucket. The wrists and fingers ache and grow stiff with fatigue. And the only result is a gill of milk in the bucket, a puzzled cow, a disheartened novice, and a row of laughing faces belonging to the instructors.

We've all been there, trying to make our hands perform an unnatural

Above: James Fennell (1784–1872), cowman on the Leveson Gower estate at Titsey, still working hard at the age of 78.

manipulation. But at last the day comes when, quite suddenly, you have the knack (which, like learning to ride a bicycle, you will never lose) and there is the wonderful joy of milk rhythmically thrumming into the bucket with a frothy head like a glass of beer. When this moment happened for Rachel, she could not help herself exclaiming, 'Good Lord! I can milk!'

Milking machines

In theory, according to Primrose McConnell in 1919 (who made no mention of milking machines), a woman could hand-milk ten cows and a man up to 15, twice a day. So, with modern herds numbering hundreds rather than dozens of cows each, your

Right: A 'modern' cowshed during World War II, with Ayrshire cows being milked by machine. This was before the installation of an overhead line system: the milk had to be emptied from the machines into pails and carried to the dairy.

labour force would be well into double figures for each milking. The introduction of machines for milking was the biggest revolution for dairy farmers.

Most farmers distrusted machines; they felt they got better results from hand-milking as long as they could find the labour to do it. And that was the crunch: the supply of agriculture labour was rapidly decreasing. By the outbreak of World War II, about 15 per cent of the nation's dairy cows would be milked by machine. Half a century later, very few people know how to milk by hand and even fewer are skilled in the art.

At first, the machines milked into an enclosed bucket and the bucket had to be carried to the dairy. The machine was a vacuum system, with teat-cups attached to the cow's teats drawing out the milk under vacuum pressure and piping it into the buckets. Then early in the 1920s a new type of machine appeared on the market that could also pipe the milk all the way into the dairy; this was known as a releaser milking machine, as opposed to the older bucket plant. But the cows were still being milked in their individual stalls in the cowhouses where they spent the winter months.

MILKING BY STEAM

A steam-powered Thistle Milking Machine was exhibited at the Royal Show at Darlington back in 1895 and it was claimed to milk ten cows in just 12½ minutes with only one man in attendance. Two years later, a splendid collection of milking machines was tested in Scotland: two were steam-driven, one was powered by water, two by oil engines and one by horse-gear.

Milking bails

The next step was to take the milking point to the cows, rather than bring in cows from fields that might be quite a way from the farmyard. This was Wiltshire dairy farmer AJ Hosier's invention of the portable milking bail, which he first devised in 1922 by building his own releaser plant on wheels so that he could tow it out by tractor into the fields and milk the cows on the spot but under cover

in his portable shed. The cows could file into the handful of stalls in the bail and he could milk anything up to a dozen cows at a time; the cows would leave the stalls as soon as they had been milked and the next batch of animals would take their place.

In 1945, with the end of a long war in sight, Clyde Higgs had a flexible system of milking bails: each bail accommodated 60 cows and each bail was under the charge of one cowman and his mate. The joy of the bails was that they could be moved to wherever food for the cows was available or where the land needed manuring. In a guided tour of the farm, Higgs described a milking bail parked at Crow's Nest for the winter. Here, the cows were 'folded', like sheep: they were put into an area of kale and confined to a patch by electric fencing which was moved daily to give them a fresh patch to munch on. A colossal amount of manure gradually covered the ground around the bail and would then be ploughed into the land to provide a good crop for the next season. Higgs's enterprise had four of these milking bails in different parts of the farm and 230

recorded English average of 710 gallons, and in addition to more milk he also had greatly improved fertility on the manured bail-land for the next season's crops. For a while milking bails were all the rage.

Milking parlours

Ten years after inventing his milking bail, Hosier went indoors and built the first milking parlour – a building specifically designed for milking the dairy herd. In effect it was his bail within a permanent building: there were stalls to accommodate the cows while they were being milked by releaser machines; the milk was piped straight into the dairy for processing; the first batch of cows moved out of their stalls and the next batch moved in.

Below: Portable Gascoigne milking bail on Lord Iveagh's Elveden estate in Suffolk in about 1950. The estate was huge and in summer the bails were taken out to the fields and moved with the herd; in winter the bails were put on concrete floors in the farmstead.

cows in milk, the total herd (including dry cows and young stock) being 690.

Each outdoor milking bail had its own bull running with the cows, and this could make life a little dangerous for the cowman – especially if it was a dairy-breed bull, as they are notoriously less good-tempered than beef-breed bulls. Higgs worked out a system for controlling his bail bulls: five yards of trailing chain suspended through the bull's nose ring. Another idea was to tether the bull to a cable by means of a runner, or to give him a mask so that he could see well enough to feed and do his duties but was handicapped if he put his head down to charge. Poor old fellow: all the fun taken out of his daily dealings with human beings.

Another drawback to milking bails was that the cowman had to go out to the bail, which might be several fields away, in all weathers, rather than just wandering across the yard to the cowhouse. But in 1946 one farmer proudly claimed that his outdoor milking bail averaged 756 gallons for 60 cows, compared with the

DOWNLAND BAILS

Bails could be delightfully Heath Robinson affairs. For example, an official war artist Evelyn Dunbar painted a scene on the Hampshire Downs in 1945 in the foreground of which a landgirl, dressed in dung-brown overalls and soft hat, is eyeballing the 'bail bull' in a field full of cows. In the background is a little yard fenced with hurdles on three sides, with a lean-to open-fronted milking shed on the fourth side, where a white-overalled worker is guiding the penned cows into their milking stations. Hard up against the yard is what looks remarkably like a converted shepherd's hut: a wooden shed on iron wheels with a corrugated iron roof, a metal chimney pipe belching steam and teetering doors swinging open to reveal straight-sided milk churns within.

Above: Mary Jane Gresswell, still milking by hand at the age of 97, on her son's Oxfordshire farm at Hinksey in the 1950s.

milked, and with the cows walking to the milking area rather than the cowman walking to the cows to milk them.

Meanwhile the milking parlour was changing too. In the early models, the individual cow stalls were in a row side by side (abreast), with the cows turning into their chosen stall head first. This was the situation on a farm where I helped with milking in the early 1970s: once the cow had stumbled up on to the low concrete platform of her stall and was bawling for her cake, you simply hooked a chain across behind her backside, stood clear in case she raised her tail, threw a scoop or two of cake into her manger with a satisfying rattle, stooped down to wash her udder, stooped again to stick the milking-machine 'clusters' on to her teats, and let the machine get on with the job of milking her while you moved to the next cow in the row. When the udder was empty, you detached the clusters with a satisfying slurp, gave the cow's teats a dip in iodine against mastitis and pulled a clanging lever to open the gate at the head of the stall so that she could amble out to the yard, or be diverted into a pen if she was 'bulling' and due for a visit by the AI operator. Then you slid back the very noisy metal entrance door (everything in the parlour seemed to be noisy) to let in the next batch of cows from the collecting yard to take their place in the stalls, while you diverted the persistent Teenager away from the feed bin along the way. You could get through a hundred cows in less than a couple of hours, unless they were feeling awkward or a new batch of freshly calved heifers was coming in for the first time and didn't understand the routine and spooked at this strange place full of shadows and clangings and the hypnotic pumping of the milking machines.

After World War II, progress on the dairy farm was rapid. For a start, in the 1950s most farms were on mains electricity (80 per cent of farms were served by the mains by 1960) and nearly all cows were being milked by machine. Most farms had a separate dairy next to the milking parlour, and were now able to use electricity rather than solid fuel as a means of making steam for sterilising everything. Most no longer used the old-fashioned cowhouse system in which the cows remained in their individual stalls all winter, being milked in situ and having all their feed and bedding brought into the cowhouse by hand and all their manure removed by hand. Loose housing became popular, with one area (the yard) for the cows to rest and chew the cud and another (the parlour) where they were

The farm I was working on was an old-fashioned family farm that had not quite caught up with the times. Most other dairy farms had long since graduated to tandem parlours, in which the cows stood on either side of and rather higher above the milker – conveniently at elbow height to avoid all that stooping – and head to tail rather than all with their back ends facing the milker. You got a bit of exercise, having to move down the pit along the length of a cow, rather than the breadth, between each one to wash down udders and deal with clusters. As early as the mid 1950s, this system was improved upon by the herringbone system: the tandem stalls were angled at about 30 degrees to the milker's pit, so you were once again faced by a row of back ends, but you didn't have to walk so far along the pit to deal with them.

By 1960 the farm dairy had progressed from using water for cooling the milk to using refrigeration, which meant that the milk could be stored in huge and expensive steel bulk tanks, ready for direct collection by the commercial dairy's milk tanker lorry. Before the bulk tank, you had to cool the milk pail by pail and then transfer it into big metal churns, which were horrible things to handle in icy weather, and difficult to manoeuvre even when you became skilled at tipping them on to the rim of the base and rolling them into position.

✖

Parlour and bail cows were usually ready and waiting to come in for milking, but sometimes a cowman or cowgirl would need to call up the cows to fetch them from the farthest corner of the meadow. Back in 1872, Richard Heath was wandering the Yorkshire Dales and noticed that, at about six in the afternoon during the summer, the cowherds would go out with great tin cases slung over their shoulder, 'uttering a shrill cry to call the cattle off the moors'. In fact the cows had such good body clocks that they would come down themselves, even if there was no hollering. Cows are creatures of habit.

Wandering in the Cotswolds in 1919, Walter Johnson had met a little, bent old man with a 'grizzled half-circle of hair and beard which ringed the thick stubble on his rarely shaven face and chin'. It was nearly milking time and the old man had strong views about mechanisation.

Noa, I don't believe in they milking machines, but they uses them on a good many farms around yur. You've always got to strip the cows afterwards, and besides, if there's anything amiss with the cow's quarters, the machine takes no notice, and your milk can't be so good.

Stripping is not as alarming as it might sound: it is the practice of drawing out the last of the milk from the udder by hand.

Below: In the mood for milking. A Devon farmer installed TV sets in the parlour to soothe his cows and increase their milk yields.

Cow Problems

Most of the problems associated with dairy cows are the result of demanding too much from their bags, practising intensive farming methods and concentrating too many animals in one place (in the interests of convenience and efficiency) so that they are vulnerable to contagious diseases – diseases that can sometimes affect humans as well.

Above: Taking precautions against foot-and-mouth disease in 1951 at Writtle, Essex.

In 1945 Clyde Higgs made sure that the milk from his farms was tuberculin tested, 'although from being a pioneer in this practice I have been converted to the need for pasteurisation in these days, and a plant is being installed at the central dairy where all milk comes from the bails'. This was a controversial move on his part: some customers detested the idea of their milk being interfered with in this way. But then he showed them a list of bacteriological tests carried out at 50 dairies producing pasteurised milk, much of which was unfit for consumption when raw.

It had been known for very many years that tuberculosis in cows' milk could lead to tuberculosis in humans, but people were still contracting the disease from milk after World War II. In September 1950 a plan was announced to rid Britain of bovine tuberculosis. Any vet working in an agricultural practice in those days will remember the enormous amount of hard work involved in the TB eradication campaign and also the huge amount of heartache for farmers whose cows failed the tests and had to be slaughtered – cows that might be the result of several generations of careful family breeding.

Several vets who practised between the wars have told me of the old way of dealing with milk fever. This alarming

Above: Bringing the cows home at milking time to Fornside Farm, St John's in the Vale, in the Lake District.

condition can result in a cow losing consciousness and even suffering paralysis, as a result of low levels of calcium in her system when the farmer insists on pulling more milk out of her udder than cows were designed to produce. It was very easy to lose one of your best cows to milk fever and some farmers found that using a bicycle pump to inflate the udder gave the cow some relief (one wonders who first thought of *that* idea). Another alarming condition was bloat: the bellies of cows on clover-rich pasture, or who had gorged themselves on lush grass in the spring after a winter on hay, would suddenly inflate (without any help from a bicycle pump) from lack of belching. Quick action was needed to save the cow and the quickest was to jab something sharp into her side to release all that trapped gas. Sometimes, just for a laugh, someone might strike a match nearby and watch the methane light up.

It could be worse. Several old cowmen and women have told me about cattle being struck by lightning. Miss Buckingham (she never divulged her christian name) was in her nineties when she told me about her childhood in my own cottage. In those days the cottage was part of a big estate and there was

Right: Amenable Ayrshire house cow, somewhere near Whitby.

a herd of Jerseys kept mainly for milk for the big house. The cows were out in the meadow beside the cottage during a mighty thunderstorm and took shelter under a huge oak tree. Ten of them were struck dead by lightning, but, said Miss Buckingham, the farmer didn't realise it, because they remained standing. It was only when none of them moved when he called that he knew something might be wrong, and it was not until he touched them that they fell over.

Aubrey Seymour, who told many a good tale about his farming life between the wars, recorded a story about two of his own cows struck dead by lightning – they had made the mistake of unwittingly standing under overhead power lines, it seems. But there was a lighter touch to the story: the drama happened within sight of the road and very soon a little posse of policemen arrived on the scene and went to investigate, marching boldly up to the victims. All but one of the men were wearing oilskins and gumboots. The unlucky odd man out was in regulation hobnail boots and, as Seymour told it, 'began to execute an impromptu dance'. The ground was still charged with electricity and he had no rubber boots to insulate himself from it.

A final tale from Seymour on the ills that befall cows concerned an old countryman called Hitchman whose cow was 'under the weather' and was being treated by the vet. Seymour enquired after the old cow's health one morning and was startled at Hitchman's answer. 'The vet says she's full o' dirt from that old field of mine and it's all 'cumulated in her Bible!' He later learnt that many of the locals referred to a cow's second stomach (she has four, and the second is the basis of tripe) as her Bible, 'resembling, as it does, a number of superimposed leaves'. Holy cow!

Sheep and Shepherds

Countless authors and journalists have described the characters they met caring for sheep in all parts of the country. Perhaps it was because shepherding was a solitary occupation and perhaps they all assumed that, because they were alone all day apart from their sheep and dogs, shepherds must invariably be deep thinkers, philosophers and poets. No doubt some of them were and no doubt others among them were able to spin a good tale to the gullible townsman who was willing to sit at their feet out on the hills and downs and marvel. Whole books have been devoted to such chance meetings with shepherds of old: shepherding must be the most thoroughly recorded of all agricultural occupations, and several men found themselves being interviewed by more than one eager author. Others could not resist photographing shepherds. Somehow a modern shepherd on a quad bike does not have quite the same spirit of romance.

The Romance of Shepherding

Those who work with cows – apart from idealised dairymaids – have never attracted the rosy aura that seems to cling to shepherds. 'The shepherd,' a well known breeder once told me, 'is half the flock. You can buy any sheep you like but you can't buy a shepherd.'

Left: Shepherd Jack Amos (1903–1997) of Kirton, Suffolk. The hurdles, which he probably made himself, suggest that the sheep were being folded in a temporary lambing area.

Right: William Sheppard, or 'Shep', a well-known and often-photographed character with a billy-goat beard who usually wore a billycock hat, brown velvet jacket, woollen waistcoat, plaid neckerchief, light corduroy breeches and leather leggings, sometimes under a smock.

The Reverend John Coker Egerton wrote about the countryside of Sussex, as he was curate and rector at Burwash on and off between 1857 and his death in 1888. He by no means spoke only to shepherds; he covered a very wide range of country folk. His broad view on shepherds in the 1880s was:

> *Shepherds are commonly credited with a good deal of wisdom, the result of much solitary and independent thinking; but the life of the shepherd of poetry is a very different one from that of the modern shepherd, whose sole business is to bring forward his sheep as fast as possible for the butcher. A hill-shepherd in Scotland, who is not engaged from morning to night in hurdle-pitching, turnip-cutting, and other matter-of-fact work, may meditate and cultivate wisdom, but our south country shepherds are much like other men, as far as my experience goes. Once, I confess, I picked up a theory from a Wiltshire shepherd that might have pleased Mr Darwin. I happened to ask my friend why shepherds set so much store by sheepdogs without tails. The question was apparently new, and the good man did not answer at once. At last he said, 'Well, sir, I do think they be truer bred to sit like.'*

Walter Johnson's *Talks with Shepherds* was based on transcripts of conversations recorded from 1899 onwards and he travelled the land in search of interesting shepherds, most of them in their seventies and eighties so that their memories stretched back almost to before Queen Victoria came to the throne. He described in detail their clothes, their dogs, their sheep and their work and he interviewed them on the Cumbrian Fells and in Surrey, on Dartmoor and on the Isle of Wight, in Lincolnshire and in Hampshire and Sussex – and even a Highland shepherd in London. The latter, interviewed in 1919, was one of the most unusual of all and his story reminds the city dweller of an almost lost world. Almost – because I can remember sheep being grazed in Hyde Park in the 1960s, albeit briefly, and only for a one-off sheepdog trial. In the 1940s the RSPCA's Exeter branch reported that when King George and Queen Mary invited children from the poorer parts of London to witness their drive-past from Constitution Hill, most of the children were far more interested in the sheep in Green Park than they were in their Majesties. They had never seen live sheep before. Some London children who were evacuated to Exeter during the war noticed sheep in the field through the train window and stoutly maintained that they were young kangaroos.

🦘

Between the wars Sussex brothers Ephraim and Fred Holden, along with farmers Charlie and Len Wady, used to collect Kent sheep from the railway station and overwinter them at Ebernoe, returning them to the Kent marshes in the spring. The journey to or from the station could take four hours, with one man walking in front of the flocks and two behind to keep them moving. In my own Sussex village in the same period, farmer Ken Liverton and his brothers would collect about 60 Kent sheep from the station and walk them back to their farm, as did most other local farmers: the lanes would be full of sheep and it often took most of the day to get home, even with the help of well-trained dogs and half-a-dozen men and boys. Ken had such a good dog that he only needed the dog and himself: he walked in front and the dog came behind the flock. The only casualty was when a cyclist with no brakes came hurtling down the hill and slammed into the bank to avoid the sheep. A disaster that had nothing to do with the lanes happened when the sheep were grazing on the golf course one winter: Ken went up to feed them on the morning of Boxing Day and found carnage. A pack of local dogs had got in among the flock and the course was littered with clumps of wool and dead or horrifically mauled sheep.

LONDON HIGHLANDER

Johnson discovered that, every summer, a flock of sheep came all the way to London from the Highlands to graze on the city's 'much trodden' commons, such as Tooting Bec, Wandsworth and Clapham Common. (The ones below are on Hampstead Heath in about 1945.) He had read in the newspapers that the flock walked all the way, but in fact they came by rail and, in the early years of what was an experiment, they had been brought to St Katharine's Wharf by steamboat. What an adventure for the sheep!

The shepherd was in his seventies but looked ten years younger. He liked London, he said, because the sheep gave less trouble amid the stress and clamour of the city. He liked his work, his pipe and his collie, which slept with him in the shepherd's hut. The collie had to meet some unusual challenges in this strange urban environment, such as pet dogs constantly barking as they frolicked in

Above: A London flock: shepherd on Hampstead Heath in about 1945

the ponds, annoying the sheep and making the dog in not the best of tempers as he was constantly being bidden by the shepherd to keep the flock together. Sometimes the shepherd had trouble with local boys teasing the sheep but two of his ewes took matters into their own hands: they would run at the boys and butt them. The shepherd's hut in London was a converted hackney coach, at least half a century old, roofed with zinc, tar and tarpaulin to keep out the rain. Londoners used to mistake it for a coffee stall and shout at the shepherd during his Sunday afternoon rest to open up and serve them a coffee. When he was ready to shift his home and his sheep to another London common, he would make the move in the early morning while the roads were still quiet and had to be accompanied by a licensed drover wearing a proper badge. At the end of the summer season, the sheep were shorn and then sold to London butchers. The Highland shepherd was appalled at how closely shepherds in the south sheared their sheep: it made the animals vulnerable to sunburn. 'The mutton is partly cooked while the beast is alive,' he declared. A word of wisdom from this Scottish shepherd: goats love tobacco and will follow you for miles for a chew.

Shepherd's Gear

Writers may have been drawn to the idea of shepherds as poets and philosophers, but a further attraction was captured by artists, photographers and realists: the shepherd in his traditional clothes, perfectly suited to his environment and his work, and the very practical tools of his calling.

Above: Shepherd Turner of Westmeston, Sussex, wearing a typical hard felt hat. The canvas cape over his greatcoat was made waterproof by being soaked in boiling oil.

Clothes

A carter's smock came only to his thighs, but a shepherd's reached below his knees. When Walter Johnson talked with Stephen Blackmore in 1912, he learnt that this famous fossil-collecting shepherd had worn a bleached linen smock all his working life and that this had been his garb on his wedding day. In 1899 Johnson had chatted with a massively built shepherd with a long grizzled red shovel beard on Gilbert White's Selborne hangers, who said that when he was a lad all shepherds wore 'draybet' smocks, with a frill on the front and sometimes a little white heart or something similar stitched on the front of the neck. 'They kept your hips waärm,' he said. The Selborne shepherd said he never wore a smock now, though in the old days even a rich old farmer always used to wear his drabbet smock when he went to Alton market.

London-born naturalist Harry Barclay Wills took a great interest in everything about Sussex downland shepherds in the 1920s, including what they wore. Nelson Coppard, born in 1863, usually wore a good corduroy suit, gaiters and a

HOG STOPPERS

Walter Johnson had often seen shepherds spread their smocks out like a tablecloth as they sat, knees apart, ready to eat their luncheon: after the meal they would catch up the crumbs with a jerk to 'make a last mouthful'.

Others used their smocks as 'hog-stoppers': to stop a pig, you got in its way and sat on your heels, using the round-frock to close the gap between your knees.

hard felt bowler hat but his father had always worn a butcher-blue smock over his corduroys, with an overcoat as well in bad weather – thick, rough, fleecy and *white* – or an old cavalry cloak. The whiteness should not surprise: many old countrymen's corduroys were also white, though George Humphrey, born in 1864, remembered that when he was a boy he and his three brothers and his father all wore buff-coloured corduroy, with corduroy gaiters lined with canvas (they could not afford leather ones), and over this they all wore blue smock frocks, 'all tuckered up proper', with big turn-down collars and with pockets big enough for a rabbit. His mother made all of their clothes.

Jack Cox remembered that some shepherds used to change from smock and hard hat into a rough sacking slop and a little cap, usually red, when they were pitching hurdles: a hard hat got in the way when a man was carrying his hurdles, which sometimes tipped the hat over his eyes. Some shepherds wore dog's-hair hats, something like a billycock but thick and very strong and heavy to wear in the sun, so they carried a cap in their pocket as well. The dog's-hair hats were so strong that you could stand on them. Some shepherds, and farmers, wore hard felt 'half-high' hats with flat crowns that they painted (usually grey) to make them shiny and waterproof.

The 'singing flautist' shepherd Michael Blann (who died at the age of 90 in 1934) told Barclay Wills that he had worn a round-frock for many years, and longer than some who felt old-fashioned in one. His wife made his smocks and the last one she made was to his own design: it was open all the way down the front, as he got fed up with pulling smocks over his head. He described the large, heavy overcoats – fleecy outside and very thick, with a big cape to keep the weather off your shoulders. His had been white and much loved: when it became almost worn out he sewed it together with twine to extend its life. These hefty white coats kept you bone

Above: A group of Norfolk shepherds near Sandringham in about 1890. They would have been instantly recognised locally as shepherds by their style of clothing.

Top left: The renowned and highly skilled shepherd Stephen Blackmore, who had only one arm (the other had been 'clean cut off' without the aid of chloroform when he was a lad in the 1830s). He had a famous collection of prehistoric flint implements gathered from the South Downs throughout his life.

dry, though the weight of a rain-soaked coat was considerable. They lasted forever and sometimes the farmer would pay for the coat so that the shepherd had no excuse for not working in bad weather.

All this talk of smocks and round-frocks and corduroys and gaiters and hats and white coats – they all cost money, and many a shepherd would simply wear whatever he could get.

Crooks

The crook symbolises the shepherd, though it was only used in some parts of the country. It was not just something for the shepherd to lean on in a picturesque pose for artists and photographers or to indicate his calling at hiring fairs. It was designed for catching a sheep by the hind leg. Some crooks were simple in shape; others were made by blacksmiths to their own pattern and the well-known crook maker at Pyecombe, in Sussex, also made crooks for bishops.

Stephen Blackmore admitted that the local Pyecombe crook was good, as long as its handle was made of hazel and as long as the hook had the right twist and was made from a gun barrel. Some hooks were of wrought iron, some of brass, though not very popular. Although hazel was favoured in Sussex, elsewhere handles might be of ash, holly, cherry or other woods, as long as the stick was straight and strong. A 'wooden crook', incidentally, was not a crook at all: it was (at least in Sussex) a yoke on which sheep bells were hung.

Above: Young shepherd at the end of the 19th century, wearing a waterproof jacket.

Bells, irons and knockers

Sheep bells were hung about an animal's neck so that its whereabouts could be known from a distance and were particularly popular on the Sussex downs but also in Gloucestershire, Berkshire, Cambridgeshire and Wiltshire. They were attached to bell-wethers – sheep specially chosen who, so the shepherd fondly thought, would each restrict themselves to a certain part of his territory. Canister-bells and clucks were generally made of sheet iron, whereas cup bells, latten bells and others were made of brass.

A pitching iron, or fold bar, was a thick rod with a heavy, tapering iron point used for making holes in the turf so that hurdle stakes could be driven into the ground. Another very useful shepherd's tool was the dirt knocker, used to remove caked mud from fleeces. It was a wooden mallet and you put the mud-and-dung encrusted ends of the fleece on a flat piece of wood held in one hand and then tapped with the mallet in the other to break up the dirt.

The shepherd's hut

The shepherd's hut was his home on wheels, which could be drawn by one of the farm horses to wherever he needed to be to keep a closer eye on the flock, especially at lambing time. A good hut was made of wood, but gradually wooden huts were replaced by painted iron ones, which were draughty and uncomfortable as well as ugly in the landscape.

The hut accumulated much useful clutter. There would be sacks on straw for the shepherd's bed (should he find any moment for sleep during the chaos and worry of lambing), a good supply of candles and a stove for heating milk for the lambs as well as his own meals. A stove pipe passed through the roof of the hut to take away the smoke. On a shelf were his essential tools and medications: shears, hammer and nails, a clasp knife, raddle, a pot of sheep-salve, a pot of Stockholm tar, a box of ground ginger, a bottle of turps and one of castor oil.

Caught out in the open, downland shepherds would snatch a snooze in a hole in a bank. Or they might choose a nice friendly thorn bush, hack some of it away and line it with dry fern, straw and sacks for a rainy day. (Is this the origin of Shepherds Bush?)

Richard Heath talked to many a shepherd all over the country and recorded his conversations with them in *The Dying Peasant*. He wrote about Sussex shepherds in 1871, describing how, in former times, every shepherd had his hut on the Downs:

Sometimes it was a cave scooped out of the side of a bank, lined with heath or straw, and covered with sods of turf or hawthorn boughs. Here in rough weather the shepherd took refuge and watched his sheep. Sometimes he would read or otherwise amuse himself. 'It was in my hut,' said one of these worthies to Mr Lower, 'that I first read about Moses and his shepherding life and about David's killing of the lion and the bear. Ah, how glad I felt that we hadn't such wild beasts to frighten, and maybe kill our sheep and us.'

KEEPING DRY

Shepherds' umbrellas were more than shower protection: they were perhaps four feet across, and you could back yourself into a bush, crouch down and hold the umbrella over and stay perfectly dry in a storm. Some shepherds referred to them as their tents. They might have been cumbersome but were well worth carrying around in bad weather: there was a cord so that the shepherd could strap the umbrella across his back like a satchel. The ribs might be made of cane or, for preference, of whalebone. The covers were originally green but usually faded to blue.

All they had to contend with was the occasional fox, ravens that picked out the eyes of a fallen ewe, and the sight of buzzards, an eagle and (apparently) wild turkeys that frequented the Downs.

Above: The shepherd's protective umbrella, demonstrated by George Humphrey.

Left: The shepherd's hut, home from home and containing everything a shepherd could possibly need.

The Shepherd's Year

In Sussex, the sheep ran free throughout the summer on the thyme-scented downland herbage by day but at night, from September, the ewes were confined with portable wooden hurdles on different areas of mustard, cabbage, kale, trefoil, rape and turnips. This was the practice of folding.

Folding, flushing and tupping

Folding not only gave the sheep a change of diet but also concentrated their manure on areas that would later be cultivated and sown with a new crop, and the treading by all those dainty little hooves helped to tighten the land as well. A fold might cover, say, a quarter of an acre and that area would need about a hundred hurdles, carried forward on the shepherd's back to a fresh area each day along with the stakes to support them.

As well as being folded, the ewes were given a supplement of crushed peas or oats to flush them for the tup, the aim being to encourage twinning. A tup is a ram; tupping is the mating of ram and ewe. The rams, with coloured raddle on their chests that would rub off on the back end of every ewe they mounted, would be turned in with the ewes at the end of the month (one ram to every 50 ewes) and the colour of the raddle might be changed from red ochre to blue four weeks later to

give the shepherd some idea of when to expect each ewe's lambs.

Throughout October and November the folding pattern continued except that they might be grazing on stubble. By the end of November the rams had been separated from the flock; by the end of January lambing time was on the horizon and from now on the ewes were kept close to home, only grazing the downs nearest the fold. By mid February they were confined entirely to the fold while the shepherd built a sheltered lambing yard.

Lambing

All in all, the South Downs sheep were thoroughly spoilt in comparison with those in the Shetlands. A typical scene was described by WP Livingstone in his detailed book describing the life of Shetland crofters before the war.

Early one morning a woman bearing a white burden in her arms went up to her cottage on the hillside, a ewe, suspicious and anxious, trotting after her. It was lambing time.

Shetland sheep, dainty and agile, are special in several ways. Like other Shetland animals, they are small: you sometimes feel that everything in the islands is worn down by the weather and keeps as low to the ground as possible in an attempt to avoid the winds. One old record mentioned that 4,500 sheep had been lost in a single winter throughout the Shetlands, so harsh had it been out on the open hills. But now, at lambing time, lots of small white, black and brown lambs were soon leaping and racing about on the hills and moors and Livingstone wondered how each crofter could identify their own sheep when the flocks were all 'mixed up

Above: Typical lambing fold on the South Downs, with neat lambing pens protected by thatched hurdles, and circular feeding cages woven by the shepherd from hazel rods.

Opposite top: Mounted shepherd rounding up Will Goodchild's sheep on a 2,200-acre estate on Wallasea Island, Essex, in 1950.

Opposite bottom: Billy Playfoot and Bill Lodge thatching hurdles for the lambing yard.

on the scattald'. The answer was simple: by the lug mark clipped or cut in the ears. Each crofter had their own mark – a hole, a slit, a chip, in a particular place in one or other ear – and claimed to be able to spot them at a distance.

Looking after the lambs was the work of younger Shetland women. Lambs tended to be born during the night and the women would be out at dawn looking for them, or spending whole nights on the hills with the flocks, and sometimes returning home bearing a weakling lamb in their arms. Weak lambs needed to be nursed and on sunny days the women knelt on the mossy turf feeding their charges from bottles, with the ewes circling around to keep an eye on them. At weaning time, a woman would bring half a dozen lambs into a grassy enclosure and hobble them in pairs, tethered by a long cord. If they were approached, they fled, 'tripping and tumbling like children in a sack race'. They quickly learnt to keep step with each other.

Right: George Chant fitting a 'jacket', skinned from a dead lamb, on to an orphan lamb to persuade the dead lamb's mother to adopt the orphan. At the time (1933) he had already been a shepherd for more than 60 years, 45 them on the same farm.

Bottle lambs and fosters

Faced with an orphan lamb, most of the old shepherds would try to encourage another ewe to foster it – usually a ewe that had lost her own lamb. But any ewe worth her salt knew perfectly well that the alien was not her own and it could take a lot of persuading before she would allow it to suckle. Once it had ingested some of her milk, she regarded it as her

own. A trick used by many a shepherd was to skin the ewe's own dead lamb and tie the skin to the foster lamb like a jacket in the hope that the ewe would be fooled by the familiar smell. An experienced shepherd in the 1930s said that this practice was unnecessary: instead, he would put the ewe in a pen, introduce the orphan and stand quietly by the pen to watch them. He found that the ewe would not attack or reject the lamb in his presence, and after a while all would be well. That was a patient shepherd. Walter Johnson had met George, a Cotswold shepherd, during the years of World War I, whose method was to take the orphan lamb and put it with a ewe and her own single lamb into a pen. Then he would hold up his stick and say, 'Go it billies.'

LAMBING YARDS

The traditional southern lambing yard was protected from cold northerly and easterly winds by a couple of long, low threshed-out oat ricks. Sheltered by the ricks, thatched hurdles were arranged in a square, two hurdles high, secured to a sturdy framework of stout ash uprights and lashed cross-poles, which supported a thatched-hurdle roof. Within this yard were short-stay ewe coops, one hurdle deep by half a hurdle wide for each ewe and her lamb, well littered with straw. A second set of yards was built on the other side of the rick wall to accommodate the animals when the lambs were a few days old: one yard for singles, another for ewes with twins.

Close by would be the shepherd's wheeled hut, fully equipped with all he would need for lambing, along with a galvanised bin well stocked with cake, and a small stack of sweet hay protected from the weather by thatched hurdles and a tarpaulin. The shepherd was well aware that he was about to face the busiest time of his year.

There might be a bit of trouble at first but soon the lambs would take a teat each. After he had held up his stick two or three times, there would be no trouble, especially once the mother could smell her own milk on the new lamb's lips. George also had a trick with weak little lambs when the weather was cold and wet. He kept a teat-fitted feeding bottle full of gin ready to give them a nip.

If a foster could not be found, or if a ewe had produced triplets and was unable to feed three lambs, the shepherd would resort to hand rearing, feeding the 'cosset-lamb' himself. More often than not, the lamb would be brought into a warm niche right beside the shepherd's hut and fed with warm milk from the bottle. Before rubber teats were available, the shepherd would fashion his own from a cork with a groove at the side to hold an elder twig, its pith removed to form something like a drinking straw, bound with a rag. Bottle-feeding required an immense amount of patience, and it is hardly surprising that bottle-fed lambs formed a strong bond with the shepherd.

Docking

All of the lambs on the South Downs would have their tails docked before they were a fortnight old. Sometimes this was done with a knife or sometimes with tailing irons. These small spade-shaped irons on wooden handles had a wedge-shaped section and were made red-hot so that the tail was cauterised while it was severed. The skin of the tail was pulled back before the cut was made, so that it would cover the wound afterwards. In some parts of the country lambs' tail pie was a treat.

Ram lambs not needed for breeding lost more than their tails at that age: they were also castrated, generally using the same tool as for tail docking, with its blade at one end and a slotted grip at the other for removing the 'stones'. An

expert could do both jobs at once: cut away the tail, remove the bottom of the scrotum and withdraw the stones in half-a-minute flat. Ian Murdoch recalled his father doing just that, with no apparent stress to the lamb. He also recalled his grandfather telling him with some glee that in his day the testicles were drawn with the shepherd's teeth.

Above: Elderly shepherd bottle-feeding lambs that were either orphans or from sets of triplets. He has made a hay crib out of cleft poles, and erected bundles of brushwood to protect the lambs from the weather.

CASTRATION

Francis Kilvert was a little shocked in 1870 when he was visiting Newchurch and entered the fold of Gilfach y rheol:

Janet issued from the house door and rushed across the yard and turning the corner of the wain-house I found the two younger ladies assisting at the castration of the lambs, catching and holding the poor little beasts and standing by whilst the operation was performed, seeming to enjoy the spectacle. It was the first time I had seen clergyman's daughters helping to castrate lambs or witnessing that operation and it rather gave me a turn of disgust at first. But I made allowance for them and considered in how rough a way the poor children have been brought up, so that they thought no harm of it, and I forgave them. ... Matilda was struggling in a pen with a large stout white lamb, and when she had mastered him and got him well between her legs and knees I ventured to ask where her father was.

Above: Shepherds often made use of a horse, especially to move their huts and hurdles or to cart roots for feeding. This is the head shepherd on the Elveden estate in Suffolk in about 1950.

Rams, riding and hill sheep

A ram is an entire (uncastrated) male sheep. Whether the verb, to ram, derives from the animal or the animal's name from the verb, I have no idea, but ramming is what rams do and any smallholder who keeps a lone ram, isolated from his flock until he is allowed to mingle with the ewes to perform his duties, would do well to hang an old tyre from a branch in his paddock so that he can take out his frustration by head-butting something less unforgiving than a brick wall. Aubrey Seymour used to grease the heads of his rams after shearing, because animals that had been lying peacefully together when in full fleece often failed to recognise their companions in the nude:

> *They would back away, twenty feet or more, and then rush head on with a horrible thud. Not infrequently one of*

the combatants had its neck broken by the impact; but animals that had had their foretops made slippery with grease generally escaped serious injury, though a short-legged ram could dislocate the neck of a taller one because the blow came below the centre of gravity.

In 1829 William Garne placed an advertisement for letting tups. The practice of renting out your rams rather than selling them had been started half a century earlier by the celebrated breeder, Robert Bakewell, and meant that the breeder could continue to use his own proven ram. The Garne dynasty reared splendid rams: the village boys at Filkins, which would later become famous as the home of Sir Stafford Cripps, used to sneak on to the farm to catch rabbits and, more excitingly, to ride the enormous Cotswold rams.

Talking of riding, shepherds quite often rode ponies during the course of their duties. Just after World War II, in a BBC radio programme about farming in Britain, a visit was made to a farm at Milsington, a few miles west of Hawick in Roxburghshire. It was a typical hill farm, with all of the land above 1,000 feet with wide grass slopes leading up to the heather, and they ran 2,000 Cheviot sheep on this wild and seemingly infinite landscape, with no fences and no shelter. There were stone walls or wire fences only in the lower parts of the farms, on what was known as the in-bye land, while the open hills were the out-bye. The Scott family had been farming at Milsington for more than a century and had 200 acres of in-bye and 1,100 of out-bye, along with an adjacent area of rented land that brought the total to 2,700 acres. The staff for this vast acreage comprised a married cattleman, a single horseman living in the bothy and one married shepherd, living in a 'really outlandish' cottage away over the hills. The son of the farmer did full work as a shepherd during the school holidays, while the daughter and wife helped at lambing. 'It is doubtful,' wrote Professor HG Sanders of Reading University, who had been advising the BBC for the programme, 'if all the work would get done if Mr Scott and his son did not get round the hills on horseback. Quite often for four or five hours at a stretch his horses have to tramp up to the knees in snow when lost sheep have to be found.'

The lone Milsington shepherd was typical of the older ones in the region who lived close to their sheep, which in the hills meant miles away from any other dwellings. You could see the old shepherds' houses dotted about the hills but they were already mostly empty and dilapidated by the time of World War II. They had wonderful views and would have a great appeal for the escapist, but they were anathema to the shepherd's wife: the postman might call once a week but no tradesmen would deliver and her children had to walk several miles over the hills to school. Sanders suggested that shepherds in the future would have their houses in the villages and would be mounted on horseback like so many cowboys, so that they could reach their sheep quickly.

Some of the older shepherds thoroughly disapproved of the horseback method, saying the shepherd ought to be living among his sheep. Others, especially those who practised folding, blessed horses: they used a horse and cart to carry all those hurdles to another field, along with hay cages and troughs, and also to move their wheeled shepherd's huts.

Winter in the Cheviots was hard for the shepherds and sometimes men perished as well as sheep. The custom was to build a circular stone wall in a sheltered part of the hills, about four feet high and made of boulders, as a refuge for the sheep when the storms came. The shepherd needed to anticipate the storm and gather his sheep into this stell in good time to make sure that they did not take it upon themselves to scatter over the hill and find individual refuges in nooks and gullies where the snow would then accumulate and bury them. If that happened, the shepherds would probe the snow with long poles, relying on their dogs to tell them where to probe. Each shepherd had two dogs and relied on them totally.

Marking

Marking irons resemble the branding irons used on cattle in Wild West films, except that they were not designed to sear the hide. They were dipped in a colour or Stockholm tar to stencil the owner's mark on the fleece. Shepherds also devised their own colour coding for the sex of a lamb or for whatever it was that the shepherd wanted to record on the fleece.

Walter Wooler, born in 1856, would make a little hollow in the ground and build a fire, with a brick on either side

Above: Lakeland shepherd marking a lamb by clipping notches in its ear.

Above: Herding fell sheep in Kentmere, Westmorland.

to support the iron bars on which his pot of pitch would be heated. Dipping his marking iron into the hot pitch, he would shake off the drips, lean over the hurdles that were tightly confining the flock and mark the wool of a chosen lamb with the letter M (the farmer's initial) in a circle. Sometimes a lamb also merited a dot of red paint, applied very precisely by a marking stick dipped into the paint can. He would mark up his chosen animals in this way before taking them off to the local sheep sales.

George Humphrey told Barclay Wills in the 1920s that his father had owned a little marking iron made from a farthing: a small hole had been drilled through the tiny jenny-wren coin and a hot pointed metal rod had been driven through the hole, then a wooden handle had been fitted to the other end of the rod. The 'mark' made with this farthing iron was a neat dot of colour or black. It was also used to mark the inside of a sheep's

ear, either to label a ewe known to give trouble at lambing time and therefore to be set aside for the butcher, or to mark ownership of a ram where rams from several flocks were kept together. On Dartmoor in 1906, an old shepherd said that his animals could be identified by 'the threepenny bit in one ear and the sixpence in the other', whereas some sheep apparently had ha'pennies or half-a-crown.

Up on the Cumbrian fells around the time of World War I, sheep would have a letter painted in red on their flanks but the use of paint was being discouraged, and the use of tar-marks was frowned upon as both types of marking lessened the value of the fleece. Hence there was a local revival in the old system of ear-marking instead. This involved cutting bits out of the sheep's ear or ears. One man's mark might be a mitre (a forked cut), another a scallop, or just a simple slice. There was quite a glossary of ear marks, with terms such as key-bitted, click-forked, three squared-holed, upper halved and so on. The theory was that each flock owner had his own unique cut or combination of cuts by which his sheep could be identified. There was a law that you could not cut off more than a third of the poor sheep's ear.

In North Wales at the same period, typical marking involved cutting off the tip of the ear or nicking its under-margin, and there had in the past been a custom of branding the animals on the nose. In the Cotswolds ear marking did not seem to be widespread, or where it was used the clippings were very small. Instead they used the letter-painting method of the Cumbrians, usually surrounding the letter with a neat circle or lozenge shape.

It's a tough life ...

All sorts of very unpleasant things can happen to sheep and perhaps it is hardly surprising that they have a reputation for a strong will to die. In 1830, two million sheep died in Britain during an outbreak of rot (liver fluke), which spread all over the country. In the 1960s, more and more Yorkshire smallholders on the Cleveland Hills were selling off their flocks and going out of business because of heavy losses in both capital and income caused by the destruction of their sheep by traffic on unfenced roads at night.

In mid summer, shepherds were on the alert for flystrike – a particularly unpleasant problem for sheep, as the blowflies lay their eggs on the animal's wool and on cuts and sores, and the hatched maggots literally start to eat their host alive, putrefying the flesh. It was vital to shear the sheep immediately. Some had their own remedies: an old Gloucestershire farmer, in the 1930s, mysteriously carried a copper George III penny with him from June to September to keep blowflies away from his sheep. A simple fly repellant was a lotion made from elderberry flowers and shoots.

There is a phrase, 'rattle your dags', which means hurry up. Dags are the clattering dung-matted locks of fleece at the back end of a sheep. In hot weather it was sensible to dag the sheep to get rid of those mucky bits before they attracted the flies, and the job was done by hand with a pair of sheep shears. You could then spot any potential problem areas and apply an appropriate potion.

COUNTING

In Sussex it might be: one-erum, two-erum, cockerum, shu-erum, shitherum, shatherum, wine-berry, wagtail, tarrydiddle, den ('den' meant a score of sheep and you were counting them in pairs). In Borrowdale, it went like this: yan, tyan, tethera, methera, pimp; sethera, lethera, hovera, dover, dick; yan-a-dick, tyan-a-dick, tethera-dick, methera-dick, bumfit; yan-a-bumfit, tyan-a-bumfit, tethera-bumfit, methera-bumfit, gigot. In Wasdale it started with: yan, tian, tudder, anudder, mimph. In Welsh it was: un, dau, tri, pedwar, pump; chweck, saith, with, naw, deg; unarddeg, dauddeg, triarddeg, pedwarddeg, pumddeg; unarpumddeg, dauaapumddeg, daunaw, pedwa-rapumdded, ugain; then you had deugain for two score, and trigain for three score. By then you were sound asleep.

Counting payment rather than sheep: in 1926 a hill shepherd aged 50 on a Scottish farm received wages of 33 shillings, plus 6s for his cow's keep, 30cwt of potatoes (worth 3s), 65 stone of oatmeal (3s), 12 bushels of barley (1s 3d), three sheep (1s), peat (1s 6d), and a new cottage with garden, byre, pigstye, carting for straw and coal; in all, say, 53s 9d. The shilling for the sheep was based on the cost to the master being 10s a head but the value to the shepherd of the produce being about nine times as much. The cow was the man's property and was cared for by him and in his master's time; its summer ration was grass and in winter it had hay, with 1cwt of cow cake at calving time. On the same farm a 27-year-old in-bye shepherd received 35s in cash, 6s for his cow's keep, 30cwt of potatoes, 40 stone of oatmeal and, again, a cottage and garden, pigstye, and carting, in all 52s 6d. A 25-year-old shepherd's total came to 53s and the steward who managed the whole farm, at the age of 70, was paid 36s in cash and, including in kind, his total was 58s.

Sheep Washing and Dipping

Sheep washing and sheep dipping are two different procedures. The aim of washing was to reduce the amount of lanolin in the fleece before shearing, making the act of shearing easier as well as resulting in a cleaner and therefore more valuable fleece to sell. It was quite a dramatic event and was often a highlight for the locals, who came to help or at least to watch and laugh.

Above: Washing sheep with the aid of two water-carrying ducts. The boy with the pole keeps the sheep submerged. The men appear to have the benefit of purpose-built 'cradles'; often sheep-washers were protected in fast-flowing streams by standing in wooden barrels.

Right: Energetic sheep-washing in North Wales – hard work for men and sheep alike.

Some people say that sheep hate water so much that they will never cross a stream, even if the grass is greener on the other side. Some people say that sheep never drink water either, which is rubbish. Shepherds on the South Downs went to a lot of trouble to create dew ponds so that their flocks could drink. In 1901, a shepherd on the North Downs said that a sheep slipping into a ditch and getting gradually dragged down into the mud by its own weight had neither the sense nor the spirit to scramble out before it became 'stogged'. What a splendid word! But with a sheep's supposed hatred of water, it can be imagined how much stress they were under during a forced swim in cold water for sheep washing. Sometimes a sheep was incapable of walking home on its own legs after the ordeal of washing and would be carried home in a cart.

Where individual farms did not have an appropriate brook and pool, the flocks would be washed in a communal one instead. Cyril Matcham's sheepwash was fed from the strongly tidal river Arun, which raised the level of 'The Splash' twice a day. Two men were suspended in barrels, anchored to posts in midstream,

TROUT TREAT

It was not wise to drink water downstream from a sheepwash, but apparently it was good for anglers: young J Arthur Gibbs, in his delightful book A Cotswold Village, said that when the stream was thick after sheep-washing the trout would come out of their holes and feed on all those lovely fat sheep-ticks that had been swilled out of the fleeces.

Dipping sheep at Rotherbridge Farm, Petworth, in 1938.

Above: Canadian servicemen help with sheep dipping.

thoroughly soaked. Another man nearby might help in the dunking with a wooden crutch. Just as the poor animal thought it was about to drown under the weight of its own sodden fleece, a lower hatch was opened and the miserable dripping sheep could make its way up a slope to safety.

There was a more elaborate system somewhere in the Cotswolds at the time of World War I. The village swimming bath (for sheep, not for people) was divided across its middle by a hinged hatch that could be swung backwards and forwards. A boy, perched on a temporary seat, had the masterly job of working the hatch by pulling a cord that ran over a pulley. He controlled the destiny of each sheep: no animal could escape from the bath until the boy's handheld watch indicated that it had served its time in the water. During the sheep's imprisonment a man would roll it from side to side in the thick cocoa-coloured waters and then use a wooden crutch to grip it by the neck and plunge its head under. Meanwhile, other men were selecting the next victim.

Washing was already less widespread by the 1930s: it was deemed to be too much labour for the returns, as washed wool fetched only a halfpenny a pound more than unwashed and a washed fleece, deprived of some of its grease, weighed less anyway. Hence it had been customary to leave a fortnight between washing and shearing: it gave the yolk, as the grease was called, a chance to rise again into the fleece and add to its weight.

Sheep dipping is much nastier: the sheep, recently shorn, are totally immersed in insecticide. In 1873, Francis Kilvert rose early on a bright and breezy morning and wandered through the rain-washed meadows and down the lane past West Hay to cross the dry bed of a brook. Before he crossed, he heard a sudden sound of water and saw a stream beginning to

rising and falling with the tide as they controlled the sheep swimming past them, grabbing the animals to rub the wool by hand and then dunking them under the water. Two others had the job of moving the sheep from the pens.

In some villages there was a purpose-built race below the village pond for use as a sheepwash, complete with its own plug (a heavy stone) so that the race could be emptied. At the end of the 19th century, there was a carefully built washpool for sheep in Gilbert White's village: a stream ran through the meadows and a brick cistern had been built near its bed, with an inlet along which the sheep were coaxed, one by one, into the water. A man stood in the pool and pushed each animal into the water, making sure it was trickle, and then broaden and deepen until a 'swift rush of brown turbid water' filled the bed of the brook. At first he thought it was a little flood from the overnight rain but a 'merry-faced peasant' came along on his way to a 'rustic festival of sheep dipping' and told him that the sudden stream was the water just released from the mill pond above. At the bottom of the hill, Kilvert and the peasant met a woman who directed them to a meadow where this festival was being held.

A group of men whose clothes were splashed and dyed by the red wash were plunging sheep and lambs one by one into a long deep trough. The sheep went in white and came out red, protected by their dipping against the attentions of the fly, and walked away across the meadow to join the flock, shaking the red wash in showers from their close-shorn fleeces.

Forty years later, Walter Johnson came across a dipping party in the Cumbrian fells. The farmyard had been divided into roughly equal areas by hurdles. In one part was a flock of shorn sheep, panting with apprehension: they had been shorn a fortnight ago and were still alarmed by that adventure. In another were a few animals that had just been through what their companions were about to experience. On one side of the yard was a permanent concrete-lined dipping bath, about six yards long and four or five feet deep, and wide enough for one sheep to pass easily through it but not to turn round along the way. The sheep entered the bath, one by one, down a steeply sloping gangway and walked (rather than swam) slowly through the blue liquid. Then the gentler slope of the concrete took the animal up again and out of the bath into the small square dripping pen for a short while before it was let into the receiving pen with the growing flock of 'been there, done that' mates.

A SHEPHERD'S HOME

In 1871 Richard Heath had visited Cheviot shepherds and Northumberland hinds. He came upon a shepherd's cottage, dreary in the rain, with a little stone passage through to a larger room containing two box beds. There was no ceiling – just canvas drawn tightly over the rafters, with the great beams exposed beneath it. The walls were rough stone and someone had half-heartedly tried to put paper over them but the wind crept behind the paper and made it 'wabble to and fro'. The wife was kneading bread on a spotless deal table and baking it in a large oven.

Above: Helping the shepherd.

The shepherd said that, when he had entered into service, he was allowed to purchase a number of sheep at his master's expense. When he married, he started with 13 sheep; he now had 42, and also a cow and two large hogs, all provided for by the master, who also gave him 13 barrels of corn (each containing six bushels) and 1500 yards of potatoes, as well as the house. The shepherd made his income out of selling his sheep's wool and his lambs, which he took to Alnwick Fair.
Another shepherd, a friend of his, lived in a new house built by the Earl of Tankerville: two large rooms with every convenience, a capital stove, good oven and boiler, all put in at the laird's expense, and a roomy dairy, a cowhouse with stalls for six, a stable for the horse and a place for the dog.

Shearing

Poor old sheep. The primitive breeds, such as the island sheep of Soay, are more like sheep were meant to be by way of a coat and nobody would try to shear a Soay. The Merino is the extreme of what humans have turned sheep into: a massive amount of wool on legs, its face disappearing into its own fleece.

When wool is highly prized, a woolly sheep is highly desirable; but in Britain today the fleece is almost an embarrassment to many sheep farmers – something that has to be shaved off and bundled up and sold for a price that is hardly worth all the effort. In Sussex in the 1920s, shearing was in late June, a fortnight after washing so that the yolk had had a chance to rise in the fleece. It took place in a sheltered yard or a downland barn with a cleanly swept floor, and the fleece needed to be dry to cut well. After shearing the ewes were kept in for a night or two to become acclimatised to the loss of their jackets. My, how coddled these southern sheep were.

Half a century earlier sheep shearing had been party-time. In June, men formed themselves into companies and appointed a captain, wearing a cap with a gold band, and lieutenant, wearing a silver band. They met at the captain's cottage or in the local pub for what was known as White Ram night, had a feast and made their plans for shearing. On the appointed morning the gang of anything up to a

Above: Taking the fleece home near Kielder.

Above: Shearing in Eskdale. The shearer is Arthur Irving, a well-known maker of shepherd's sticks with ram's-horn handles.

FARWELTERED

A typical problem with sheep, especially the breeds with broader backs, is what in Lincolnshire would be described as a 'farweltered yow' – a ewe on her back and unable to rise because of her heavy fleece. You sometimes find such a sheep in the meadow, looking utterly helpless: she will try for a while to roll on to her side but eventually she simply gives up (typical sheep) and dies. One of the main reasons for a sheep getting itself on to its back in the first place is itchiness: it just wants a good rub. In some parts of the country, shepherds would provide their sheep with something to rub on while they were upright, to save them the bother of rolling about on their backs. This was the roller-wattle, simply a roller bar at back height between two uprights, or a rubbing rail supported by two pairs of crossed sticks driven into the ground.

Above: Shearing by hand in Ambleside around 1900. Note the tar pot in the alcove, ready to dab on any cuts or nicks, though this calm shearer looks too competent to need it.

score of men assembled at seven, had breakfast and set to work, clipping with hand-shears and plenty of laughter but working hard all the while, until it was time for a pause to light up a clay pipe and gulp down some mild home-brewed swanky (ale) or lemon oatmeal water brought out by the farmer's daughter. Dinner was brief because the main event of the day was the sheep-shearing supper, held in the barn or the big farmhouse kitchen, with much food, merriment and singing. At the end of the shearing season the whole gang would get together in the pub for Black Ram night, which was payday as well as a good old booze-up. It was a bit like childbirth: you managed to forget just how hard and exhausting

Above: Shearing gang at Newtimber, Saddlescombe, in 1886. The gang included the shepherd's wife (foreground, by a heap of wound fleeces), a dozen shearers, a winder, two sheep catchers (background) and a tar boy.

the labour had been, until next time. A shearer in the 1920s told Barclay Wills that it was a 'back-aching ol' job, but we knows as 'twill come. The wool grows, an' mus' be sheared off, an' there 'tis!'

The gang included catchers, whose job was to fetch sheep from a nearby pen when the shearers were ready for them, and winders, whose job was to roll up the fleeces as soon as they came off the sheep. There would also be a tar-boy, clutching his pot of Stockholm tar and running to any shearer that shouted for him: a dab of tar would be applied, by finger or by stick, to any little nick that the shearer might have made on a wriggling sheep's skin, to ward off flies. Jack Hazelgrove had been a tar-boy to the Clapham and Patching gang in Sussex in the 1880s. He told Barclay Wills that they used to start work on the farms at six thirty in the morning, which might mean leaving home at four. He explained that the tar was not just dabbed: it was put on with his finger, and as the tar dropped on the sheep's

wound he would turn his finger over and spread the tar. Sometimes he was given wood ashes to use instead of tar: he would drop a little ash on the wound and spread it gently with his finger. When it was time for a refreshment interval, the tar-boy's job was to fill each man's mug with beer. In the meantime, as well as running about with his tar pot, he would help the winder, and gradually he learnt how to shear and graduated to being a 'colt' on the team. If the gang was working on a large flock that needed more than one day, they would take enough food for a couple of days and sleep in a barn.

The selected sheep would be caught in the pen by its hind leg, drawn backwards to the shearing cloth and thrown on its side with a vigorous jerk. (One reason for the shearing cloth, quite apart from keeping the fleece clean, was to make the job of tidying up afterwards easier.) Stooping to his work at the start, the shearer would stand to do the head and side, raising the sheep on its haunches. Doing the back, he would hold the sheep's head between his knees. Finishing the back end and hind legs he would kneel over the animal, putting one foot across its neck to hold its head down. Most sheep gave in more or less gracefully to all this indignity, or, rather, resigned themselves to it, but the occasional ram might need holding by two men.

In the 1940s the Milsington flock of Cheviots were clipped at the beginning of July. Earlier in the 19th century all of the farmers in a district would join together and go round to each one's flock, in turn, but by World War II they usually did only their own flocks, with the help of their own men. At Milsington, farmer Scott hired three or four professional clippers and worked with them himself, paying the men by the score of sheep clipped (a good man could clip a hundred in a day). All of the sheep had to be brought down from the hills to the homestead for clipping, and the opportunity was also taken to sort out animals to be culled and to mark the remainder, with a stock mark in one ear and an age mark in the other.

Before World War II there would usually be several men on a farm who knew how to shear, but after the war it was more likely to be the work of professional shearing groups. By the 1940s, shearing in most parts of the country was generally done by machine rather than by hand and in the major sheep districts the travelling shearing gangs were on the job endlessly from the end of May to the middle of July – experts all, and fast.

Old farmers said that hand-shearing left a better looking animal and also the wool grew better than after shearing by machine, so most continued to hand-shear an animal if it was to be shown. This was particularly the case with lambs being taken to a sheep fair. Each lamb would be restrained by a sheep bow, a forked branch driven into the ground: the lamb's head was placed in the fork and a thin iron rod on a chain fastened to the fork by a bolt was slid across between two holes to lock the lamb in place. A piece of sacking was put over its head to keep it calm while the shepherd cleaned its body down with a stiff brush and then carefully trimmed its short coat to make it look smart. The clippings were good for stuffing cushions.

Just after World War I, a Cotswold shepherd told Walter Johnson that he could clip 30 sheep a day and do it well. He was contemptuous of those who boasted they could do it faster, and even more contemptuous of machines:

The machine yunt no use. Ship gets restless, and then you must be quiet like, and whistle to 'en. Us be obliged to study them, and 'tis no good getting narky and out of temper with 'em. I'll tell you something. Thur was a chap called Jim Stanley, a friend of the guvnor's, and what does he do but persuades the guvnor to let him use the machine instead of the shurs. Now this yur Stanley was very rough, and I caught him knocking a ship about. I had just opened the ship out at the breast with the shurs, when he begins to strike the ship.

Stanley banged the sheep on its hind quarters and then punched its sides and shoulders to 'larn' it. A week later, the sheep was found dead in the field with a crushed liver, 'all black jelly inside', from the thumping.

ROOING

In the Shetlands, and with other island sheep, it was a matter of rooing rather than shearing. Rooing is hand-pulling the naturally loosened fibres and you know when the time is right because the sheep begin to look quite a mess, with clumps of wool trailing from their fleeces. In the middle of June, the crofters of the 1920s would round up the ewes with the help of half a dozen excitable collies (Shetland sheepdogs, of course) and pen them in a kru – a square concrete enclosure. The sheep's legs were tied and the kneeling women would swiftly pluck off the wool. Pluck is perhaps the wrong word: the wool was already loose and simply came away in their hands, pushed up by the new wool that was growing through the follicles. The wool would be twisted, thrown into kishies and taken back to the croft, leaving the ewes looking thoroughly sheepish and even smaller than before.

Sheepdogs

There were two common types of sheepdog: the collie and the shaggy Old English. The collies were more popular in the west and north, and the Old English in the south, especially Sussex.

Left:A northern hill shepherd and his mutt on the steps of the shepherd's hut.

Below: Scottish contestant WR Little at sheepdog trials in London's Hyde Park in 1955.

In 1917 Walter Johnson met a Sussex shepherd near Eastbourne whose dog was 'a woolly-faced, stumpy-tailed, bluish-grey creature, of the kind commonly called Old English'. Its master declared that it was good on the open down, and clever enough to ensure the sheep did not trespass on adjacent fields of clover or corn, and that it bore the heat better than any collie. Just across the water on the Isle of Wight in 1920 he found that the island shepherds all preferred the old bobtails to collies: 'Collies get so durty,' they explained. In the Cotswolds a year earlier, Johnson had rather surprisingly met a flock of Southdown sheep, not 'Cotsalls', and their shepherd had collies but did not much care for them; he said they were not hard enough and would not stand if a big Cotswold sheep made a dash at them. 'Give I an old English dog,' he said firmly. But on Dartmoor in 1906 Johnson had seen at first hand the superb work of collies, travelling smoothly at high speed to cover huge distances on the moors, highly intelligent, wonderfully trained by their master (who, incidentally, had the sense to be on a pony for doing his rounds) and invaluable for the massive scale of the 'drift' to gather all of the farmer's moorland animals, however far they might have wandered. A century earlier, the drift had been so organised that on one day bullocks would be gathered, on another ponies and on another sheep, and involved much shouting and hooting by men on horseback and yelping by their assorted dogs as moor men from several farms worked to drive the stock together, then pick out their own animals from the throng and drive them home.

Shepherd Charlie Wilds, of Goodwood, with his faithful rough collie.

Barclay Wills also noted the Sussex shepherds' preference for bobtails or rough-haired dogs in the 1920s, repeating Johnson's observations (perhaps he talked to the same shepherds) that the bobtails were better at ensuring the sheep did not wander into adjacent crops. He was told that bobtails might feel the heat as much as most dogs but that they disregarded cold and wet and worked through it, whereas collies would endeavour to take shelter from drenching rain, preferably under the shepherd's overcoat. Well, to me that makes a collie pretty intelligent!

It seems that most Sussex shepherds would keep a bobtail for fold work and a collie for racing about on the downs. There was also, once upon a time, a breed of Sussex sheepdog that was smaller than the Old English and was brown rather than blue.

Stories of the work and escapades of sheepdogs are legion, and in 1946 *The Countryman* made the mistake of inviting its readers to write in with their own. They ranged from the credible to the unbelievable, and from the practical to the very soppy indeed. HR Tanner, living in Cornwall, made some general observations of dogs at work on market day in the local country town, which with all its unusual distractions must have been quite a challenge for any farm dog. Tanner's letter was a reminder that not all farm dogs are sheepdogs:

A herd of cattle are being driven to the auction by a man with the aid of his dog. A dozen times the drover whistles the dog to one side or the other to prevent the animals rushing down some side street. Danger point passed, the dog comes at once to his master's side. An impatient, inconsiderate motorist sounds his horn; the cattle rush ahead, to be stopped at once by the panting dog. A snapping town-bred terrier excitedly jumps in front of the cattle and again their progress is halted. A peculiar whistle by the drover and instantly the dog shows his angry, bared fangs to the terrier, who runs off. No dog does this work by instinct alone; it has to be taught, and many fail ever to be of the slightest use.

It was not just in the towns that other people's dogs could be a nuisance. In 1952 the National Farmers' Union discussed dogs at its annual meeting in the context of the country's expanding sheep population, which had increased by five per cent that year. It was felt that the expansion could have been faster if the problem of straying dogs could be solved. Clyde Higgs illustrated the problem on a personal scale: an acquaintance of his had a poodle that refused to go for walks on its own, so he bought a bull terrier. After that he had no problems, as he just let the two dogs spend all their time roaming about together. He seemed to have no thought that two dogs makes a pack, and if they happen to get in among sheep they might start playfully chasing the sheep but play quickly turns into serious hunting and the results would be catastrophic.

BUTCHERY

While rampant dogs might cause carnage in a flock, many another sheep would end up as a carcass by accident. In 1875 Walter Johnson was in Lincolnshire, where occasionally it was necessary for a shepherd to kill a sheep with a broken leg if he was too far from a butcher or slaughterhouse. The local blue-coated butcher in the village would do the job of dressing the carcass rather better than the shepherd might manage, and Johnson described one such man, almost 80 years old and usually to be found in the pub but still capable of doing a good job on dressing a sheep. He would follow the age-old custom of cutting a fancy pattern, something like a leaf or herring-bone, on the rind of the carcass while it was still warm, and he had no idea why he did so except that his father had done the same before him.

Pigs, Poultry and Goats

Pigs and poultry have only been farmed on a large scale in recent decades, especially since World War II. Before then, they were largely farmyard or backyard livestock; many a farmer's wife made herself some useful housekeeping money from her poultry, and many cottagers fattened a couple of pigs at the end of the garden and kept a few chickens. While hens were kept for their eggs as well as ending up in the pot, poultry also includes ducks, geese and turkeys, kept in small numbers and fattened up for the table or, except in the case of turkeys, for their eggs. Surprisingly, goats never became widespread farmyard animals in the accepted term in Britain, unlike many other European countries, being more often kept by cottagers in their backyards or pegged out to graze on the common.

Pigs

Pigs took the fancy of a few specialist breeders, especially among the aristocracy, even in the 18th century, and out of the hotchpotch of vague local types several real breeds of pig had been developed by the 19th century. There seemed to be something of a colour prejudice: from Cornwall to Sussex they liked very big black pigs; in northern counties they liked white pigs; and in the Midlands they liked coloured pigs in combinations of ginger and black.

Above: Large Black pigs in a quiet Devon lane.

Left: Mr IL Stent, of Cocking Causeway, with a very big Sussex pig.

Many of the new breeds had an exotic ingredient: Siamese and Cantonese pigs had been imported in the 18th century to help British pigs to produce more piglets and, above all, more lard. Fat was good; it was a warming body fuel for those carrying out lots of hard physical work, but not for the growing number of British people who, thanks to the industrial revolution, were becoming a lot less physical and a lot more sedentary.

Pig producers

Pigs that were taken more seriously than the common cottager's garden pig went through recognised production stages. In the 1880s pig-keepers were advised to castrate young male piglets at four to five weeks old, and to spay the girls at the same time unless they were to be kept for breeding; spaying made the sows capable of being readily fattened. Piglets were weaned at eight weeks old. The next stage in the young pig's life was to be a store pig, running in a large yard or paddock to get plenty of exercise and with a ring in its nose to prevent it from rooting up the grass. (The usual

way of ringing a pig was to put a piece of wire through its nose and twist the ends of the wire together.) The store pig was fed liberally on succulent foods along with maize porridge fortified with brewers' grains or kitchen waste. Lots of pure drinking water was provided and Pringle's *Livestock of the Farm* also advised giving store pigs an occasional cold-water bath: he had seen people washing them down with a hosepipe, which the pigs thoroughly enjoyed. Cottagers often reserved the soapsuds from their weekly wash and used it to wash down their pigs.

The store pig graduated to become a fattening pig and that was the end of its free outdoor living. The first stage of fattening was for porkers, which were pigs that had been well fed from weaning and would be killed when they weighed 48–56 pounds. Porkers were confined to the sty so that they did not waste energy on exercise, and the tastiest porkers were fed on skim-milk or buttermilk mixed with barley meal, oatmeal or maize meal or even boiled rice. Porkers were ready for the butcher at the age of four or five months. Baconers had a longer life: they were kept in warm housing and fed three times a day until they were ready for the butcher at anything from 12 to 20 months old, depending on type.

In the early 1870s there were said to be about 2.3 million pigs in England and Wales, but it's a fair bet that nobody counted all those cottage pigs. In 1908 there were 2.8 million pigs on agricultural holdings, specifically not including cottage pigs, and the commercial fattening of them was concentrated in the dairy and orchard areas and in eastern England's potato and bean areas. The breeding and rearing of pigs, for selling on to the fatteners (both commercial and cottager), was largely carried out by smallholders and

Above: Tethering the sow – a new idea in the 1940s. Care had to be taken that the sow did not suffer from harness sores and that the chain was long enough for her to reach her shelter, here an old truck body.

family farmers. The agents between the rearers and the fatteners were one-man pig dealers, travelling between the two by pony and trap and generally operating out of reach of the authorities who wanted to control the movement of pigs in order to control outbreaks of swine fever. The authorities also had problems with cottagers: in theory the sanitary regulations said you could not keep pigs near houses or roads, but local inspectors really did not want to deprive a cottage wife of her family's home-reared pork and bacon by condemning her pigsty at the end of the garden.

The figure dropped to 1.7 million pigs during World War I, shot up to 3.2 million in 1924 and, with various ups and downs in between, to 3.8 million in 1935 before crashing down to 1.3 million in World War II. In the 1920s, recovering from World War I, there was a big trend towards outdoor pig-keeping, with commercial herds being folded on kale, turnips and other arable crops. But despite the advantages of fresh air and sunlight and a varied diet for these omnivorous animals, there was the downside of cold muddy winters and a pig's need to sleep under cover (unlike folded sheep). So the

DRENCHING A PIG

Drenching is dosing an animal with liquid medication, such as Epsom salts as a purgative, or a de-worming medicine. The aim is to ensure that the liquid goes directly into the throat so that it is swallowed rather than spat out. With cattle, drenching was often done from a glass bottle, but pigs were much more likely to bite the bottle so all sorts of alternatives were used. The most common was an old boot from which an inch of the toe had been sawn. The pig's head was raised, the sawn-off toe end of the boot was placed in the pig's mouth and the dose was delivered into the sole of the boot so that it ran straight down the pig's open throat.

trend turned towards indoor pig keeping. By now pigs were proper livestock, not just kept in ones or twos to eat up kitchen waste, and Britain turned to Denmark to see how they did these things over there. Farmers began to specialise in pig production, feeding large numbers of pigs confined to large buildings under the care of a pig herdsman, and it all became rather like factory farming. Pigs were no longer individual animals that enjoyed human company, looked you in the eye as an equal and enjoyed having their backs scratched as you passed.

Pig marketing

That high pig population in 1935 was made possible by the inauguration of a pig-marketing scheme in 1933. The 1932 report of the Re-organisation Commission for Pigs and Pig Products said that home production was only contributing about one-eighth of the country's bacon and ham and that an expansionist pig policy must aim to increase the home-grown share of that market. Two marketing boards were formed in 1933: one for pigs and one for bacon. Pig farmers suddenly became much more professional, absorbing the complications of carcass grading for weight and quality. When the war broke out, pig-keeping in Britain was more highly developed than it had ever been, but the widely adopted system of keeping large numbers of pigs under intensive

Right: An English pig market just after World War II.

systems and depending on mainly imported concentrates for feeding them was not a good idea in war conditions.

In the late 1940s Admiral Arthur George Talbot, who had served valiantly in both world wars, retired to become a pig farmer. It is surprising how many serving men wanted to take up farming of some kind, with absolutely no experience, and even more surprising when they had been sailors. But Arthur George wanted to change his sea legs for the certainties of wellies and mud and he found some land in Dorset, where he kept a large herd of outdoor sows and reared piglets for the butcher. I have vivid memories of visits to Arthur George's pigs when I was small, and in particular of being nipped by a cheeky piglet with needle-sharp teeth, which gave me a healthy respect for the whole race of pigs. Above all I remember the warm, friendly smell of the pigs and the continuous grunting conversations between the sows and their squealing, playful offspring. Arthur George won prizes for his pigs and for their carcasses, but then the farm got hit by swine fever and he turned to market gardening.

Pig killing

Many of the older generation in rural areas can still remember having a pig at the bottom of the garden before World War II. The problem was that someone had to kill it and many are the gruesome tales told about how those cosseted pigs met their end. Long after slaughterhouses had to meet strict regulations and ensure that animals were stunned into unconsciousness before being slaughtered, cottage pigs were still being killed in the garden by a local man with a knife who did pig-sticking as one of his many jobs around the villages

BRED FOR ROUND 'ERE

Many breeds (once breeding became more organised in the late 18th and 19th centuries) were known by county names – wonderful characters, some now extinct, such as the Lincolnshire Curly-coated pig, the Old Gloucester and Suffolk Dun cows, and Blue-faced Leicester and Derbyshire Gritstone sheep. Many were even more local and were named after much smaller areas, especially the sheep – the Castlemilk Moorit, the Clun Forest, the Bampton Nott, the Swaledale and the Wensleydale – and among the pigs at least one breed was named after a mere village: the Rudgwick Black in Sussex. The glorious ginger Tamworth pig in

Gloucester Old Spots piglets (left), and (above) the wiry Lincolnshire Curly-coat, a breed no longer seen in Britain.

Staffordshire was rumoured to have exotic 18th century origins that included boars from the West Indies and West Africa or from the jungles of India, all mixed up with red pigs from Barbados and Portugal and lean, unruly razor-backed pigs from Ireland and Wiltshire. It was a fact that many British pigs changed radically in the early 18th century, when it became fashionable for the aristocracy to introduce Asian blood into their show-winning pigs, and most of today's breeds still have traces of Siamese and Chinese ancestry.

Right: The family pig meets its destiny. Local Milland pig killer Tom Collins and helper with cottagers Dick and Mary Pay and their small daughter Daisy. This was a common scene in farmyards and cottage gardens right up to World War II.

THE PERFECT PROVIDER

It was often claimed that you could find a use for every part of the pig except its squeal: it gave you fresh pork, salted bacon, cured ham, lard and sausages; it gave you pigskin leather for saddles, gloves, bags and (originally) footballs, and bristles for brushes; and it gave you lots of lots of pretty potent manure – an average of a ton a year per pig. It was the perfect animal for the would-be self-sufficient family and had the added advantage of being an omnivore: you could feed it with just about anything.

and farms. Basically the family pig had its throat slit and then the family all pitched in to help with the bleeding, scalding and butchering. In 1945, determined to reveal country life in all its aspects, *The Countryman* published detailed eyewitness accounts of pigs being killed on farms and at cottages. One woman remembered:

At the first squeal we girls used to run as hard as we could to see. Hurrying across the field we gathered round the bench on which the pig lay. A man made a slit in its throat and the blood rushed out spurting into a pail – they make the black puddings with the blood. When the blood did not pour out fast enough another man worked one of the pig's legs up and down and the blood came faster than ever. All the time the pig's squeals were gradually growing fainter … It took about half an hour for the pig to die. I liked to see it then but I could not see it now.

On the farm it was more businesslike but was also the excuse for a bit of a party. One man had been part of a pig club of eight, all working on the same farm, and remembered that the events of the year were buying, ringing, parting out and

killing. They would know all the pigs and keep an eye out for the best ones, judging when they might be ready and encouraging the foreman to boil up plenty of potatoes to feed them up. In September they would have a draw for their chosen eight pigs and the day was allotted when everybody agreed the animals were fit to 'come down' – generally a Sunday morning, as perhaps the only day when the whole group could be together. A

PIG'S MILK

In theory, pig's milk should be good for you: the milk of the pig is as close to the milk of a human being as any farm animal is likely to produce. The problem is that, whereas goats and sheep have two teats and cows have four, pigs have many more. And sows only like to let down their milk for about seven seconds, which is why piglets go a bit crazy at suckling time. So, to milk a sow, you would have to be nimble enough to milk all those teats at high speed, just supposing the sow would tolerate such an insult in the first place. There is a splendid 19th century engraving of a sow hoisted in mid-air by a harness contraption in preparation for milking, but the idea never caught on.

Above: Local officials inspecting pig carcasses, 1954.

barrel of beer would have been tapped and the jar filled in readiness to slake thirst. Everybody was laden with baths and buckets to carry home their allotted bits and pieces. The young butcher, wearing a leather apron, would arrive full of banter and smiles and accompanied by his beefy mate, who carried buckets of water back and forth for washing out the carcass. After each pig was 'stuck', it was laid out with its trotters stretching fore and aft and was surrounded with straw. Burning straw singed the carcass's skin, and then it was scrubbed before the butcher set about his delicate work. Each of the eight clubmen carried off various tasty bits and hung them on his allotted hook, then fetched the pig's belly in his bath and took it home to his wife, who would be waiting with a neighbour to clean the chitterlings. When the pig had been thoroughly cleaned, two stakes were put under the bench and four men carried the carcass to the stable for hooking up. 'And down the long road from the farm, men with baths and bloody morsels on hooks may be met at any time.'

PIG CLUBS

Pig clubs and cooperatives were still being formed in the late 1940s, under the auspices of the Small Pig Keepers' Council based in Henley-on-Thames.

The minimum membership was four pig owners in a club, and the maximum in a cooperative was 100 members or 50 pigs. The advantage of belonging to a club was that members could draw a bigger ration than domestic pig keepers and could make use of bulk trading to buy necessities cheaply. The clubs also ran a form of insurance against pig deaths and disasters.

Poultry

Most of the poultry reared in Britain were given housing and free access to some kind of a run. The merriest were the farmyard fowl pottering about in the yard and the nearest paddock. The least cheerful were fowl being fattened for market: they were shut up in coops within a warm house and often in the dark.

In Pringle's book *Livestock of the Farm* it was stated firmly that poultry were generally considered 'of so little importance as scarcely to be worthy of notice'. Yet in 1885 the British were importing nearly 2¾ million eggs a day. The returns for that year showed that there were nearly 16 million assorted poultry in Britain: 12.4 million chickens, 2.2 million ducks, 885,000 geese and 475,000 turkeys.

Cramming

Mlle Millet Robinet, a 'high authority' on poultry management in the 1880s, advised that 'cramming' was the most effectual and economical means of fattening chickens for the table. This was an early battery system: each bird had its own compartment within a long narrow wooden box set on legs and with the base of the box (or coop) having rounded spars running lengthways on which the birds perched, their dung dropping through the bars down to ashes or dry earth to be removed by a scraper every two days and stored as manure. The partitions within the coop were only eight inches apart, so the bird could not turn round. At feeding time the attendant (usually a woman) put on an apron, removed one bird at a time from its compartment through a sliding roof, put the fowl on her knees with its rump under her left arm to support it, opened its beak with her left hand and used her right hand to cram a homemade feed pellet 'carefully' with her forefinger well into the gullet. She then pressed the pellet down with thumb and forefinger into the crop and fed more pellets in the same way. This process continued for two or three weeks, or for a few days longer for 'extra fat' poultry. 'With good management,' said the French lady, 'you may go on for thirty days; after this the creature becomes choked with accumulated fat, wastes away, and dies.' A bird nearly ready for the table had to be fasted for 12 hours before being killed. What follows is not for the squeamish.

Mlle Robinet advised that the victim should be held carefully, 'not hung up by the heels, which would suffocate it', and its mouth should be opened. Then, either the underside of the tongue was cut with sharp scissors, or a pointed knife blade was 'thrust into the palate till it pierces the brain'. A third alternative was to pluck a few feathers from the left side of the head just below the ear and make a 'good incision' at the spot. Whichever of these methods was used, the bird was fastened up by the heels immediately afterwards so that it bled freely, 'for on this the whiteness of the flesh depends; but during the death-struggle let it be held by the head'.

Turkeys and ducks

My parents used to have a turkey in a run at the bottom of the garden, which would mysteriously disappear around Christmas time, and as a small child I never connected its fate with Christmas dinner. Dorinda Jeynes's family used to rear turkeys at Bremridge in Devon in the 1920s and as Christmas drew near the family would decide whether to have turkey, goose, duck or chicken for their dinner, all home grown. It was not too much of a wrench: they had been looking after the turkeys and geese since the summer and the birds did seem to be consuming a lot of feed and making their houses and runs very slippery and dirty, and there was always the fear that they were about to hurt or kill themselves, as they sometimes managed to do, before their time. Dorinda's mother had the job of killing the birds for market, which she

detested but knew that at least the job would be done properly. They were hung by their feet to a line in the back court and bled to produce white flesh to appeal to the butcher; they were plucked, gutted and neatly tied, then in due course loaded into hampers and baskets and taken by pony and trap to Crediton to be sent on to Exeter market by train. The proceeds from the sale of poultry, at Christmas or any other time, went to the farmer's wife and so did anything from the sale of eggs, butter and cream.

On a nearby smallholding, Mrs Heard reared ducks and she had a habit of dosing them with cod liver oil: the authorities said it was good for children and she reasoned that it must therefore be good for calves, pigs and ducks as well. The authorities had warned that the stuff might taint eggs but Mrs Heard's ducks were for the table, not for egg production, so she dosed them and they did well; she

Above: Towel-drying a turkey at Newdigate, 1938.

Above: Group of turkey pluckers in 1909.

Below: Higgler collecting from a farmer's wife in 1905. Higglers traded in eggs and poultry.

upped the dose and they did even better. When they had finally been killed, hung and roasted, the meat tasted so strongly of cod liver oil that it was fed to the dogs.

In 1870, George Dew wrote in his diary on 24 October that he had taken the early train from Kirtlington to do his rounds as Relieving Officer at Bletchingdon, Weston on the Green, Islip, Oddington, Charlton on Otmoor, Fencott and Murcott. He wrote at length about the last two miserable hamlets and was impressed by their Aylesbury ducks, 'as white as snow and altogether beautiful creatures', gossiping among themselves in several muddy pools. Two years later he noted hundreds of the

white Aylesbury ducks at Fencott and Murcott. 'They were of all sizes and some just fit for the table. They usually send them to London.'

The smallholders in these two hamlets were still noted for their duck rearing when Arthur W Ashby wrote about the area in 1917. Men with an acre of land could earn about £1 a week, hatching ducklings under hens and selling their ducks at Smithfield market. The locals made no effort to organise their supply: it was all managed by the Smithfield salesmen, who sent out crates to the smallholders to be packed with partially plucked duck carcasses and collected by carriers, who took the crates to Bicester railway station. The salesmen paid the carrier and the railway company for their services, and gave the producer the net return after those costs had been paid and after they had deducted their own commission.

Chicken fatteners, higglers and geese

At the same time as Dew was finding duck rearers in Oxfordshire, Richard Heath was finding chicken fatteners

in the Heathfield area of Sussex. Many of the labourers and small farmers kept perhaps a dozen or so broody hens and bred chickens, living chiefly in places remote from the villages and preferably on the commons and heaths. They specialised in obtaining large broods of chicks in the early spring, aiming for the spring chicken market in London when prices would be two or three times as high as at other times of year. In 1864, it seems, more than 163 tons of fatted chickens were sent to London from Heathfield by one carrier – that was the combined weight of 101,547 fowls fed and fatted in the parishes of Heathfield, Warbleton and Waldron. And that carrier was not the only route; probably half as many birds again were being sent up by different routes to London and to Brighton and Hastings. Heath said you could scarcely go along any road in the vicinity without meeting one of the higglers who collected the chickens from the commonside cottages. He described the higglers as

… lean sinewy men or youths,
carrying an enormous wicker cage,
full of chickens, on their shoulders,
and a stout staff in their hands.
Trudging along at one pace, they bear
the burden of life in a brace though
somewhat moody fashion.

In the neighbouring county of Surrey, they did things differently on the commons. The squatters here kept geese in large numbers, some of them belonging to the cottagers and some simply being minded by the cottagers for others.

Poultry farmers

In the early years of the 20th century, young Fred was working in a bank but dreaming of chickens. During World War I he joined the Artillery and saw service in France. On demob, he did what he had always wanted to do: he started a poultry enterprise. For the first few years he and his wife had to work from six in the morning until ten at night, seven days a week. All that hard work meant that, over the years, he built up a good little business – until, that is, bacillary white diarrhoea hit his little farm in 1927 and wiped out 6,000 chicks. Two years later 3,500 of the growing birds were wiped out by coccidiosis. In those days there were no cures for either of these problems.

Above: Plucking geese in 1911.

Then in 1932 fowl-pox reduced the farm's winter egg yield to zilch and killed most of the birds. Fred bravely established new strains and increased his flocks for winter production. Oh dear. This was the 1930s: the next blow was the depression and, with Britain importing heavily, the price of home-produced eggs hit a record low of just a shilling a score. But Fred's whole life, and all his capital, was tied up in his birds, and he was not alone: many like him had answered the call of the land and were floundering in the mud. At least Fred had a warm glow from all the prizes he won at shows.

In 1936 another disease came out of the blue: fowl paralysis. Nothing either cured or prevented it and Fred lost 3,200 birds and had to kill another thousand. He kept trying: he built up his numbers again, at great cost, but again they went down with the disease. He could not pay his feed bills and his creditors started to strip the farm of its new laying houses and other equipment. He sold his car and went bankrupt; he was 50 years old with no job, no money and no training. He became a salesman for a firm making vacuum cleaners and, when the war started, became a temporary civil servant.

Above: Feeding with Christmas in mind.

During World War II Mr and Mrs JT McClure were running a family mixed farm in Northern Ireland, worked entirely by family members and giving all of them full-time employment. Among the children, John drove the tractor, Lily looked after the dairy, Isa helped with the foddering, 'himself' looked after the dry stock and gave general supervision, and his wife was responsible for the poultry, with the help of daughter Ruby. The farm was in the parish of Ahoghill, a few miles from Ballymena, and Mr McClure had taken it over from his uncle in 1912. By the 1940s he had doubled his land holding to 52 acres, with a further separate 52 acres of conacre (land hired out to him on an 11-month let for one season only, with sanction of the government). He grew various crops but the mainstay of the farm was his herd of milking Shorthorns, about 30 or 40 cows and heifers. They also had poultry, at a time when it was impossible to be in Northern Ireland for more than a day or two without realising that poultry played a large part in the region's farming. There seemed to be hens in every grass field, and during the war Northern Ireland was sending over enough eggs to meet the whole egg ration for Greater London. Usually the farmer's wife looked after the poultry and many of the women reckoned to pay for all of their housekeeping needs from poultry sales. Poultry numbers increased in Northern Ireland during the war (in contrast to pigs, which reduced drastically) and nearly all of them were free-range birds, very happy on oats and chat potatoes with just a small proportion of rationed imported foods, which were allowed at only a quarter of an ounce per bird. The McClures usually had about 700 birds, or as many as a thousand from time to time, and they would put a poultry house in the middle of a grass field and allow the birds to range freely. After no more than two years the house would be removed and the field ploughed up for arable crops.

Britain was still importing one-third of the eggs it needed in the 1930s but by the late 1950s it would be almost self-sufficient in egg production. In the late 1940s, nearly all British laying hens were managed in extensive range systems, in fixed houses or movable folds on pasture. This was labour intensive, and it also meant low egg yields in winter, as egg production depends on length of daylight. Before World War II the intensive battery hen system had been introduced, in which the hen's environment was controlled by the farmer in every respect, including the amount of light. During the war there were heavy restrictions on feedstuffs and the battery system barely survived, but when concentrates were again readily available after rationing of them ceased in 1953, the industry expanded rapidly. By 1960 more than a third of British hens were in batteries rather than free ranging. Another one-third were housed in deep-litter systems, which had been introduced from the United States in 1948 and spread rapidly.

Left: Packing and grading eggs in Devon's South Hams.

Another American idea was the broiler industry, which originated there during the war and spread to Britain in 1953. The first broiler houses here raised flocks of fewer than a thousand birds. Then after a few years some of the producers got together to run co-operative packing stations, with a minimum delivery of 10,000 birds in each batch. By 1960, about a hundred million broilers were being marketed per annum.

As a young man Walter John Guest, born in 1886, began a carrier's business from Loddiswell to Plymouth, using two horses and a wagon on a journey that took seven hours each way. During World War I he got himself a Fiat van with solid tyres. In 1911 he had started to collect butter and eggs from local farmers and eventually he started buying their milk as well. He bought a pub and the businesses grew steadily. When he died in 1943, his daughters Sheelah and Iris continued the egg and poultry side of the business, which grew and grew. By the 1950s broilers and battery hens were being kept in larger numbers in the South Hams and the family built a big new packing station, employing 30 people on egg grading and poultry processing and another five out collecting from nearly a thousand customers during the week. By the late 1960s, smaller farmers were giving up their hens and by the mid 1970s the firm was collecting only from large producers, about ten of them, twice a week – and they were picking up as many eggs from these ten as they had previously collected from a thousand small farmers. Two of the large producers had 10,000 hens each. The family also set up their own egg production unit to balance any shortfall from their producers. It had become a considerable business but things were changing. Bulk tankers were collecting milk that used to be put out in churns so the milk side of the business disappeared. And then in the late 1970s new European regulations would be the last straw. It was too much, so in 1983 they closed the business. But in the meantime hadn't Walter John Guest's little horse-and-wagon enterprise hatched a big one!

COD LIVER OIL

Cod liver oil was known as bottled sunshine: it was widely used in poultry rations in winter, especially for birds that had been kept out of direct sunlight and were missing out on the boost that sunshine gives to vitamin D in the body. Cod liver oil increased egg production and increased chicks' resistance to disease.

Goats

It seems strange that, in spite of their potential, goats have generally been regarded in Britain as backyard animals for cottagers and commoners, to be pegged out on verges and odd patches of rough land, rather than kept in herds as farm livestock.

Above: Prize-winning nanny goats Sunshine and Sunbright with a young billy, Meteor, and their stockman. The goats were from the herd of Sir Humphrey de Trafford, Bt, in the 1890s.

Right: Many smallholders and cottagers kept a few goats, usually staking them out on tethers so they could browse safely over limited areas.

Even though some interest was expressed in goat breeding towards the end of the 19th century, it seemed to be restricted largely to 'the wives and daughters of the men pushing forward the frontiers of the British Empire', according to Alan Mowlem, writing in 1988.

Of these ladies many were left at home with often a good education but in a society that frowned upon working women. Those with country backgrounds or leanings found the goat an ideal subject with which to develop this interest into small-scale farming and food production. Thus the pastime of goat keeping and goat breeding became acceptable and even today is largely the province of women.

Mowlem, who is a practising authority on commercial goat farming in Britain and has always been generous with his knowledge, noted that interest in goats did accelerate during the two world wars as part of the campaign to encourage home food production, but somehow, unlike pigs and poultry, goats were largely overlooked after World War II and the average herd size for goats remained at two or three animals. It was not until the 1970s that more interest was taken in them, partly because many more people were taking holidays on the Continent and developing a taste for the foods they found there – including goat's cheeses and yoghurts. I have to say that, having lived in Greece for two years as a small child immediately after the war, goat's milk has never been my favourite food: in those days dairy hygiene was appalling and all Greek goat dairy products were decidedly goaty, while goat meat was generally from aged animals and as tough as old boots. It is all very different today and goat's milk is recognised as a very healthy food.

Markets

Farming can be a very lonely life and it is not surprising that most farmers seized every opportunity to mingle with other farmers by going to the markets, fairs, sales and the shows. It helped them to get their own problems into perspective, to learn about new ideas and techniques and, most important of all, to catch up on all the gossip. Oh yes, and it gave them a chance to buy and sell, but that was almost incidental.

In 1927 there were 414 agricultural markets and auction marts and 250 agricultural fairs in the Midlands alone, including livestock markets, corn markets, wholesale fruit and vegetable markets, egg and poultry markets, meat markets, fish markets, cheese and butter markets, wool auctions, hide and skin markets and numerous retail markets. The annual agricultural fairs were gradually disappearing, or turning into pleasure fairs. The agricultural producer found that the properly equipped weekly markets that had taken the place of the annual fairs offered much greater convenience and efficiency.

Getting There

For some time after the railways were built, livestock might still be taken to market in droves. On a long walk, especially in warm weather, they were bound to lose weight, which meant a waste of valuable meat. For example, the heavy stall-fed bullocks of east Norfolk were said to lose an average of four stone (each stone being 14lb) on the five- or six-day road journey to Smithfield market in London.

Once the railways came, all the hassle of the drove and all the bother of finding fodder and water along the way was overcome. The cost of sending animals by rail might have been greater than the old droving charges but the animals arrived in much better condition and so they were worth more. They could leave the farm on Saturday and be in the salesman's lairage that very evening, to be fed and rested so that they were fresh for the market on Monday morning. By the mid 1870s the great majority of farms were near enough to a station to get their animals to their destination within a day at the most. Country stations, even village ones, had lairage and loading facilities and for the next few decades wagons loaded with livestock were a common sight on the rails.

The railway changed farmers. For a start, it gave them access to a much wider market: goods could be put on a train to anywhere in the country and get there still fresh; they could even send something as perishable as milk up to the cities in time for breakfast. A farmer could easily collect bulk goods such as fuel

Above: Country milk heading for the cities. Porters loading churns into a goods waggon on the North Staffordshire Railway.

Right: Livestock and farm implements being transported in open railway wagons from Milnthorpe to Cheshire. Taking livestock by rail used to be common; today the animals generally travel by road.

Market day

and fertiliser from the nearest railway station by horse and wagon, and could just as easily send prize livestock to the big shows. What is more, he himself could travel on that train and his horizons were hugely widened. Life was so much easier by rail.

The canals offered another means of bulk transport that opened out new markets for some farmers. They could send their meat, dairy produce, straw and hay into the cities, and in return they could collect manure from city stables. But the trains were quicker.

The railways brought the beginning of the end to rural isolation: country people could travel so much more easily and so much further than on foot or by pony and cart or, later, by bike. And the railways brought things *into* the countryside: daily national newspapers, cheaper coal, manufactured goods, fashions, ideas and, eventually, commuters. Oh yes, the railways changed a lot more than just the farmer.

Bill Tull started going to Petersfield market as a lad in the 1920s and told me proudly in his eighties that he had never missed market day since, even though by then there was not a live animal in sight. In Bill's youth, it had been very different: the square on market day was full of cattle, sheep, pigs and poultry adding their various voices to the bedlam of dogs barking, carthorses clattering, men joking, women gossiping and children enjoying themselves.

George Sturt (1863–1927) described his memories of Farnham market in an unpublished article written in the 1920s:

Within living memory it was no uncommon thing to see the flocks of sheep, and the cattle beyond them, stretching far up the street; while, nearer at hand, there were pens for pigs and poultry, standings for ploughs and all manner of farming tackle. The

Above: Market day in Petersfield, Hampshire, in about 1880. Today the market square is empty of livestock: market days are filled only with stalls selling fruit and vegetables, fish, plants, clothes, haberdashery and the like.

Above: The Old Market in the main street of St Ives, Huntingdonshire, in 1890.

gathering of men who have a little corn to sell and much gossip to unload before they go home. After the auctions are over they adjourn to this old meeting-place – scarce half a hundred of them all told; and there for an hour or two they stand at their corner, chatting and driving hard bargains, and unconsciously preserving just so much of the old traditions as may stir up in the onlooker a warmer affection for England's changing life. Like a picture of superb summers long since past … so the market lingers on into our day, not without intrinsic merit of its own, yet chiefly notable for the much life that went to the making of it in earlier days.

present writer remembers especially the pigs; for it was into his boyish ear (one school half-holiday) that a wretched porker delivered an agonised shriek, upon being lifted in the usual way from its pen by hind leg and ear, and carried off under its purchaser's arm.

But all that sort of thing has disappeared. Long ago two enterprising auctioneers began holding weekly auctions of 'stock' in another part of the town; and the old market, shorn of its glories, is now only a small

As late as 1946 R Glave Saunders was writing about cruelty at Britain's cattle markets. Most of the older markets were too small, lacked shelter for the animals from bad weather and from extremes of temperature and were by no means rigorously supervised. Veterinary inspectors were present for only part of the time, police officers and the very limited number of RSPCA inspectors did their best, but the drovers, often badly paid, ignorant and largely drawn from the 'down-and-outs', soon got to know when there was no one about. What did they care? Just doing my job, mate.

There were countless incidents of animals suffering from broken legs and other serious injuries simply because no one provided loading and unloading ramps at the market. Often no provision was made for feeding, watering and sheltering any animals left over at the end of the day. Most animals spent an average of five or six hours in the market anyway and sometimes had to suffer from children who seemed to come to the marketplace for the sole purpose of teasing them in their pens,

THE OUTDOOR CLUB

Among the farmers there would mingle a few London merchants – corn merchants, hop merchants, manure merchants – and assorted local trades such as wheelwrights, timber merchants, coal merchants, millers and brewers. There would be provincial corn factors bargaining softly to the sound of rustling corn being poured out of sample bags into the palm of the hand and overflowing on to the flagstones. Sometimes there would be a gaudily painted new cart or farm implement by way of advertising its maker, and the whole scene at the market glowed with colour; even when the market itself was moribund it was still an outdoor club for farmers and their friends.

prodding them and even whacking them with sticks. Cows would arrive at the market unmilked, their udders bulging, and would remain unmilked until they were sold. Diseased cows were frequently up for sale, regardless of the threat of contagion to other cows.

Sheep fairs

Old Raggitan was the name that Walter Johnson gave to a Lincolnshire shepherd he met in 1875. He was a short, wiry and rather bent man, perhaps 70 years old at the time, with bushy eyebrows and a round bullet head. His favourite job, once a week, was selecting which sheep and bullocks should go to market and then taking them to town. He would choose the stock on a Thursday and put them aside for a good rest. At two or three in the morning on the Friday he would mount his cob, summon his lad and his

dog, gather his drove of animals and find a couple of boys to help along the way. The drove would usually include a dozen bullocks and a few hundred sheep, many of them strangers to each other and often joined by a few other animals from smallholders along the way. The journey on the road was about nine miles, with many a side lane, byway and open gateway to tempt them away from the drove, and the occasional drama of meeting another flock in the lane and sorting out the ensuing chaos. The closer they came to the market town, the more alert Old Rag had to be, with droves arriving from every direction. But at last his bullocks would find a place in the stalls and the sheep in their pens, and the cattle would have a circular piece

Below: Findon Sheep Fair, traditionally held on the second Saturday of September and packed with sheep here in the 1930s. Barclay Wills chats to William 'Old Shep' Sheppard in the foreground.

Inset: George Chant and George Humphreys, two well-known Sussex shepherds, at Findon Fair.

Above: Brough Hill Horse Fair in Westmoreland, 1950, was an annual magnet for horse-dealers and gypsies from all over the country.

Below: Bampton Horse Fair in Devon, 1925, with a group of free-running Exmoor ponies rounded up from the moor, broken to the halter and ready for sale.

of paper pasted to their rumps, bearing their number. Potential customers would come and talk business with him before the cattle auction began around a large circular enclosure. The sheep were sold by the penful and then arrangements were made about payments and dues, and the purchased animals brought together in new droves for the homeward journey. By the time that journey had been made and the animals settled in, it was already dark before the shepherd could relax with a meal by the fire and discuss the next day's work with the lad.

Another of Johnson's shepherding friends was a Sussex man not far from Arundel. Stumpy and square, with broad shoulders, grey eyes, round ruddy face, small nose and short, rounded white beard, he was a well-travelled man who visited sheep fairs for miles around and had been to the main livestock shows all over the country though he had passed up the opportunity to go to Paris, Chicago and South America with his animals. His sheep had been exhibited at the Royal Show and the big county shows, and he had won the occasional second and first prizes with his compact little Southdowns.

He was 83 years old when Johnson met him in 1918. By then the sheep generally travelled to the shows by train, but in the early days of the shepherd's career the journeys were made on foot along the roads. The flocks would cover eight to ten miles a day and there would be a boy with a light cart bringing up the rear to pick up any footsore or weary sheep and give them a rest for while. The route was carefully planned so that the shepherd could sleep each night in a village inn while the sheep were pastured in a local field by previous arrangement. Eventually, after several days of travelling, they would reach the fairground. His sheep safely penned, he would have time to gossip with a wide variety of shepherds from faraway villages whom he might meet once a year at this fair.

Without a doubt, one of the fairs that

the old shepherd would have visited was at Findon. In 1896 the Reverend John Goring wrote a stiff letter to Harry James Burt, who had written to local flock owners asking if he could sell their sheep for them by auction at Findon Fair instead of the time-honoured method of private bargain. Findon Fair soon became an auction sale for sheep and the largest in Sussex, all under the management of Harry James Burt.

Clem Fowler joined Burt's firm and recorded his memories of Findon Fair from 1917, when the sheep would 'come over the hill like small clouds in the mist of dawn'. They were often driven to the area from their home farms the day before to lie up in local fields by previous arrangement. After the sale, drovers from the Chichester area made up droves of up to 3,000 sheep, which they drifted over the Downs in various directions, dropping off lots here and there at the farms of various purchasers. In 1925 Fowler suggested that his firm should organise rail transport for long-distance travellers if the fair was to survive. The sheep were driven over the Downs to Steyning station and put into large sorting pens in the market there. In that first year, Southern Railway provided a special shunting engine and there were 30 consignments of sheep, requiring 56 trucks to transport them to their final destinations. At its height, the auctioneers loaded 80 trucks and it took them two days. Even in 1947 they filled 50 trucks. But in 1928 the first lorry came on the scene and by the mid 1950s road transport had taken over from rail. In 1958, an exceptional year, a total of 16,700 ewes and lambs and a thousand rams were sold at Findon Fair – and that is a lot of sheep for a small downland village.

Right above: Showing off at Tunbridge Wells in 1938.

Right below: Goat ladies at a show between the wars.

SHOWS

The fancier heavy-horse breeders loved to have their best animals competing at the shows. The preparation was considerable – all that grooming and hoof polishing and cleaning of the harness to a peak of perfection, quite apart from all the training involved to ensure that a horse stood proud for the judges and did not take alarm at the hustle and bustle of the show ring.

One does wonder how the precious horses and other prize livestock got to the shows, though. The Royal Show, for example, moved to a different part of the country each year, reducing the travelling distance when it happened to be closer to your farm, but the major central shows stayed in faraway places like London and Glasgow. Until the railway network was adequate, the show animals would either have walked or have been put into wagons drawn by horses or oxen on a long, slow journey that could take several days – heavy, plodding, work-a-day oxen drawing a wagonload of fancy show-offs along the road to glory.

It was in 1839 that the new Royal Agricultural Society had decided to hold its first country meeting and it chose Oxford as the venue because of its central situation. More than 20,000 people came to the show at Oxford and naturally Cambridge wanted to be the host the following year, but in 1841 it was felt that a manufacturing district should be chosen: Liverpool. Thereafter they devised a rotation of districts. Bristol, the north-east, Middlesex, North Wales (actually Shrewsbury), northern England and South Wales were scheduled to take their turn until it was realised that railway connections to South Wales were lacking – and they knew that railway access was vital, so they opted for the Midlands district instead. It was part of the specification that the showgrounds should be accessible from a railway terminus. Rotation through the different districts of England and Wales continued until in 1963 the Society finally found itself a permanent base at Stoneleigh, which remains the venue for the Royal Show to this day.

Farm Processing

Most farmers rather resent losing some of their profits to a middleman between themselves and the consumer; they really don't like too much of a margin between wholesale and retail prices. Today there is much talk today about added value – about farmers earning a larger share from their produce by processing it in some way on the farm.

Above: Bottling milk at Poplars Farm, Bradford, in the 1940s. Milk trickles through the cooler into the bottles, which are then capped by machine.

Below: A farm cheese press at Driver Farm, Simonsbath, in Somerset.

For example, instead of selling their livestock they might have their animals slaughtered and process the meat on the farm to sell in their own farm shop as farmhouse sausages, or rather than selling raw milk in bulk they might convert it into farmhouse cheese and ice cream – just like their recent ancestors used to do.

In the dairy

It had long been a tradition that the farmer's wife was in charge of the farm dairy. Most of the milk was converted into something less perishable, particularly butter and cheese, especially in parts of the country where access to urban markets for raw milk was difficult.

With the growth of the railway system, more and more farmers could transport their milk in liquid form for sale in the cities. The change to selling liquid milk made life a lot easier for the farmer: there was no longer the worry and bother of the uncertainties of cheese production, and also sales were instant – the milk was simply put into churns, hoisted into a horse-drawn cart and delivered to the station. There was no wait between extracting milk from the cows and producing something that could be sold. With cheese, you might have to wait for several weeks, or even months, before the product was ready for the market.

It was not just the more accessible markets for raw milk that challenged the farmhouse dairy and ensured that the days of the farmer's wife's nice little earner were numbered. Science began to catch up with instinctive skills and cheesemaking techniques were improved. Bit by bit, the homeliness of cheesemaking was giving way, and when cheese factories became established that really was almost a death knell for farmhouse cheeses. It all started across the Atlantic. In the 1860s, American factory-made cheeses were beginning to

Above: Woman at work by her farm dairy in Wensleydale.

compete with home produce and in 1870 the Royal Agricultural Society of England responded by setting up its own cheese factory. Within six years there were ten such factories, processing the milk of some 8,000 cows. One factory employing five men could process the produce of cows from 30 farms, each of which would in the past have employed its own cheesemaker.

The dairymaids and the farmers' wives could not hope to match the factories. By the outbreak of World War I, only farms in remote areas were still making and marketing their own butter; and by the outbreak of World War II only about a thousand farms were still making their own cheese.

Farm cheesemaking

Avice Wilson was born in Chippenham and worked at Cocklebury Farm as a landgirl during World War II. She later became a dairy technologist and knows all there is to know about cheesemaking.

Describing cheesemaking at Cocklebury in the 19th century she explained that, immediately after milking, rennet (an extract of calf's stomach) would be added to the warm milk to encourage the formation of curds. The curds were broken up gently by hand, the whey was ladled off and the curds were pressed by hand to remove more whey. Then they were scalded, salted, placed into moulds, compressed again by hand, wrapped in cloth and compacted in a weighted press. That was just the first stage: the rest of the process took several weeks before the cheeses could be transferred to the cheese loft for storage. The loft at Cocklebury was large enough to store up to eight tons of cheese a year, the produce of 40 cows.

Farm buttermaking

Buttermaking was sheer hard work. I know, I've done it: you churn and churn and churn, thinking you are getting nowhere and getting all hot and flustered

FAIR ROSAMUND

Francis Kilvert had a soft spot for dairymaids. His diaries made frequent references to them when he went 'villaging about' on his pastoral duties. At Whitsun in 1874 he went through the meadows to John Knight's dairy to drink whey when they had been making cheese:

'At the dairy it was butter morning and Fair Rosamund was making up the sweet rolls of rich golden butter. Mrs Knight says the butter is so golden at this time of year because the cows eat the buttercups. The reason why the whey is so sweet and wholesome in May and June is because the grass is so full of flowers and young sweet herbs. When I go to the Common Farm to drink whey I think of my grandmother, my mother's mother Thermuthis Ashe, then a fair beautiful young girl, and how she used to come across the meadows from the Manor house to this very dairy and drink whey here every morning during the sweet May month.'

A Yorkshire milkmaid out in the field with her Shorthorn cows.

until, quite suddenly, the precious yellow flecks begin to appear in the milk and quickly bump together into a big lump. My mother remembered her childhood in Argentina, where the gauchos had a much simpler method: they put milk into saddlebag flasks, rode about all day chasing steers and by the time they came back to the ranch in the evening the flasks were full of butter.

Churning used to be by simply swishing your hands and forearms in the milk continuously until it 'came'. Various hand-operated churns were devised, either by rotating or rocking a barrel or by turning paddles in the liquid. Once you heard that encouraging bumping noise as the buttery bits came together, you separated the lump from the buttermilk and then squeezed it to remove every drop of liquid, or it would quickly go rancid. Some farms had little butter mangles; the rest of us used hands and wooden spatulas. The butter was washed and pressed again, and the process repeated over and over until you had a beautiful golden lump of solid butter, salted to taste. At last came the artistic bit: you patted it into shape with a couple of butter pats, weighed it and impressed a pretty pattern with the farm's own stamp.

Buttermilk

On the Ayrshire farm of the well-known dairy cattle breeder Willie Dunlop of Gree, they used to make a lot of their milk into butter and cheese. The milk was churned in 200-gallon churns by horsepower or by steam power, and the butter was sold four days a week in summer and three in winter. The residual buttermilk was sold in Glasgow for baking and for porridge: the men had to leave home at four in the morning with the pony and milk-cart and would not get back to the farm until three in the afternoon. From 1915 Dunlop gave up the buttermilk run and instead sold whole milk to the city, which meant an even earlier start: shipyard workers wanted their milk at six and they wanted it still warm from the cow when they poured it on their porridge. But Gree was too far and it was a relief when one of the first creameries in Scotland started up locally. A private dairyman bought an old mill, where he collected milk from all the individual farmers and then drove it into Glasgow in bulk, firstly with horses and later lorries. In due course the farmers formed a co-operative and bought out the dairyman, and the system continued until the formation of the Milk Marketing Board in 1933.

Meat

George Dew went to Steeple Aston one February evening in 1877 and recorded in his diary that he had some 'American beef of good quality. Brought over in the joint.' In 1870 he had enjoyed some Australian potted beef at the same house: it was a treat, as the importation of meat from

ASSES' MILK

Mrs Bennett had lived in Ivy Cottage, near Bremridge in Devon, between 1911 and 1930, where she and her family made do on eleven shillings a week. The children all looked well (it helped that they had a very productive vegetable garden) but the neighbours were surprised to learn that, before they had come to Ivy Cottage, one of Mrs Bennett's boys had been reared on donkey's milk. He was quite different from all the others – much taller, darker, a really 'fine' fellow'.

Australia was in its very early days. By the mid 1870s, though, chilled beef was coming in from North America and by the 1880s frozen meat from Australia, New Zealand and South America was rapidly challenging the home beef producers. When Dew ate his potted Australian beef, imported meat from all sources accounted for only 10 per cent of all meat consumed in Britain. Between 1870 and 1874 only about 30,000 hundredweight of beef

Below: The well-stocked butcher's shop.

Right: Travelling Sussex cider-makers grinding apples (left) and putting the pulp into old sacks for loading into the cider press (right).

(chilled and frozen) came in from abroad each year, but for the period 1875 to 1879 it rocketed up to 350,000, of which about 93 per cent came from the United States. They had imported Britain's beef breeds with enthusiasm and shipped them back again as frozen joints.

By 1950 the cattle industry in Britain had been directed almost exclusively towards milk for more than ten years, so much so that there was hardly any British beef left to eat and what there was tended to be a by-product of the dairy industry, which is to say that it was more likely to be from dual-purpose milk-and-beef breeds than from the pure beef breeds on which Britain had built its fame as a beef-eating nation and which it had exported all over the world. The home beef industry had been sacrificed on the shrine of milk, or, as Professor Allan Fraser put it in 1950: 'We have, to a certain extent, discarded the substance of beef for the shadow of milk.'

TINNED UNICORNS

Potted meat might not have suited a Sussex woman in John Coker Egerton's village in the 1880s. The shopkeeper showed her some of the best tinned meats and she retorted, 'No, no; none of them things for me; they be all lions and unicorns, they be.'

Cider

There were ancient cider apple trees in my cottage garden in the 1970s and in the overgrown garden of a derelict farmhouse up the rough track through the woods. Here and there along the track were scattered apple trees, mostly with small, sharp fruits of no identifiable variety but generally marking where once there had been a cottage or a small farmstead long ago. In these parts, cottagers as well as farmers had made their own cider; and in autumn, when the ripe fruit had fallen to the ground and was beginning to ferment, you could smell its richness and almost taste the cider they would have tasted, and imagine the cottagers visiting each other to help with the brewing and the tasting, getting unsteadily merrier as they wandered along the track.

The farms surrounding the Cornish village of Quethiock in Victorian times were typical of many parts of the countryside: each farm had its own orchard, and most of the trees were cider apples. Most of the farms had their own cider-presses but there was also a communal one in the village, courtesy of the squire: a small thatched building to which people brought their own sacks of ripe apples and squeezed the fruit into a 'cheese' between two hefty granite stones. Local children took turns to operate the handles of the press, and usually brought with them some long straws to suck up unfermented juice that dripped into a wooden barrel.

Moses Barnicot, of Tregony in Cornwall, described his own method of making cider between the wars:

We don't make but a very little cider here, but when we have plenty of apples we throw them in an iron boiler and scrat 'em with the butt-end of a stub. Then we lay the pummy on a thin layer of reed, or oaten straw, at the bottom of the press; turn the ends of the straw in, and spread another layer on top; and so we keep piling up, like cheese, till the 'mock' is finished.

Then the press was wrung down and the thick brown juice ran into the tub. The rest of the juice was left to rack off into a hogshead to ferment for a fortnight before being decanted into another barrel. A few weeks later it was ready for drinking. The oat straw was said to give the cider a good rich colour and, mixed in with some of the pressed apple, called pomace, was fed to cattle and pigs.

A group of farmers were swapping cider tales in the pub in 1945. One talked of some home-brewed cider on his own farm that had turned out to be 'lovely stuff, smooth': they drank the lot and then discovered the bones of half-a-dozen rats inside the cask when it was being cleaned. Another farmer added that his father had always put a piece of steak into their home-brewed cider, to mellow it. 'The meat used to disappear in a few weeks. He said the cider fed on it.'

A third used to make a lot of cider on his farm, in two large vats with wooden lids covered with straw. One year a Large White sow disappeared. 'It was the talk of Monmouthshire. We hunted all over. Everyone had a different theory to account for it, but it was never found until next year when we had emptied the big vat and came to clear it out and there we found the sow's skeleton white and clean at the bottom.' She had climbed up a ramp and walked on the lid, which tipped up and slid her into the cider; the lid tilted back into place and no one knew. It was the finest cider they had made in years.

Below: Loading apples into the loft

Tailpiece

I n the 1980s I was told that the neighbouring farm had been sold to someone who wanted to farm wallabies. It didn't happen. Twenty years later I was told that a field on the same farm had been sold to a man who wanted to farm emus. That didn't happen either, but it would not have been altogether surprising if it had.

In the 1940s, a Hertfordshire man used to travel almost daily by bus from Bennington to Ware. He was always on the lookout for a barn owl that used to sit on a gatepost along the way but one morning he saw something so strange that he stopped the bus. Sitting on its haunches, a kangaroo was peacefully surveying the countryside. The passengers eventually decided it must have been an escaped mascot of the New Zealand Forces, but they might have been wrong about its origins.

Since the 19th century, quite a few kangaroos had found a home in private collections on farms and big estates – along with wallabies, bison, zebu bulls, water buffalo, ostriches and other potential farm livestock, including, I am reliably informed by the highly knowledgeable Clin Keeling, 'two hogs from the Havannah with navels on their backs' at Horton Hall in Northamptonshire in the 18th century, or so the menagerie list of the period claimed.

Throughout the centuries some farmers, or, more often, wealthier landowners have always had an eye for the unusual, the innovative, the exciting: the animals that will make their friends and neighbours sit up and take notice, the techniques that will make their fortune or at least improve their income, the inventions that will make their lives easier and get the job done more quickly. So there has always been change on the farm. The difference is that, within living memory, those changes have been far faster, on a far bigger scale and far more influential than perhaps in any time before ours. They have left us panting, not able to absorb the changes gradually and very often unable to see them, let alone understand them, since most of us are now so divorced from farming.

Those two world wars were major spurs to change – especially towards intensification and full mechanisation, which meant a drastic reduction in the amount of human labour employed on the land and a dramatic increase in the speed with which farm operations of all kinds were carried out. The revolution in agriculture during the 20th century brought many benefits to consumers, the retail trade and to larger farmers, but the downsides have perhaps slipped in unnoticed by many.

A smaller workforce in the countryside has increased the loneliness and the sense of being beleaguered by the urban

majority, putting rural workers and landowners on the defensive and denting their sense of humour. There has been a big loss in the old sense of companionship in work and I wonder whether the present generation of farmers and farmworkers will be able to reminisce as richly as their grandparents. They will have had far fewer shared experiences, and far less time to stand and stare and smell and to feel part of the land and the landscape. Will they, like the men in their eighties in my village now, be able in their own old age to potter about and meet up casually with their old workmates for a gossip about their younger days, or will none of them have stayed in one place for long enough to

become part of such a longstanding group of close friends?

It is all too easy to view the past as a better place, a place in which the scale of things was more human, more personal, more accessible, when you could make your own implements and repair them simply with bits of wood and nails and string because they were so easy to work out. It happens in all walks of life, of course. Whereas a boy in the 1930s might have happily made his own crystal wireless set, his counterpart today is highly unlikely to make his own television. And whereas a typist in the 1960s would have been able to repair a manual typewriter with nothing more than fingers or perhaps a small

Above: Making hay in Langdale.

Opposite: Shepherd Charles Townsend caring for lambs in the snow.

Above: The original ploughman's lunch. Surprisingly, this man is wearing a smock as late as 1938.

screwdriver, how many today could even think of doing the same with a computer? Mechanics has given way to electronics, and it is the same on the farm. The equipment has become complicated, expensive to buy and maintain and often incomprehensible even to the most practical of farmers.

The transponder around a cow's neck is surely a sign of the times, relying on the computer to recognise the cow, give her an appropriate ration and fix the clusters to her teats in the milking parlour, rather than relying on the experienced eye of a stockman who knows her name, what her temperament is like, how soon she is due to calve and whether her udder is in good health because he has checked it himself, visually and physically, when washing her down before milking.

Life has become easier in many respects on the farm: sheer hard physical labour and drudgery have all but disappeared along with the monotony that so often accompanied it, but instead there is more pressure and stress in everyday farming. The younger generation do still seem to relish their work, especially if they have an interest in things mechanical, but farmers who used to seem so independent, doing what they thought was best for their land, their animals, their farm and their grandchildren based on their own rich experience, now find themselves being told what to do and how to do it by governments, committees, pressure groups, scientists and journalists. Their independence is being rapidly eroded and, to the chagrin of some, they are being bribed to become park keepers rather than producers.

There has been a worrying impact on the landscape and on the natural world in the past half a century, though this is something humans have done to their environment since the first of them tried to clear an area to grow crops, or allowed their animals to graze too much in one place. But one of the most worrying trends of all has been the burden placed on livestock. We have bred animals way beyond what nature intended, particularly in the dairy herds where cows produce unthinkable volumes of milk far in excess of the needs of the single calf for which their udders were designed, placing them under enormous physical stress and, yes, emotional distress. We have kept animals in conditions of quite appalling deprivation, giving them (so it is argued) all the comforts of warmth, shelter, food and security that they could possibly need but denying them the ability to express far too many of their natural instincts. By ratcheting up the scale of things, keeping them in enormous herds and flocks, we have lost sight of the animal as an individual and thus lost the mutual respect that used to exist. Yes, in days gone by there were many acts of cruelty, but largely through ignorance, for which today there is no excuse.

Somehow, in ensuring a better working life for the farmworker and the farmer, we have passed the burden on to the livestock and are working them to death. Perhaps we should listen to the voices from the past, take time in the rush and hurry of modern life to step back a little and consider just where we are heading on the farms of the future.

Acknowledgments and Picture Credits

The author would like to acknowledge, above all, the many farmers and farmworkers who have shared their memories with her over the years; and also those who, a generation or two or three ago, recorded the memories of their own period, as well as those who have made a special study of their own village or family. Numerous village groups in recent years have published histories of their parishes and these personal recollections of farming in days gone by have been invaluable as well as entertaining and sometimes heart-rending. The author is particularly grateful to the villagers of Bremridge, Buriton, Castlemartin, Cocklebury, Loddiswell, Milland and Quethiock.

Special thanks are due to those who have given permission to quote from their books and to the several authors who have proved very difficult to trace to seek such permission. The author and publisher have done their best to find them or their descendants and would welcome information so that full credits can be given in future editions. Details of the source books are given in the Bibliography, overleaf.

Old photographs play a major role in this book and thanks are due to all those who gave permission for their reproduction. Again, every effort has been made to locate the original sources but, again, in some cases we have failed and would appreciation information for future editions. Acknowledgement is made to the following known photographic sources, both private and public, with the relevant page number.

Avoncroft Museum of Buildings (46b); Percy Bedford (133); Rennie Bere (148); Millman Brown (87b); Buriton Heritage Bank (34); Cambridgeshire Archive Service/Huntingdonshire County Record Office (236); David Cole (173); Countryman (160); CW Cramp (37t); Fred Crossley (137l); Peter Ditchfield (115, 185); Michael V Dixon (5t, 73b); WM Dodson (220t); EH Donovan (4–5b); Dorset County Museum (39, 51); Mary French (33, 62–3b); Friends of the Lake District (37b, 68, 69, 71, 76, 100t,b, 190–1, 205, 212b, 247); Getty Images (7, 10–11b, 13, 19, 20, 26, 27, 31, 32, 35, 40b, 41, 49, 62t, 63t, 70t, 74b, 80, 90–1b, 94, 95, 98, 107b, 108, 117, 120, 122t, 129, 140, 143, 151, 153, 158, 161t,164, 169, 175t,b, 183, 188, 189, 195, 206, 212t, 213, 216t,b, 227, 228t, 229, 234t, 238t,b, 240t, 248); Mr Goulding (8b); Dr Habberton Lulham (88t); Hampshire Record Office (47); George Hepworth (28b); Hereford City Library (86); Prof. JH Hutton (93); Illustrated (187b, 204); AF Kersting (45b); Lackham Agricultural Museum (46t); Leicester Museums, Arts and Record Office (64, 99b, 178, 181b); WP Livingstone (131t); Loddiswell History Group (59, 82, 138, 231); Mansell Collection (196, 203); Mary Evans Picture Library (38l,r, 78, 104t, 142, 163r, 181t, 225); Milland Memories Group (36, 42, 43, 44, 48, 121t, 134, 139, 150, 159b, 180b, 224, 243); Museum of English Rural Life (1, 9, 11t, 12, 14–15, 16b, 17, 18, 24, 50, 52, 53, 61, 65, 75, 79, 84–5t, 89t, 92, 96t,b, 101b, 102t, 105, 109, 111t, 118–9, 122–3b, 126, 128t,b, 131b, 132, 141, 144, 145, 146, 157b, 159t, 165, 170t, 171t,b, 174, 177, 179t,b, 184, 186–7t, 190, 199b, 208b, 210, 219, 221, 222, 223t,b, 228b, 232b, 233, 234b,239t, 241, 245); National Museums of Scotland (121b, 152b, 170b); National Trust Photo Library (23); North Lincolnshire Council (162–3b); Norwich Central Library (197); Old Pond Publishing/David Kindred (Titshall collection) (6, 99t, 127, 154, 180t, 194t); Oxford Mail & Times (45t); Jesse Packham (196 inset); G Parsons (176); Holmes Pegler (232t); Petersfield Museum (235); Pitstone Green Museum (4t, 84b, 226); Eleanor Porter (22t,b); W Pouncy (182); EH Pulbrook (97, 137r); C Reid (148t); Lilian Ream Exhibition Gallery (57t, 58b, 83, 88b, 106–7t); Redcliffe Press (240b); Royal Photographic Society/Social & Science Picture Library (Gal collection) (106b, 110, 114, 130, 135, 198, 208t); Ryedale Folk Museum (104b); Glyn Slattery (54); Sutc Gallery (192, 242); Mr Taunt (89b, 149); Mr Vasey (85b); Doug West (200t); Stuart West (29, 30); West Sussex Record Office (Garland collection) (3, 8t, 10t, 28t, 40t, 55, 56t 57b, 58t, 60t,b, 66l,r, 70b, 73t, 74 87t, 90t, 101t, 103, 111b, 113, 124–5,136, 147, 152t, 155t,b, 156–7t, 161b,167, 168, 193, 194b, 199t, 20(201, 202, 209, 211, 214, 217, 220b, 230, 237t,b, 239b, 244, 246); Avice Wilson (166); Wiltshire Archaeol and Natural History Society (172); Women's Farm & Garden Union (25, 56b).

Bibliography

Alderman, Denis (ed.) *Castlemartin ... a chuckle and a cackle* (2000, self-published)

Allison, Philip (ed.) *The New Forest: a photographic record of 100 years of Forest life* (1979, Pioneer)

Astell, Joan *Somerset Scrapbook 1920–1940* (1985, Redcliffe)

Barton, FT *Cattle Sheep & Pigs* (early 20th c., Jarrold)

Beckett, Arthur *The Spirit of the Downs* (5th edn, 1930, Methuen)

Bertelsman, Gwen *Lakeland Life in the 1940s and 1950s* (2003, Halsgrove)

Brigden, Roy *Harvesting Machinery* (2003, Shire)

Briggs, Martin S *The English Farmhouse* (1953, Batsford)

Bryner Jones, C (ed.) *Live Stock of the Farm* (1920, Gresham)

Burdekin, TA (ed.) *A Victorian Farmer's Diary: William Hodkin's Diary* (2003, Derbyshire County Council)

Eden Fisher & Co. *The Country Gentlemen's Catalogue 1894* (reprint 1969, Garnstone Press)

Chapman, J and Seeliger, S *Enclosure, Environment & Landscape* (2001, Tempus)

Chivers, Keith (ed.) *Harnessing the heavy horse for the 21st century* (1988, Shire Horse Society and RASE)

Christian, Garth *Tomorrow's Countryside: The Road to the Seventies* (1966, John Murray)

Coburn, Mary Amy *George and Henry* (1992, Wheathampstead Local History Group)

Coe, Brian *A Victorian Country Album: The Photographs of Joseph Gale* (1988, Guild)

Coker Egerton, John *Sussex Folk and Sussex Ways* (1884, Trubner/Chatto & Windus)

Davidson, HR *The Production and Marketing of Pigs* (1948, Longmans, Green)

Davis, Bob *Water Under the Bridge* (2004, self-published)

Devine, TM *Farm Servants & Labour in Lowland Scotland 1770–1914* (1984, SAC)

Ditchfield, PH *Country Folk: A Pleasant Company* (1923, Methuen)

Ditchfield, PH *Rural England: Cottage and Village Life* (1912, Dent; revised edn 1993, Bracken Books)

Dixon, Michael V *Farming Times* (1991, SB Publications, Market Drayton)

Duncan, Ronald *Jan's Journal* (1954, Museum Press)

Egerton King, Maude (ed.) *A Cottage Wife's Calendar* (c1919, reprint 1975)

Eglon Shaw, Bill *Frank Meadow Sutcliffe* (1974/1985, Sutcliffe Gallery, Whitby)

Ewart Evans, George *Where Beards Wag All* (1970, Faber & Faber)

Fenton, Alexander *Scottish Country Life* (1976, John Donald, Edinburgh)

Fraser, Allan *Farming for Beef* (1950, Crosby Lockwood)

Fream, William *The Complete Grazier* (15th edn 1908, Crosby Lockwood)

French, Mary *A Victorian Village* (1979, Glasney Press, Falmouth)

Garne, Richard *Cotswold Yeomen and Sheep* (1984, Regency Press)

Garner, Frank H *The Cattle of Britain* (1944, Longmans, Green)

Gibbs, J Arthur *A Cotswold Village, Or, Country Life and Pursuits in Gloucestershire* (1898, Jonathan Cape)

Goddard, Nicholas *Harvests of Change. The Royal Agricultural Society of England 1838–1988* (1988, Quiller Press, London)

Grant, Ian and Maddren, Nicholas *The Countryside at War* (1975, Jupiter)

Grey, Edwin *Cottage Life in a Hertfordshire Village* (1935, St Albans)

Hagan, G *Dry Docking* (1975, self-published)

Hammond, Nigel *Rural Life in the Vale of the White Horse 1780–1914* Nigel (1974, Countryside Books)

Hargreaves, Cyril *Father's Derbyshire* (1978, Moorleys Bookshop, Ilkeston)

Harvey, Nigel *A History of Farm Buildings* (1970, 1984 David & Charles)

Hauxwell, Hannah with Cockcroft, Barry *Hannah: The Complete Story* (1991, Random)

Heath, Richard *The English Peasant* (1893, Fisher Unwin)

Hennell, T *Change in the Farm* (1934, Cambridge University Press)

Horn, Pamela (ed.) *Oxfordshire Village Life: The Diaries of George James Dew (1846–1928), Relieving Officer* (1983, Beacon Publications, Abingdon)

Hughes, Annabelle and Johnston, David *West Sussex Barns & Farm Buildings* (2002, Dovecote Press, Wimborne)

Jefferies, Richard *Landscape & Labour* (1872–1887; ed. John Pearson, 1979, Moonraker Press)

Jefferies, Richard *Hodge and His Masters* (1878–1880; ed. Henry Williamson, 1946, Faber and Faber)

Jekyll, Gertrude *Old West Surrey* (1904; facsimile 1978 Kohler & Coombes)

Jennings, Louis J *Field Paths and Green Lanes* (1877; 5th edn 1907, John Murray)

Jerrome, Peter and Newdick, Jonathan *The Men with Laughter in Their Hearts: Photographs from the 1930s by George Garland* (1986, Window Press)

Jeynes, Dorinda *Back Along, Up Bremridge* (1989, United Writers Publications, Penzance)

Johnson, Walter *Talks with Shepherds* (1925, George Routledge)

Jones, Doug (ed.) *Buriton in Living Memory* (2003, Buriton Heritage Bank)

Keeling, CH *Where the Zebu Grazed* (1989, Clam Publications)

King, Peter *Women Rule the Plot* (1999, Duckworth)

Kitteringham, Jennie *Country Girls in 19th Century England* (1973, History Workshop)

Knappett, Rachel *A Pullet on the Midden* (1946, Michael Joseph)

Leicestershire MARS *Farming in Focus: Photographs of Leicestershire Agriculture 1860–1940* (1989, Leicestershire Museums, Arts & Records Service)

Lewis, Mary (ed.) *Old Days in the Kent Hop Gardens* (1962, West Kent Federation of Women's Institutes)

Live Stock Journal Annual 1926 (1926, Vinton & Co.)

Livingstone WP *Shetland and the Shetlanders* (1947, Thomas Nelson & Sons)

MacLellan, Angus (ed.) *Stories from South Uist* (1961, Routledge & Kegan Paul)

Martin, EW *The Shearers and the Shorn* (1965, Dartington/Routledge & Kegan Paul)

Massingham, HJ *The Faith of a Fieldsman* (1951, Richard Clay)

McConnell, Primrose *The Agricultural Note-Book* (9th edn 1919, Crosby Lockwood)

Morgan, David *Harvesters in 19th century England* (1973, in *History Workshop Vol. I*, Routledge)

Mowlem, Alan *Goat Farming* (1988, Farming Press)

Munby AJ *Diary* (1862–1865, vols 14–25, ms at Trinity College, Cambridge)

Museum of East Anglian Life *The Farming Year in Suffolk* (East Anglian Record Office, Ely)

Newby, Howard *The Countryside in Question* (1988, Hutchinson)

Olivier, Edith *Wiltshire* (1951, Robert Hale)

Orwin, Christabel S and Whetham, Edith H *History of British Agriculture 1846–1914* (1964, Longmans, Green)

Owen, Brendon *One From the Plough* (2001, Gazebo)

Parish, WD *A Dictionary of the Sussex Dialect* (1875; ed. Helena Hall, 1957)

Partridge, Michael *Farm Tools through the Ages* (1973, Osprey)

Payne, Shaun and Pailthorpe, Richard (eds) *Barclay Wills' The Downland Shepherds*, ill. Gordon Beningfield (1989, Alan Sutton)

Peacock, Alf *The Revolt of the Fields in East Anglia* (1968, CP History Group)

Peters, JEC *Discovering Traditional Farm Buildings* (2003, Shire)

Pitstone LHS *In Pitstone Green there is a Farm* (1979, Pitstone Local History Society)

Plomer, Wm (ed.) *Kilvert's Diary 1870–1879* (1944, Readers Union/Cape)

Porter, Eleanor *Yeomen of the Cotswolds* (1995, Images Publishing, Malvern)

Porter, Valerie *Southdown Sheep* (1991, Weald & Downland Museum/Southdown Sheep Society)

Porter, Valerie *English Villagers* (1992, George Philip)

Prebble, John *The Highland Clearances* (1963, Secker & Warburg)

Pringle, Robert Oliphant *Live-stock of the Farm* (1st edn 1874; 3rd edn 1886 ed. James Macdonald, Wm Blackwood, Edinburgh)

Pulbrook, Ernest C *English Country Life and Work* (1922, Batsford)

Reitzel, William (ed.) *Autobiography of William Cobbett* (1947, Faber & Faber)

Robertson Scott, JW *The Dying Peasant* (1926, Williams & Norgate)

Rogerson, Sidney and Tunnicliffe, Charles *Both Sides of the Road* (1949, Collins)

Royal Agricultural Society of England *Journal of the RASE 1963* (1963, John Murray)

Russell, Rex C *Cottagers & Cows 1800–1892: the Cow Clubs in Lincolnshire* (1987, Barton Branch WEA)

Sampson, Reg *Life Stories of Bygone Days* (Loddiswell History Group)

Sanders HG and Eley G *Farms of Britain* (1946, Crosby Lockwood)

Seymour, Aubrey *A Square Mile of Old England* (1972, Roundwood)

Silver, Brian *Fernhurst Pictures and People* (1999, self-published)

Sinclair, James (ed.) *Heavy Horses: Breeds & Management* (5th edn 1910, Vinton)

'Stonehenge' (JH Walsh) *The Horse in the Stable and the Field* (1862, Routledge)

Sturt, George *The Bettesworth Book* (1st edn 1901; 2nd 1902, facsimile Caliban Books 1978)

Thomas, Maurice *Do you remember what Granny told you about the Women's Land Army* (tr. Tricia Holmes 1999, copyright Reginald John Chapman, Abthorpe)

Tilley, Michael F *Housing the Country Worker* (1947, Faber and Faber)

Tyrer, Nicola *They Fought in the Fields. The women's land army: the story of a forgotten victory* (1996 Sinclair Stevenson)

Veterinary Department of the War Office *Animal Management* (1923, HMSO)

Ward, Tim *Herefordshire on Old Postcards* (1987, Reflections of a Bygone Age, Keyworth, Notts)

Watson, James AS and More, James A *Agriculture: The Science & Practice of British Farming* (7th edn 1944, Oliver & Boyd)

Wentworth Day, J *The New Yeomen of England* (1952, Harrap)

Wentworth Day, J *Poison on the Land* (1957, Eyre & Spottiswoode)

Wilson, Avice R *Cocklebury* (1983, Phillimore)

Winstanley, Michael *Life in Kent at the Turn of the Century* (1978, Wm Dawson & Son)

Winter, Gordon *A Country Camera 1844–1914* (1966, Country Life)

Woodforde, James *A Country Parson 1759–1802* (1985, Oxford University Press)

Woods, Stephen *Dartmoor Farm* (2003, Halgrove)

Wright, Philip *Traction Engines* (1959, Adam & Charles Black)

Zeuner, Diana *Heavy Horses* (2004, Shire)

252 •

Index